ETHICAL ARTIFICIAL INTELLIGENCE FROM POPULAR TO COGNITIVE SCIENCE

This book offers a unique interdisciplinary perspective on the ethics of 'artificial intelligence' – autonomous, intelligent (and connected) systems, or AISs, applying principles of social cognition to understand the social and ethical issues associated with the creation, adoption, and implementation of AISs.

As humans become entangled in sociotechnical systems defined by human and artificial agents, there is a pressing need to understand how trust is created, used, and abused. Compounding the difficulty in answering these questions, stakeholders directly or indirectly affected by these systems differ in their motivations, understanding, and values. This volume provides a comprehensive resource to help stakeholders understand ethical issues of designing and implementing AISs using an ethical sensemaking approach. Starting with the general technical affordances of AISs, Dr. Jordan Richard Schoenherr considers the features of system design relating data integrity, selection and interpretation of algorithms, and the evolution processes that drive AIS innovation as a sociotechnological system. The poles of technophobia (algorithmic aversion) and technophilia (algorithmic preference) in the public perception of AISs are then described and considered against existing evidence, including issues ranging from the displacement and re-education needs of the human workforce, the impact of the use of technology on interpersonal accord, and surveillance and cybersecurity. Ethical frameworks that provide tools for evaluating the values and outcomes of AISs are then reviewed, and how they can be aligned with ethical sensemaking processes identified by psychological science is explored. Finally, these disparate threads are brought together in a design framework.

Also including sections on policies and guidelines, gaming and social media, and Eastern philosophical frameworks, this book is fascinating reading for students and academics in psychology, computer science, philosophy, and related areas, as well as professionals such as policy makers and those working with AISs.

Dr. Jordan Richard Schoenherr is an assistant professor in the Department of Psychology (Concordia University), an adjunct research professor in the Department of Psychology and member of the Institute for Data Science (Carleton University), and a former visiting scholar at the US Military Academy (West Point). His primary areas of interest are decision-making, ethics, and learning, with application in metacognition, the health professions, and the ethics of artificial intelligence.

ETHICAL ARTIFICIAL INTELLIGENCE FROM POPULAR TO COGNITIVE SCIENCE

Trust in the Age of Entanglement

Jordan Richard Schoenherr

Routledge
Taylor & Francis Group

NEW YORK AND LONDON

Cover image: © Getty Images

First published 2022
by Routledge
605 Third Avenue, New York, NY 10158

and by Routledge
4 Park Square, Milton Park, Abingdon, Oxon, OX14 4RN

Routledge is an imprint of the Taylor & Francis Group, an informa business

© 2022 Taylor & Francis

Library of Congress Cataloging-in-Publication Data
Names: Schoenherr, Jordan Richard, author.
Title: Ethical artificial intelligence from popular to cognitive science:
trust in the age of entanglement / Jordan Richard Schoenherr, PhD.
Description: New York, NY: Routledge, 2022. | Includes bibliographical references and index. |
Summary: "This book offers a unique interdisciplinary perspective on the ethics of artificial
intelligence (autonomous, intelligent, and connected systems, or AIS), applying principles of the
social cognition to understand the social and ethical issues associated with the creation, adoption,
and implementation of AIS. Also including sections on policies and guideline, gaming and social
media, and Eastern philosophical frameworks, this is fascinating reading for students and academics
in psychology, computer science, philosophy, and related areas, as well as professionals such as
policymakers and those working with AI systems"– Provided by publisher.
Identifiers: LCCN 2022005694 (print) | LCCN 2022005695 (ebook) |
ISBN 9780367697983 (paperback) | ISBN 9780367698003 (hardback) |
ISBN 9781003143284 (ebook)
Subjects: LCSH: Artificial intelligence–Moral and ethical aspects.
Classification: LCC Q334.7 .S36 2022 (print) |
LCC Q334.7 (ebook) | DDC 174/.90063–dc23/eng20220421
LC record available at https://lccn.loc.gov/2022005694
LC ebook record available at https://lccn.loc.gov/2022005695

ISBN: 978-0-367-69800-3 (hbk)
ISBN: 978-0-367-69798-3 (pbk)
ISBN: 978-1-00-314328-4 (ebk)

DOI: 10.4324/9781003143284

Typeset in Bembo
by Newgen Publishing UK

Tempora mutantur, nos et mutamur in illis

CONTENTS

PREFACE

This book is the product of rants, digressions, and coincidence. Growing up in a small country town, I was torn between forests and libraries, fields and museums, science and science fiction. My mother was (and is) a proud luddite with an interest in the social sciences. My father was fascinated with technology, teaching me to solder circuits and exposing me to computers. As a student, I was pulled between ethics, anthropology, and cognitive psychology. Each time an instructor described research, I considered how it was relevant to my daily life and what the ethical implications were. When teaching psychology, I wanted to make these same links for my students. Unbeknownst to me, I had drifted into cyberpsychology. As I consulted outside academia, I emphasized the importance of understanding both the ethical and psychological dimensions of our work and how they could be applied to organizational design. In writing this book, I have attempted to speak to a broad interdisciplinary audience … and justify my cumbersome, well-travelled library of books.

This book reflects a synthesis of popular science, cognitive science, and ethics. While attending either conference or consulting, I often found that I translated core concepts and concerns of one group to another. I wanted to create a primer that allowed people, within (and between) disciplines, to have a common basis for discussion, something that could be used to inform a project or guide a class. Of course, covering each discipline in a comprehensive manner would take a group of scholars rather than one person. To that end, I have tried to consider core issues and approaches from several disciplines to provide a framework for understanding autonomous, intelligent, and connected systems. Notable absences include anthropology, ethnography, and sociology. While these approaches can offer dynamic accounts of sociotechnical systems from multiple perspectives, I felt that including them would have been a bridge too far.

Finally, a note on terminology. For the sake of brevity, I use AISs for autonomous, intelligent, and connected systems to reduce confusion in an interdisciplinary world already saturated with acronyms. As I argue, these three features must be considered alongside human interpersonal processes to begin to assess the ethical affordances of AISs. I also adopt the term 'affordances' because it emphasizes the interactive nature of the individual and the environment. Ethical affordances reflect the outcomes of the interactions of agents. They are ultimately abstractions based on the values, norms, and conventions of the agents involved. We perceive these affordances when there is intersubjective agreement. Otherwise, they remain hidden. Rather than differentiating technical and functional levels of design, I have opted to use the term 'technical affordances' to cover both the technical (e.g., code) and functional aspects (e.g., prediction, classification) of AIS design. I also repeatedly reinforce the distinction between social issues and ethical issues. Here, ethical issues reflect concerns stemming from conflicts that arise within formal ethical systems whereas social issues reflect concerns stemming from norms, conventions, and categories used within a society. Whereas ethical issues reflect more general, abstract concerns (e.g., Is discrimination acceptable?), social issues are more concrete, embedded within a sociocultural context (e.g., Is discrimination against a given social category acceptable?).

ACKNOWLEDGEMENTS

Although many thanks are reserved for inquisitive students and colleagues, I would especially like to thank Drs. Sylvie Houde, Dean Verger, and Stephen Hare for feedback on early versions of the manuscript; Corrina Cai for insight into the Mass Effect videogame reward system and for creating the corresponding figure; and my colleague Dr. Robert Thomson, Army Research Laboratories, the Army Cyber Institute, Behavioural Science and Leadership Department for the opportunity to work as a visiting scholar during 2019–2020. Finally, many thanks also go to the countless anonymous reviewers who have (thanklessly) contributed their time and effort in reviewing the articles that informed the development of this book and to Jen Hinchliffe for her fastidious editorial services.

1

INTRODUCTION

We live in an age of entanglement. Whether willingly or unwillingly, our daily lives are inextricably bound to technologies. In most developed countries, people often start and end their day by checking their mobile phones, throughout the day they query the Internet to find information, humour, lust, and love. For many people, failing to interface with technology in this manner is almost unimaginable. At the same time, consequential decisions about our lives are being made with, and by, these technologies, often without our knowledge. Browsing any consumer website creates a profile of your habits and the seller uses this profile to infer your preferences and influence your behaviour. Social media collects your information in much the same way and places you in an echo chamber of images and thoughts that conform to your own (Quattrociocchi et al., 2016).

Technologies might change but human psychology remains much the same. The foundation of any human society is trust. Trust enables us to create responsibilities, assign them to individuals, and collaborate in the integration of the resulting products. When you make an online payment, you are trusting that the company does not overcharge you, that the product arrives on time and as described, and that the transaction is secure. When you work for a company, you trust that they will pay you on time and in the appropriate manner. In the background, trust is distributed between human and nonhuman agents. There is no person sitting around taking your money and depositing your pay cheque into your account. Technology is acting as an intermediary at almost every stage. Over time, we have progressively placed more trust in nonhuman agents, often without realizing it.

How did we come to accept this reality? Have we truly accepted it? The key to understanding is not in looking at what is new but what remains constant. Humans are an adaptive species. The rapid spread of humans across the globe can likely be attributed to a mental toolkit that has evolved over hundreds of millennia, allowing

DOI: 10.4324/9781003143284-1

us to adapt to novel environments. This is evidenced in the intuitions we have about people, places, and processes.

To psychologists and cognitive scientists, the term 'intuition' provides a deceptively simple explanation of human thinking. It gives us the sense of a homogenous process that many people think of as reliable. Many interrelated concepts capture this idea. In the problem-solving literature, this is referred to as *einstellung* (Luchins, 1942) wherein we use the same solution despite a change in the structure of a problem. In the decision sciences, their is broad recognition that we must understand how we make choices within a complex environment using heuristics, simple rules that use a subset of information to render judgments (Gilovich et al., 2002). We assume that humans encode features of the environment, identify a familiar pattern in whole or in part, and then select from the available response alternatives. Often, only a single response is considered (Klein, 1993). These same processes affect our moral judgment. When we feel uncomfortable, this visceral response alerts us that something is wrong. Yet, we do not often take into account the basis of these moral judgments and we often rationalize them rather than examine the dynamics of our current social and physical environment (e.g., Haidt, 2007). Our moral sense might be a useful tool, but it is not always reliable.

One of the reasons that we rely on these intuitions stems from our mental limitations. Humans have a limited amount of attention and working memory, a limited capacity, short-term store that keeps information active for brief intervals. The reliance on simple rules, allows us to scan our environment more broadly for threats and opportunities, but at a cost. The more complex or novel our environment, the more features and agents we need to consider. Although humans have co-evolved with our technologies – tools, fire, language – our fate has become increasingly entangled in a larger set of human and nonhuman agents. Making ethical choices in these complex is not a simple task. Rather than assuming that there is a optimal solution, we might only be able to achieve those that are satisfactory (Simon, 1956).

1.1 The Age of Entanglement

Natural scientists often refer to the current geological epoch as the Anthropocene, or the age of humans. This epoch is defined by how humans have reshaped their environment in an unprecedented manner, resulting in fundamental changes to the Earth and its structure. Humans are intimately bound to our technologies, often without realizing what those technologies represent. When most people think about technology, they think of material artifacts: stone tools, saws, pulleys, cars, computers, and WiFi. They often fail to recognize that many technologies – and arguably all – are conceptual. Consider languages and mathematics: they are symbol systems that allow us to encode, store, and manipulate information, which can allow us to coordinate, regulate, and monitor others in a distributed network of trust. Ancient cuneiform tablets were used to keep transactional records, shifting the focus from a flexible, fallible memory system to a concrete record (Schmandt-Besserat, 1978). Over time, much like we come to trust friends, or friends of friends that we trust, we can transfer trust from individuals or groups of individuals with credibility, to the technologies that they create (e.g., Schoenherr, 2017). In many cases, the reason why a technology is adopted becomes lost, with adopters focusing on the symbolic meaning and status granted to technology owners and users (i.e., prestige technology; Hayden, 1998). In our minds, humans, symbols, and artifacts become entangled in a process of co-evolution. As more technologies become available and complex, and as we shift away from material technologies to virtual technologies, the technologies become more cognitively inaccessible. We become dependent on trust that is defined by both the function of technology as an instrument and as a marker of status.

The modern world is defined by algorithms. Machine learning, artificial intelligence, and neural networks (i.e., AISs) have evolved substantially in recent decades, from tangles of wire in a laboratory used for theoretical demonstrations (Figure 2.2), to highly specialized, restricted tasks such as virtually unwrapping fragile ancient texts (Rosin et al., 2018; Seales et al., 2016) and the prediction of susceptibility to disease of domesticated technologies such as simple, ubiquitous processes such as autocorrect in word processors (Rayson et al., 1998), virtual assistants, and image editing software, for example, Google's DeepDream software (Figure 1.1). Whereas many of the tasks performed by AISs might not appear to represent ethical and social challenges, the centrality of AISs in our daily lives can radically alter how we interact with the world and each other, creating novel social and ethical issues.

FIGURE 1.1 Google's Deep Dream software conversion of an image (left) into one that includes animal-like distortions (right). Photo of arches in Aspendos Amphitheatre, Istanbul, Turkey.

Source: Photo Credit: Jordan Richard Schoenherr.

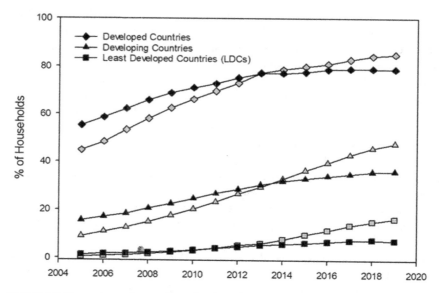

FIGURE 1.2 Percentage of users from developed, developing, and least-developed countries for households owning a computer (grey) and having access to the Internet (black).

Source: Data obtained from International Telecommunication Union (ITU). Available at www.itu.int/en/ITU-D/Statistics/Pages/definitions/regions.aspx.

I refer to this as the *Age of Entanglement*, emphasizing the growing interdependencies of humans and nonhuman agents.

Like other 'ages', the Age of Entanglement is defined by large-scale human-created changes to the environment comparable to the industrial revolution.[1] In contrast to the notion of an 'Information Age' which starts with the development of the transistor computer (Castells, 1996), the creation of the World Wide Web and the general accessibility of the Internet must be seen as a catalyst for change, restructuring the boundaries of knowledge. Technologies such as smartphones have the potential to radically change societies, increasingly the accessibility of information and services (e.g., Estache et al., 2002; Jin, 2017; Katz & Aakhus, 2002). However, digital divides remain in terms of both computer ownership and home Internet access (see Figure 1.2). Similarly, data from the International Telecommunication Union (ITU) also suggest a male bias toward Internet use globally (6.9%) which is especially pronounced in Africa (16.9%) and Arab countries (14.0%) although still present in Asia-Pacific (7.0%) and Europe (5.0%). Nevertheless, by bypassing normal communication channels, interconnectivity can empower previously marginalized communities within a society (e.g., the Arab Spring; Howard et al., 2011). There are also dark sides to this digital revolution, allowing for increased availability of illicit materials and accessibility of immoral activities on the 'dark web'. Moreover, seeing the influence of social media and the accessibility of information, countries also seek to control what information (and disinformation) is available to its citizens.

The creation of the Internet itself does not constitute entanglement. Entanglement implies *interdependency* between entities – human and nonhuman agents – based on trust. Data does not constitute information unless it reduces our uncertainty. Data cannot reduce our uncertainty unless we attend to, and trust, the source. As humans increasingly trust the results of Internet search engines, the content of websites, and would-be celebrity 'influencers' on social media, they become entangled, creating a sociotechnological system. We are often unknowingly and involuntarily digitized, rendering us digital citizens or data subjects. Data breaches provide an increasingly common demonstration of this: the loss of personal information such as demographics, passwords, and finances can lead to more significant cybercrimes such as identify theft and financial ruin. Data aggregation has become a ubiquitous phenomenon where information can be pooled together into data lakes, sold and shared, and turned into derivative datasets even when the primary dataset has been removed (Section 3.4.2). Such data can have important consequences. Loans can be denied, arrests can be made, and access to dating websites can be restricted. Thus, the Age of Entanglement follows the Information Age with the introduction of the Internet.

The Age of Entanglement has been heralded by some. For instance, Kurzweil (2005) speaks of a new epoch that '… will result from the merger of the vast knowledge embedded in our own brains with the vastly greater capacity, speed, and knowledge-sharing ability of our technology. This epoch will enable our human-machine civilization to transcend the human brain's limitations' (p. 21). Crucially, this 'Epoch' brings with it both promise and peril:

> The Singularity will allow us to overcome age-old human problems and vastly amplify human creativity. We will preserve and enhance the intelligence that evolution has bestowed on us while overcoming the profound limitations of biological evolution. But the Singularity will also amplify the ability to act on our destructive inclinations.
>
> *Kurzweil, 2005*

A similar concept was proposed at the World Economic Forum, Society 5.0 (Nakanishi, 2019). In contrast to eras defined by hunting-gathering (Society 1.0), agrarian production (Society 2.0), industrialization (Society 3.0), and the current Information Age (Society 4.0), an 'Imagination Society' (Society 5.0) reflects the integration of physical and information environments, and (ideally) balances social and economic issues.

Whether humans will, can, or should, fully integrate with nonhuman agents is an open question. Humans have always been integrated with their technologies. The use of sophisticated symbol systems, such as art and language, allowed us to represent and communicate information about entities that are not immediately present within the environment. The tools created through natural and artificial selection allowed us to modify our environments, enabling us to survive and thrive.

However, simply because this *has* been the way does not mean that it *should be* how we proceed. As with any technology, such changes pose important social and ethical issues in terms of how technologies are created, distributed, used, monitored, and regulated. Unlike our ancestors, we can use the patterns of the past to predict possible futures. Many possible relational configurations of human–AIS interaction must be identified and evaluated.

The technical affordances of these systems raise important ethical questions. How our information is acquired, processed, shared, used, and reused to make consequential decisions that will affect us and others, reflect the critical ethical affordances of these systems. Systems differ in terms of their *intelligence* (their ability to complete a task), *autonomy* (the extent to which they can independently accomplish a task), as well as their *connectivity* (how the intelligence required to complete a task is distributed within a network). How a pocket calculator differs from a webcrawler or from a drone, and how these systems are used, can have dramatic implications for how they will impact our lives as individuals. Moreover, how these systems supplement or replace human agents creates larger social issues outside of AISs themselves, including questions of human autonomy and well-being.

1.2 Trust and Ethics in the Age of Entanglement

Humans are a social species. Our sociality allows us to share knowledge and distribute tasks within both small and large social networks. Doing so allows us to reduce the time required to learn, survive, and find mates. By doing this, we are trusting others: trusting that knowledge is accurate and that tasks will be complete. Despite considerable reflection on its definition (e.g., Fukuyama, 1996; Hardin, 2002), trust is ultimately a folk concept that is likely defined by perceived familiarity, interpersonal cohesion, shared social identities and expectations, and conformity to social and cultural norms. Formally, trust likely reflects the triadic relationship between two individuals in a particular domain, i.e., Agent A *trusts* Agent B to X. Here, X might be anything, from safely driving a vehicle, to returning borrowed money, to providing accurate information. Ethical frameworks (hereafter, ethics) provide a foundation of trust. In contrast to morality, which typically reflects an agent's intuition, ethics provides a systematic approach to interpersonal interactions. However, whether the kind of trust and ethical frameworks that apply to human agents translate to non-human agents remains a topic of debate. Algorithms, 'machines', and 'artificial intelligence' might not be regarded as true *agents* that one can have relationships with.

Such an account suggests that there are categorical differences between the ways we trust a hammer or a computer and how we trust a person. This has an intuitive appeal, but it ignores the fact that some people treat other human groups in qualitatively different ways to the way they treat members of their own group. Humans, and human relationships, continue to evolve. Despite its ancient origins, ethical inquiry continues to evolve and engage. Following more general observations in the history of science and technology, new technological and social arrangements present affordances that are often poorly understood. Scholars in the humanities and social sciences have recognized that values permeate science and technology, thus determining which paths are pursued (e.g., Kuhn, 1962/2010; Merton, 1942, 1957; Mitroff, 1974; Shapin, 1989, 1994). We must also recognize that AISs do not simply reflect software and hardware. Interdisciplinary work by, and participation of, specialists and the general public is necessary to identify and respond to these issues. Ethicists have begun to examine domains created and inhabited by AISs. In an early account, Mason (1986) identified four ethical issues presented by the information age: privacy, accuracy, property, and accessibility (PAPA). More recently, ethical frameworks emphasize the social implications of technology (e.g., FATE: Fairness, Accountability, Transparency, and Ethics), with other scholars providing comprehensive surveys of social and ethical issues (Kizza, 2013; Stamatellos, 2007; Tavani, 2007). The fact that computing platforms can perform an inestimable number of tasks means that ethical inquiries into this area have already been, and will likely continue to be, quite fruitful for the foreseeable future.

In themselves, scientific and technological innovations are neither good nor bad. Ada Lovelace pointed out the limitations of Charles Babbage's Analytic Engine:

> It is desirable to guard against the possibility of exaggerated ideas that might arise as to the powers of the Analytical Engine. In considering any new subject, there is frequently a tendency, first, to *overrate* what we find to be already interesting or remarkable; and, secondly, by a sort of natural reaction, to *undervalue* the true state of the case, when we do discover that our notions have surpassed those that were really tenable.
>
> The Analytical Engine has no pretensions whatever to *originate* anything. It can do *whatever we know how to order it to perform*. It can follow analysis; but it has no power of anticipating any analytical relations or truths. Its province is to assist us to making available what we are already acquainted with.
>
> *Lovelace, 1843; italics in original*

Asimov (1983) echoes this sentiment later, noting that: 'We must not view science and technology as either an inevitable saviour, or an inevitable destroyer. It can be either, and the choice is ours' (p. 119). Clarke (2005) has similarly remarked that:

> [o]ur big challenge ... is to get [information and computer technologies (ICTs)] to solve real life problems without creating any new ones. In the early part of the last century, Mahatma Gandhi proposed a simple test for the effectiveness of any development activity: find out how the last man would be affected by it. We should adapt this as a test for ICTs in development: how will the last man, woman, and child be reached, touched and transformed by these marvellous communication tools?

These remarks highlight the growing recognition that human agency and a recognition of social context are critical to understanding the value of AISs. To this end, we must understand human–technology interaction as a sociotechnological system (Cooper & Foster, 1971; Pasmore et al., 1982; Walker et al., 2008). Thus, prior to reviewing the basic distinctions developed in philosophical ethics and social-cognition features of ethical sensemaking, I will examine the social and ethical issues presented in popularized discourse on the science of AISs.

1.3 Ethical Sensemaking: From Popular Science to Cognitive Science

Making sense of the world requires that we examine multiple perspectives. When evaluating AISs, we must go beyond the technical affordances of these systems (i.e., their hardware and software) and recognize how these systems are perceived and understood by those who will directly or indirectly be affected by them. This book provides an interdisciplinary overview of the promise and problems of AISs. Each chapter summarizes basic concerns that are presented through disciplinary and non-disciplinary lens. Due to the breadth of perspectives covered here, each domain can only be covered in a comparatively simple manner. Here, my hope is that a focus on basic concepts and issues, even if oversimplified, can facilitate crucial discussions that need to occur between the public, the humanities, the social sciences, and the computer sciences. Rather than presenting a wholly positive or negative picture, the book examines the values and ethics from each of these perspectives.

Although there is significant overlap between topics covered in each chapter, the book is divided into broad sections that can be read individually or sequentially. In Chapter 2, the basic features of AISs are described. Rather than reviewing the specific computational models that define AISs (e.g., Bayesian, neural networks, production systems), high-level functions and features of AISs that are relevant to their interactions with humans are reviewed. Topics related to research integrity, such as the validity and reliability of these systems are examined, along with how the autonomy, intelligence, and connectivity of AISs relate to social and ethical issues.

Chapter 3 changes focus by observing AISs in the context of popular science. Following approaches adopted from the humanities, this chapter considers the public representation of AISs. It examines how 'machines' (both physical and virtual) have been viewed historically and how they are currently represented. By considering popular science, we obtain insight into how the public understands AISs and what representations are available to the public within popular media, for example, magazines, news articles, comic books. Here, a major theme is between an overly optimistic and pessimistic view of the capabilities of AISs, along with attempts to persuade the public to accept (algorithmic preference) or reject (algorithmic aversion) AISs. Throughout this section, I consider evidence from studies of cyberpsychology that support and refute these concerns.

Chapter 4 outlines philosophical ethics frameworks. Although ethical frameworks often represent formalizations of moral reasoning within a society, leading to highly influential philosophical traditions, an examination of philosophical traditions allows us to understand the deeper issues associated with AISs. The chapter first presents the distinction between descriptive and prescriptive norms and reviews the burgeoning enterprise of the creation of guidelines and principles related to 'ethical AI'. Following this discussion, a cross-section of approaches to understanding ethical issues is provided from the three dominant ethical traditions: consequentialism, non-consequentialism, and virtue theory. In addition to those developed in the Western tradition, a brief overview of Eastern traditions is also provided. The chapter highlights the importance of understanding the distributed nature of responsibility as well as the contributions that transrational traditions and moral irrealism can contribute to the ethics of AISs. It suggests that virtue theory provides an overarching framework for understanding ethics.

Philosophical tradition represents ways of thinking, feeling, and responding to the world, and in this vein, Chapter 5 reviews the underlying psychological processes associated with ethical sensemaking. Psychological science provides a bridge between the intuitions of non-experts, the formation and application of ethical norms developed by philosophers, and the affordances of AISs. Rather than assuming that logic alone should or can determine the application of human values to AISs, ethical sensemaking is defined by affect, reasoning, decision-making, and social cognition. Here, this chapter argues that if a virtue theory approach is adopted, ethical sensemaking provides a more specific account of what it means to act virtuously.

Chapter 6 examines the basic structure of ethical systems and reviews multiple value-sensitive design frameworks that can be applied to AISs. An overall ethical design framework is provided, which brings together the need to take into account both the technical affordances of AISs by developers and the perceptions of the public. Here, I argue that additional emphasis should be placed on understanding the process of knowledge translation and to having designers engage with stakeholders. In addition to the traditional 'users', the framework reinforces the need to take into account the communities affected by design, with designers functioning as a nexus between technical and nontechnical communities.

In the final chapter, I summarize the preceding chapters and attempt to synthesize key issues. I highlight the critical importance of the three technical dimensions of AISs (intelligence, autonomy, and connectivity). Despite the utility of virtue theory both in terms of its flexibility and cross-cultural availability, I reinforce the need to include social ethics and 'transrational' ethical frameworks to accommodate the diversity of concerns raised by stakeholders as well as the technical affordances of AISs. Specifically, the issues of autonomy and connectivity introduce the need to understand the nature of distributed responsibility that is often deemphasized in Western approaches to ethics.

Note

1 Others have earlier noted large-scale changes due to deforestation.

2

THE ESSENCE OF AISs

Features and Functions of Autonomous/ Intelligent Systems

Understanding the world requires that we parse it into features and categories, allowing us to learn and make predictions. In terms of technological artifacts, we perceive the environment in terms of *affordance* (Gibson, 1977, 1979/2014). For J. J. Gibson, an affordance represents a way of interacting with the physical environment in terms of the functional properties of an object. Norman (1999, 2013) provided a more tractable formulation, defining affordances as functional representations of stimuli, i.e., what someone can *do* with something. Crucially, affordances are not an intrinsic feature of a technology. Rather, they require someone to *conceive of*, and *perceive*, them in a certain way: when I *perceive* a cutting edge of a stone, I can use it as a knife or scraper.

Problem-solving tasks illustrate the nature of affordance. These tasks provide participants with items that perform a typical function and assess whether they can use them in a novel manner. For instance, in the Candle Problem, participants are provided with a candle, matches, and a box of tacks (Duncker, 1945). They are instructed to fix a candle to the wall while avoiding spilling any wax on the floor. Here, participants must *see* the tack box as a shelf on which the candle can be placed, using the tacks to pin the box to the wall. Similarly, humans continually find new affordances in computers that we did not initially perceive.

Rather than automatically identifying novel affordances, most people experience *functional fixedness* – they remain fixed on a typical function of an object and fail to identify new uses for it (e.g., Adamson, 1952). This is not surprising. As we repeatedly interact with an object in the same manner, often mimicking or imitating others, typical uses will come to mind more readily (Defeyter & German, 2003; German & Barrett, 2005; German & Defeyter, 2000). If a technological artifact or object performs a task in a satisfactory manner, there is little need to consider alternatives.

DOI: 10.4324/9781003143284-2

Objects can also be defined in terms of their anti-affordances and disaffordances, design features that can constrain or undermine decision-making, respectively (Section 6.1). For instance, websites might require cookies to access content that users might automatically accept without reflection, or they might contain figures or images which people with visual impairments cannot read. Prior to considering ethical and social issues that might arise through stakeholder interaction with AISs, we must first consider the affordances and anti-affordances that define these systems.

Affordances of AISs. By adopting the term AIS, I've made a conscious decision to not use the more common term artificial intelligence. The term 'artificial' obscures the fact that these systems have been made *by* humans and have a real impact on the world, both in terms of their input (e.g., natural resources that are used to create and run these systems; 'user' data that reflect real individuals and groups) and output (e.g., decisions on whether to be awarded a loan; the environmental impact of energy consumption). Similarly, the term 'intelligence' must also be qualified. Here, 'intelligence' is typically considered in terms of a specific task performed by a system, for example, accurate pattern recognition, classification, and recommendations. This differs from human general intelligence, which can map patterns across domains (e.g., an atom is like a solar system), create novel solutions (e.g., creativity), and navigate often ambiguous social environments of conflicting sociocultural norms (e.g., Gardner, 1983; Sternberg, 2000). Intelligence is often further constrained in terms of autonomy: while a system might perform some tasks, humans remain the arbiters of the utility and reliability of the output, to varying degrees. Thus, much of the 'intelligence' of AISs remains directly or indirectly that of their creators and users.

The abilities, or intelligence, of AISs provide many potential benefits, including operating in physical and virtual environments that are inaccessible to humans, reducing cost relative to human labour, automatically translating between languages, and filling human roles where no people are available. At the most fundamental level, AISs are believed to have two principal benefits: increases in both the speed and accuracy of problem-solving *relative* to humans (Russell & Norvig, 1995/2010). For instance, the introduction of counting machines that would later form the core of IBM enabled the rapid intake and analysis of individual information by using punch cards (Sobel, 1981). Modern-day search engines can quickly identify relevant websites in milliseconds, facilitating personal and professional research.[1] Consequently, intelligence must ultimately be qualified *relative* to a domain and assessed in terms of successful prediction as well as the number and kinds of errors.

The technological affordances and trade-offs of computing systems have long been recognized. In the May 1967 issue of *Popular Science*, C. P. Gilmore writes:

> Some people are afraid that computers are so smart they'll take over some day. I'm not. I've got a reason for my optimism. I've used a real computer in my home ... for example, to figure out whether I should convert the heating system of a house I'm thinking of buying to another kind of fuel, and to

see when it would be most economical to trade in my car. I worked on one program – a set of instructions for the computer – to have it do my income tax. And when I got bored, I played games. My computer can play tick-tack-toe, blackjack, nom (an ancient Chinese game), and dice (in which a random generator rolls make-believe dice electronically). My computer can do arithmetic like a super genius – 165,000 calculations a second. But in some ways, it's not very bright: It can't begin to do the simplest problem until I tell it how in great detail.

Gilmore, 1967, p. 90

Gilmore goes on to note that '[c]hances are my computer looks a lot different than you imagine' (1967, p. 90) going on to describe the distributed nature of the system. Concluding the article, he notes that 'When computers start going into homes on a regular basis, users won't actually have to know how to program at all. The computers will have in their memories certain *library programs* … with more garden-variety class of library programs, you won't even have to know how to write a program. But you'd be missing a lot if you didn't' (p. 210; italics in original). The potential benefits of these systems were also tempered with a commentary that followed the article by Dr. John McCarthy (Stanford University), who cautions us by noting that: '[n]ot knowing how to program will be like living in a house full of servants and not speaking their language'.

AISs have made significant advances in a number of narrow domains (e.g., face and speech recognition, autocompletion; see Sze et al., 2017) leading to optimism for their application in consequential domains such as stock market predictions (Kara et al., 2011; Soni, 2011; Zhang & Wu, 2009) and healthcare delivery (Reddy et al., 2019; Yu et al., 2018). For instance, AISs were developed to predict which patients would develop respiratory symptoms during the COVID-19 pandemic (Jiang et al., 2020) as well as predicting their survival rate (Yan et al., 2020). Despite this promise, concerns have been raised regarding the efficacy of these systems and the methodologies used to assess them (see Box 2.1).

The specific technological affordances associated with AISs will ultimately vary depending on the type of approach that is adopted (e.g., 'deep neural networks', regressions, Bayesian approaches; Domingos, 2015). However, three general affordances define these systems: Intelligence, Autonomy, and Connectivity. In Gilmore's account of early computers, we can see that computers were *intelligent* in that they could perform many activities quickly, however they lacked the *autonomy*, which led to them not 'being very bright' unless they were told how to perform a task by the operator. These systems also have an element of *connectivity* with commands being sent to a central processing computer. These three features can also be used to evaluate contemporary AISs and allow us to better understand the social and ethical issues that are raised with their use and the extent to which we can or should trust them.

2.1 Technical Affordances of AISs: Intelligence, Autonomy, and Connectivity

AISs are likely one of the most complicated technological artifacts humans have created. For early pioneers such as Alan Turing, there were no upper limits to the abilities of machines: 'It is customary to offer a grain of comfort, in the form of a statement that some peculiarly human characteristic could never be imitated by a machine. I cannot offer any such comfort, for I believe that no such bounds can be set'. When judging the abilities of these systems, we need to identify criteria that allow us to assess their performance in comparison to humans. At a high level, we can consider how best to select the data and input used to develop these systems relative to the problem, the AI model, the task and output of the system, and the implementation context (e.g., OECD, 2021). However, by assessing the intelligence, autonomy, and connectivity of machines, we can establish a starting point for understanding the kind of agency that AISs can possess and how they can be judged from the standpoint of ethics.

2.1.1 Intelligence: Classification, Predictions, and Creativity

Computers and cognitive models of humans minds have often been mutually influential (Gigerenzer, 1991; Gigerenzer & Sturm, 2006; Leary, 1990). In human studies, two broad methods of categorization are frequently used to distinguish between types of AISs: their ability and their functionality. Ability can be understood in terms of the kind of intelligence: domain-specific (Narrow or Weak AI), domain-general (General or Strong AI), and super intelligence. The first kind of intelligence reflects *domain-specific* intelligence. These systems can learn, identify, and respond to patterns *within* a given domain such as text and speech perception, image processing, playing games (e.g., chess, Go, Jeopardy), and face recognition.

Domain-general intelligence reflects a theoretical ability for an AIS to operate *across* domains, just like humans. Abilities that define this kind of intelligence include abduction, analogical reasoning, creativity, imagination, and mental simulation. A key feature of general intelligence is that it can produce novel solutions to problems or identify novel problems. Although possible, there is persistent skepticism in terms of whether this kind of human-like intelligence is feasible in an AIS (e.g., Bringsjord, 1992; Larson, 2021; Moody, 1993; Penrose, 1989).

Finally, *artificial superintelligence* reflects the most speculative form of AISs. Such intelligence would vastly surpass human abilities (Bostrom, 2014). Much like some kinds of intelligence in nonhuman animals (e.g., Allen & Bekoff, 1999; Shettleworth, 2009), superintelligence might be *qualitatively* different in terms of the kinds of operations or patterns that it could detect. In an analogous way to the manner in which humans cannot see infrared or ultraviolet light unaided, humans would simply not be capable of understanding, monitoring, or regulating AISs due to a radical difference in speed, dimensionality, or representation.

Adopting distinctions based on human standards, anthropomorphizes AISs in a manner that might not be principled. For instance, these systems are often understood in terms of human cognitive processes such as 'attention', 'intelligence', 'memory', and 'learning'.[2] Rather than discrete processes, they instead reflect networks in the brain (e.g., connectome; Sporns, 2011) that are often defined by separable processes, such as distinct attentional networks (Fan et al., 2002) and learning systems for implicit and explicit learning (e.g., Ashby and O'Brien, 2005; Ashby et al., 2011). In humans, we must additionally acknowledge that these systems have emerged through stochastic evolutionary processes to process specific classes of stimuli within our environment, including social stimuli (e.g., Cosmides & Tooby, 2002; Gardner, 1983; Sperber, 1994; Mithen, 1996).

Rather than assuming that human-like intelligence is an appropriate standard, researchers have also adopted general biologically inspired models. Neural networks (including early perceptrons and connectionist networks) use neuron-like units[3] that are organized into layers, learn with feedback, and adjust the strength of connections between units. For instance, Kathleen Booth (Birkbeck College, 1958/ 1959) developed one of the first neural networks to simulate *animal* pattern recognition. More radical departures from human intelligence have also been considered. One widespread example is that of 'swarm intelligence'. Swarm intelligence has been used as the basis for operating collections of drones, using the dynamical patterns of behaviour for animals as varied as insects, birds, and fish as models (e.g., Ahmed & Glasgow, 2012; Bonabeau et al., 1999; Neshat et al., 2014; Sharkey, 2006).

From Champs to Chumps? Assessing the intelligence of an AIS requires selecting circumscribed domains, ones in which there are a finite number of outcomes that can be assessed to determine the relative accuracy of human and nonhuman agents. Consider chess. Chess is a complex game defined by 1044 possible legal moves (Simon & Schaeffer, 1992). Despite the vast problem space, chess can be used to examine expertise and problem-solving abilities because it is nevertheless a finite pattern recognition problem (Gobet & Simon, 1998; Gobet & Waters, 2003; Simon & Gilmartin, 1973). One player must identify their current position (state), their opponent's position (state), the set of the next probable moves for both players, and a set of possible steps (sub-goals) to take them from their current state to the goal state.

In chess, as well as other games, we find that AISs can defeat human players. A comparison of human and AIS chess players using expert performance ratings demonstrates that, over time, AISs have met and surpassed human players (Figure 2.1). AIS victories over human players such as IBM's Watson in *Jeopardy!* and Google's DeepMind AlphaGo in Go reflect more recent demonstrations of the intelligence of these systems. However, Watson's lackluster performance in the medical diagnostic context (Strickland, 2019), and general performance limitations of AISs during COVID-19 (see Box 2.1), demonstrate the need to moderate our expectations. Expert systems like Watson also face another barrier beyond the intelligence: the extent to which human's trust their abilities and accept their responses.

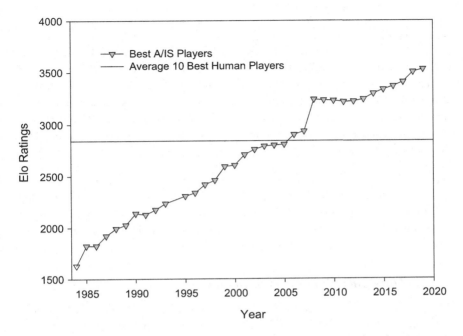

FIGURE 2.1 Annual performance of the best AIS compared to the 10 best human players of all time.

Note: Elo ratings are a measure of the relative skill of players in a zero-sum game. The Elo ratings system was developed to assess chess expertise. Human ratings obtained from www.chessmetrics.com/cm/CM2/PeakList.asp?Params=. AIS ratings obtained from https://wikivisually.com/wiki/Swedish_Chess_Computer_Association#cite_note-1

Despite the challenge of games like Go and chess, perhaps the ultimate challenge facing AISs is to understand humans. There is a long history of predicting human accuracy and response time using mathematical models, most notably psychophysics (e.g., Fechner, 1860/1964; Gescheider, 1997/2013).[4] Such early models, however, were focused on establishing lawful relationships between objective changes in the world and subjective experience, rather than explaining human behaviour (Schoenherr, 2020b). In contrast to the reasonable efficacy of these models, humans are comparatively poor judges of their own perceptual abilities, often being overconfident in novel domains (Kruger & Dunning, 1999) and underconfident in familiar domains (Koriat et al., 2002; Scheck & Nelson, 2005). These results have even been observed in expert domains such as medical decision-making (Millington et al., 2018; Schoenherr et al., 2018).

Similar results have been found in the prediction of human intentionality. For instance, Western participants, who are more likely to devalue the importance of contextual factors, assume that the individual is responsible for their actions (i.e., the fundamental attribution error; Gilbert & Malone, 1995; Krull et al., 1999).

Moreover, there can also be considerable inconsistency in the attitudes an individual expresses and the behaviours in which they engage (Glasman & Albarracin, 2006). In contrast, psychographic approaches attempt to identify reliable sets of variables that can predict human behaviour (Wells, 1975). In the context of human–computer interaction, small-scale demonstrations have revealed associations between personality traits and behavioural traces (e.g., keyboard and mouse movements, Khan et al., 2008; Saati et al., 2005; mobile phone use, de Oliveira et al., 2011), and extracts from conversations (Mairesse & Walker, 2006). With the introduction of 'big data' and AISs, psychographic profiling has been vastly improved. For instance, the patterns of likes on Facebook were able to predict intelligence and sexual orientation even when users did not explicitly associate themselves with these social networks (Kosinski et al., 2013). Subsequent studies have also provided evidence that AISs can be more accurate at making these predictions than friends (Youyou et al., 2015). At least in some domains, AISs might be capable of providing effective predictive models of human behaviour.

2.1.2 Autonomy: Computers as Agents

As machines become progressively more intelligent, we can grant them greater autonomy and responsibility. We can allow them to remind us of important events, pay bills, compute our taxes, drive cars, and detect malicious software and websites. Autonomy reflects a general problem associated with technology, rather than one associated with AISs. For instance, Greek mythology presents a variety of examples such as the bronze giant Talos that was forged by Hephaestus (Mayor, 2020), whereas the Jewish myth of the Golem presents a creature animated from clay that is 'a passive servant laboring for its master [and] a threatening and ominous figure' (Cooper, 2017; also see Rosenberg, 2008). Consequently, we must consider a principled means to determine how, when, and where to trust them (Lee & See, 2004; Sholes, 2007).

Role-Based Autonomy Models. Early frameworks often considered the roles that would define human and computer interactions. An early such account was provided by Sheridan and Verplanck (1978). They note that a computer can *extend* a human operator's ability, *relieve* the human operator allowing them to allocate their attention to other tasks, *back-up* the operator to avoid error (or bias), or *replace* the human operator. Roles have also been defined in terms of the extent to which humans are 'in the loop', i.e., human-in-the-loop, human-on-the-loop, and human-out-of-the-loop. These relationships can be understood in terms of the role of humans in actively monitoring and regulating the activities of AISs. A human-in-the-loop relational model assumes that humans have the highest degree of control (Dautenhahn, 1998). In this case, no matter how intelligent they might be, AISs are not intended to have full autonomy. For instance, robot-assisted surgery allows physicians to perform complex procedures with greater precision, flexibility, and control, for example, minimally invasive procedures (Barbash, 2010). Nevertheless, unless the system malfunctions, a physician still retains control over each step in the procedure (Yang et al., 2017).

When human involvement is minimal, AISs act as a supervisor and intervene when the operations of a system deviate from the expectations of the operator, i.e., humans-on-the-loop (HOTL). The HOTL relational model assumes that comparative strengths of human and nonhuman agents can be combined when performing a task with a reasonable degree of responsibility conferred onto an AIS. More extreme levels of autonomy grant an AIS full autonomy, placing humans out of the loop (HOOTL). These approaches already influence system design, such as adaptive cruise control and lane-centre steering in transportation and scheduled scans and real-time protection in anti-virus/firewall software (e.g., Schirner et al., 2013).

Dimension-Based Autonomy Models. Like intelligence, autonomy is not an all-or-none concept. Rather, it reflects a continuum of control relative to a domain, wherein we need to determine whether an agent (human or nonhuman) has the competencies to perform a specific task. To that end, we must assess the relative intelligence, complexity, and consequentiality of the task relative to an AIS's abilities to determine whether we should trust an agent.

Most existing autonomy frameworks are defined along a single continuum based on the decreased involvement of humans. For instance, an early scale of autonomy proposed 10 distinct levels from no computer assistance to full autonomy, wherein the system 'ignores the human' (Wickens et al., 1998). In contrast, the U.S. National Highway Traffic Safety Administration defines four levels, allowing the vehicle to (1) perform one or more control functions, (2) perform a combination of control functions with the driver, (3) having the ability to take control at any time or a limited time, or (4) with full self-driving capabilities where there are longer lags required to assume control (e.g., Goodall, 2014).

In a more recent unidimensional approach, the Society of Automotive Engineers (SAE) International has developed a 6-Level driving automation feature scale (SAE J3016™) that suggests a dichotomy between driver support features wherein a vehicle merely assists the driver (Levels 0 to 2) and automated driving wherein a vehicle can drive autonomously under most or all conditions (Levels 3 to 5).[5] Similar frameworks have also been developed in the context of healthcare delivery (see Table 2.1; Yang et al., 2017). For instance, at the lowest level of autonomy, an AIS might mediate the interaction between a patient and a clinician, however the clinician has direct control over the system. In contrast, progressively higher levels of autonomy are granted as we delegate pattern recognition, facets of a procedure, and strategy selection to these systems.

Multidimensional and Multifactorial Autonomy Models. Autonomy also requires considering the interaction between humans, AISs, and their environments. Consider AISs such as unmanned aerial vehicles (UAVs) and autonomous weapons systems (AWS). In certain situations, autonomy might not be desirable due to the potential consequences of failure such as if an AWS misidentifies a target and kills innocent civilians. In other situations, autonomy might not simply be desirable but a required feature of a system. In environments that make communication difficult (e.g., where solids and fluids can interfere with the propagation of signals), AISs *must* be designed to be relatively autonomous. For instance, UAVs must have

TABLE 2.1 Levels of Autonomy in Healthcare Devices

Autonomy Level	Description
Level 0: No Autonomy	Human operator has direct remote control over system.
Level 1: Robot Assistance	Minimal assistance provided for guidance, movement, and identification to facilitate activities of human operator.
Level 2: Task Autonomy	Specific tasks in a procedure are delegated to a system by human operator.
Level 3: Conditional Autonomy	Strategies for task completion are identified by system and provided to human operator.
Level 4: High Autonomy	Decisions and responses are made by system with supervision of human operator.
Level 5: Full Autonomy	Entire process of pattern recognition, strategy identification, and response selection is performed by a system with human operators receiving.

Source: Adapted from Yang et al. (2017).

some degree of autonomy to adjust to local conditions that might give rise to disruptions in communications with a human operator. Similarly, events can occur with sufficient speed such that they are beyond an operator's response threshold. For instance, if a vehicle identifies pedestrians who have illegally crossed a road, sending a signal to a human driver and waiting for their response could result in the pedestrians' deaths. As operational autonomy increases, so do the requirements of ethical autonomy, so much so that these systems need a form of ethical regulation (Section 6.2.1).

One of the more influential models of autonomy was provided by Parasuraman and colleagues (Parasuraman et al., 1993; Parasuraman & Riley, 1997; Parasuraman et al., 2000). Rather than viewing autonomy as an all-or-none feature of human–computer interaction, they consider autonomy in terms of four processes: information acquisition, information analysis, decision and action selection, and action implementation. System designers must then select the degree of autonomy that a system should have relative to the human operator in performing each of these tasks. This then requires consideration as to how automation affects the complacency, mental workload, situational awareness, and skill degradation of human operators as well as the reliability of the system and the consequences of automation.

More recently, Huang and colleagues (Huang et al., 2005; Huang, 2006; Huang et al., 2007) developed the Contextual Autonomous Capability for Unmanned Systems Model. The model consists of three dimensions, including mission complexity, environmental complexity, and human independence. Mission complexity is defined by such factors as the number and variety of subtasks, the number of times a decision will need to be made (i.e., decision points), the degree of collaboration and coordination required, and the situational awareness required of

BOX 2.1 THE DOCTOR IS OUT? AIS PERFORMANCE DURING THE PANDEMIC

The pandemic caused by the novel coronavirus (SARS CoV-2 – COVID-19) presents a stress-test for the application of AISs. Over the years, evidence has mounted that algorithm and statistical forms of prediction can be as effective, or more effective under some conditions, relative to human diagnosticians (Grove et al., 2000; Meehl, 1954). While medical expertise includes the ability to communicate and collaborate with other healthcare professionals, patients, and guardians (i.e., collective competence), arguably the most mportant features are pattern recognition and decision-making (Norman et al., 2018). Consequently, AISs have been an increasing focus of consideration and concern in healthcare delivery, including counseling, diagnosis, and treatment (e.g., Jiang et al., 2017; Yu et al., 2018). However, there is only limited success (Kandula & Sharman, 2019; Lazer et al., 2014; Lee et al., 2018; Somashekhar et al., 2017), users remain resistant to its use in specific circumstances (Longoni et al., 2019; Ross, 2017) and it introduces numerous legal and ethical issues (Rigby, 2019; Schoenherr, 2021c; World Health Organization, 2021).

During the pandemic, hundreds of such tools were marshaled. Three broad reviews (von Borzyskowski et al., 2021; Roberts et al., 2021; Wynants et al., 2020) reached the same consensus: the tools were largely ineffective at providing insight or managing the clinical cases associated with COVID-19. For instance, following an assessment of 232 prediction models, Wynants et al. (2020) concluded that 'almost all published prediction models are poorly reported, and at high risk of bias such that their reported predictive performance is probably optimistic' (p. 2). However, when viewed in the light of evolutionary theory, the failure of numerous variants is not surprising. Instead, it suggests that we must have more modest expectations and view the potential of these systems with healthy skepticism.

Instead of assuming that AISs should be autonomous, it is likely the case that we should identify more effective means of collaboration as the combination of human and nonhuman competencies might prove effective (Schoenherr, 2021c). Supporting this, Wang et al. (2016) developed a deep learning system to identify the presence or absence of metastatic breast cancer and compared it to expert responses. The system was assessed in terms of its performance on slide-based classification (whether cancer was present or absent) as well as lesion-based detection (whether all lesions within the slide could be detected while maintaining a low number of false-positives). When examined separately, the human experts marginally outperformed the AIS in both the slide classification task (0.966 > 0.925) and lesion detection task (0.733 > 0.7051). However, when combining the predictions of the pathologist with the results of the deep learning system, diagnostic accuracy increased further (0.995). Although the change might appear small (Δ0.07), this reflects a reduction in pathologist diagnostic error from 3.4% to 0.52%. Results such as these demonstrate that humans will continue to have a role in complex decision-making tasks for the foreseeable future. Inasmuch as teamwork can be effective when we maintain accurate knowledge of others' abilities (i.e., transactive memory; Wegner, 1987; Wegner et al., 1991), human–AIS interaction must come to be defined in terms of understanding the competencies and capabilities of AISs and humans within a given domain.

the system. In contrast, environmental complexity reflects the static and dynamic features of the environment, the degree of noise (e.g., weather, electromagnetic), urban or rural conditions, and the operational environment (e.g., enemy fire, presence of decoys and civilians). Finally, human independence is defined by the extent to which an operator must intervene, the workload of the operator as well as their skill level.

Discussions of autonomy raise important concerns about the nature and extent of trust that we can place in these systems. Even if a system is intelligent and can act autonomously, humans might fail to effectively interact with the system due to a lack of trust, leading to algorithmic aversion. For instance, repeated nudges from a user's PC to update software might be disregarded due to an inability to understand why these updates are required, or could be viewed cynically if users believe that updates to privacy policies might change how their data are used.

2.1.3   Connectivity: Trust and Distributed Processing

Implicit in discussions of AIS intelligence and autonomy is a third technical affordance: connectivity. Interconnectivity is a fundamental feature of human intelligence (i.e., the connectome; Sporns, 2011). A key feature of early neural networks (i.e., connectionist networks) was parallel distributed processing (PDP; McClelland, Rumelhart, and the PDP Group, 1988; Rumelhart et al., 1986). PDPs require multiple layers of units that are activated in parallel (e.g., levels related to basic perceptual features, letters, and words). As Gilmore's (1967) account of early computing in the Introduction suggests, distributed process has been a feature of the earliest computer systems, the definitive characteristic of the Internet (Leiner et al., 2003/2009), and ubiquitous distributed storage and processing, referred to as 'cloud computing' (e.g., Wang et al., 2010).

Connectivity is also embodied in the Internet of Things (IoT). The IoT reflects the distributed network of devices (e.g., smart phones, smart homes, security cameras, etc.) that are connected via the Internet. They allow people to remotely adjust the temperature of their house from their mobile phone or check on their pets when they are on an international trip. Despite their convenience, these systems also create security vulnerabilities: unscrupulous individuals could use the recorded videos or metadata to monitor an occupant's behaviour. On a larger scale, these concerns are also relevant for industrial control systems (ICS)[6] used for manufacturing and critical infrastructure (e.g., power plants) and smart cities defined by sensors (e.g., CCTV cameras) and control systems (e.g., traffic lights; see Section 3.7). In the case of ICS, these systems often use old operating systems that were not designed to be integrated with a network and could be easily exploited.

Beyond ICS and smart cities, drone swarms represented another form of connectivity. In a drone swarm, each individual drone performs its function independently while coordinating all their activities collectively. For instance, in the context of search and rescue, a set of drones could be released in an area, each searching a specific grid while sharing information (e.g., weather conditions, environmental features). In military applications, a collection of relatively inexpensive drones might be able to overwhelm a target by its sheer number, exceeding the human ability to respond (Section 3.8).

Whether in terms of cloud computing, ICS, or drone swarms, connectivity necessitates trust. Systems must trust the source and the integrity of the information. Humans must trust that they can distribute responsibility between their cognitive processes and those of artificial agents. However, trust can ultimately be misplaced and exploited. Consequently, the dimensions of intelligence, autonomy, and connectivity must be examined, along with our knowledge and goals, to determine the nature and extent of trust.

2.2   The Mechanical Turk: Inside the Black Box

Despite the increasing accuracy of AISs in performing both simple and complex tasks, concerns have started to grow in terms of *how* these systems solve problems. Both the intelligence and trustworthiness of these systems have been a repeated focus of debate. In addition to concerns over who has the power to access data and make decisions (e.g., Bucher, 2018; Crawford, 2021), the risks of allowing AISs to operate autonomously also loom large. For instance, accidents involving self-driving vehicles have been prominent in the media (Bogost, 2018; Greenemeier, 2016; Klein, 2016), leading to the creation of specific report mechanisms by the Department of Motor Vehicles in the US to monitor their failures (Department of Motor Vehicles, 2020) and public concern. For instance, the American Automotive Association's annual survey (AAA, 2021) found that only 14% of respondents would trust riding in autonomous vehicles, with the majority indicating that they were either unsure (32%) or afraid of riding in an autonomous vehicle (54%).

2.2.1   *Data and Design*

AIS development reflects a multi-stage interactive process that requires defining a problem, selecting data for training and testing, choosing an appropriate algorithm, and comparing its results to a standard. For instance, Domingos (2012) describes learning as selecting a *representation* of the problem in terms of an algorithm (e.g., decision trees, neural networks, propositional rules, regression), selecting an *evaluation function* to assess the performance of an algorithm (e.g., cost/utility, likelihood, accuracy/error rate), and *optimization* by selecting from among the available functions (e.g., gradient descent, linear programming; see Figure 2.2).

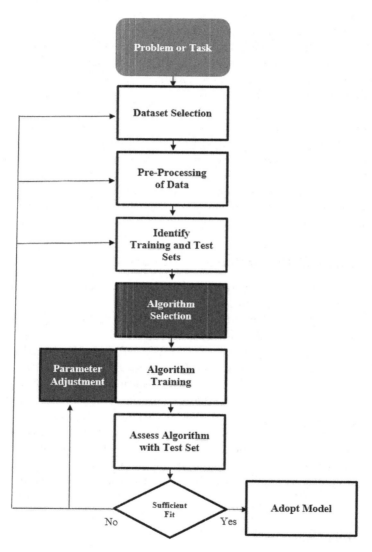

FIGURE 2.2 Main decision-points in the design process for a supervised learning algorithm.

Source: Adapted from Ayodele (2010).

Even if AISs are complicated and require vast amounts of data, many of the problems that define their use are old. A number of these issues relate to data integrity and construct validity, which reflect concerns of scientific integrity in the physical, social, and data sciences. For instance, Friedman and Nissenbaum (1996) identified three potential biases that can affect AISs: pre-existing biases within the data set, technical biases, and emergent bias. They note that '[p]reexisting bias has its roots in social institutions, practices, and attitudes. Technical bias arises from technical constraints or considerations. Emergent bias arises in a context of use' (p. 332). Acknowledging that emergent biases can occur after development and during implementation is critical for an ethics of AISs, in that systems can be developed in one context and used in another, leading to unforeseen consequences.

Construct Validity. The quip that there are 'lies, damn lies, and statistics'[7] reflects a misunderstanding of how meaning is imbued in numbers and how numbers create meaning. When we use numbers, there is (hopefully) a lengthy decision-making process concealed within 1s and 0s. That meaning is always relative to how they were assigned to objects or events within the world. A basic assumption of classical measurement theory is that our data is defined by three sets of factors: the true score, bias, and random error. The *true score* represents the actual performance of an individual or object in an ideal state. In contrast, bias represents factors such as individual response biases (e.g., personality, information processing strategies, application use), instrument bias (e.g., miscalibration), as well as biases that might be attributed to the physical, social, or virtual environment (e.g., environmental stressors, disaffordances of design). Finally, there is also the possibility that, once all biases have been accounted for, there are still truly random errors that reflects idiosyncratic features of a measurement context.

Understanding the nature of a 'true score' requires that we clearly define the construct (phenomenon) we are trying to study, for example facial recognition, consumer behaviour, combat capabilities, credit worthiness, or diagnostic accuracy. Demonstrating construct validity is a perennial task in all sciences. Researchers must question whether they have clearly defined a construct, operationalized that construct in such a manner that they can create testable hypotheses, and examined their data to determine whether their hypotheses are supported. The quality, quantity, and diversity of evidence can then be used to make a validity argument. In this way, researchers must constantly make value decisions in terms of what to include in their design and measurements (Messick, 1995) and must not assume that merely having quantitative evidence proves their argument (e.g., Quantitative Fallacy; Box 4.1). As K. C. Cole notes, 'One person's data is another person's noise'. However, these arguments are always relative to the context (Kane, 1992) and can be misinterpreted or misrepresented through the process of knowledge translation (Schoenherr & Hamstra, 2016).

Consider a credit score. To be valid, a credit score must reflect 'creditworthiness'. Creditworthiness would typically be defined in terms of the likelihood that an individual would not default on a loan repayment provided by a lender. Developers of the score could assess the borrower's past ability to repay a loan as a predictor of future payments as well as information from other individuals who were in similar circumstances. But what makes an individual *worthy* of credit? This approach leaves unexamined *why* an individual was unable to repay a loan in the past and might not critically evaluate whether specific variables (e.g., sex/gender, race/ethnicity, socioeconomic status) introduce bias into understanding the true creditworthiness of an individual. A credit score might be developed in a particular context as a pragmatic tool (i.e., to allocate finite resources) but if this is used by other actors or overgeneralized, we can no longer claim that the score has validity.

Assessing the Accuracy of AISs: A Fitting Conclusion. When we attempt to ascertain the validity of a model, a straightforward means is to assess how the behaviour of our model matches data obtained from the real world. Philosophers have often highlighted an issue embedded within the process of induction as we progress from data to theory (e.g., Goodman, 1955; Hume, 1748; Quine, 1951). To understand this problem, consider the three data points in Figure 2.3. How should all three points be connected?

At first, we might adopt a familiar approach and connect all the points together with three lines, 'A' (Figure 2.4). The relationships are clear and straightforward. Alternatively, we might introduce another criterion: use the shortest lines possible. In this case, we now have a different relationship, 'B'. Crucially, this second pattern also is clear and straightforward. Finally, we might develop a theory that suggests a more complicated relationship between the entities we have observed and those we have yet to observe. One such relationship is 'C'. Despite being a decidedly more complex pattern, it might be preferred due to bold predictions.

FIGURE 2.3 Graphical representation of three data points obtained in a hypothetical experiment.

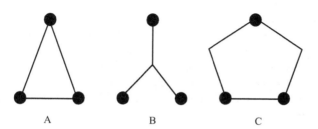

A　　　　　　　　B　　　　　　　　C

FIGURE 2.4 Graphic representation of the underdetermination of theory by data.

Note: Three data points can be connected in multiple ways. Three possible relational structures are shown.

In the philosophy of science, this problem is referred to as 'underdetermination of theory by data'. For Duhem (1954) and Quine (1951), the underdetermination hypothesis assumes that multiple (equally valid) theories can be provided to account for data. This might seem like an esoteric issue, but it raises problems for AISs. Namely, model developers are often satisfied that their model fits the data and can perform a task without conducting empirical research to observe if better fits are available. In some cases, additional data can help us eliminate erroneous hypotheses, given that some solutions that initially appeared to account for the pattern of data are simply wrong. By selecting the simplest explanation, we can also eliminate models and theories that are unnecessarily complex, i.e., an eliminative strategy. Similarly, the introduction of constraints can reduce the number of possible solutions that are assessed. However, multiple models might remain available to us. Consequently, although there might be trade-offs between functionality and social and ethical issues, we can imagine many possible solutions in the problem space for any task, with a smaller subset of these satisfying the requirements of ethical design.

Model developers are often only concerned with 'fit', given a particular data set. Measurements of 'fit' require their own justification and the context in which we are assessing 'fit'. For instance, if we are developing a model using a particular training set, we might seek to identify one that fits these data points with the highest degree of accuracy. Indeed, we could simply introduce parameters until we perfectly fit the data, but in the process we fail to generalize to other results, i.e., overfitting.[8] Like making a shoe that perfectly fits one customer's foot (e.g., men's size 15), we might disadvantage others in the process (i.e., everybody else!), thus demonstrating that a model fit does not in itself validate a model, rather the nature of the data (e.g., population, variance, sample size), how fit is measured, and the theoretical importance of the parameters and variables must also be taken into account (e.g., Barrett, 2007; Hayduk et al., 2007; Kenny et al., 2015; Yuan, 2005; see Appendix for a simplified discussion in the context of regression).

Understanding the error rate and how it translates into the operations of a system must be accounted for when assessing the reliability and trustworthiness of AISs. At a basic level, error rates increase as a function of the length of the program: the longer the program, the more errors will be present (Royce, 1970). Providing evidence to support this claim, an early study by Hatton (1997) obtained results that were 'fascinating and deeply disturbing' (p. 24) in that the more computation that was required using statistical packages, the more errors were present in the data set. In a recent meta-analysis, Horner and Symons (2019) examined 11 frequently cited studies of error rates. They found that the average error rates obtained in each of these studies varied from a low of 0.005 to a high of 0.03. Thankfully, there are numerous available methods that can be used to detect biases and errors (Symons & Alvarado, 2016; Symons & Horner, 2020).

Errors must also be contextualized. The failure of an autonomous mobile robot (AMR) to select the appropriate products for a shipment from the warehouse significantly differs from a UAV firing on a non-target or the collision of a self-driving vehicle with a pedestrian or other vehicles. A failure to optimally select a product differs from a failure to detect a virus or the loss of life associated with the use of lethal force. In that AISs are not aware of the qualitative differences in the nature of these errors, designers and developers must determine the fault and defect tolerance of their hardware and software systems relative to the properties of the system and the tasks that are being performed (e.g., Albert et al., 2000; Breuer et al., 2004; Torres-Huitzil & Girau, 2017).

Data: Missing, Poisoned, and Blackened. Discussions of model fitting also highlight the importance of data integrity. For some, data is the new oil. Unlike oil, it can be used and reused. Like oil, it can contain impurities in terms of errors and biases. In her review of the effects of algorithms on selection, Eubanks (2018) notes that some estimates suggest that as many as 4% of cases of child abuse are malicious, i.e., made in bad faith to erroneously create issues for the parents (Trocmé et al., 1998). Similar results have also been observed for allegations of sexual assault (e.g., estimates vary between 2% to 10%; Heenan & Murray, 2006; Lisak et al., 2010; Lonsway et al., 2009).[9] If data is used in the absence of accounting for these biases it can produce erroneous recommendations, fail to allocate appropriate resources, violate individual rights, and fail to identify and support actual victims.

In addition to errors of commission, errors of omission are equally, if not more, problematic. Failure to provide social services to those in need, denial of loans to applicants, failure to detect potential offenders within a population, and denial of admission into university programs are equally concerning as they may reinforce existing biases (Eubanks, 2018; Ferguson, 2019; O'Neil, 2016). For instance, failure to report physical and mental abuse, discrimination, and harassment that might result from social norms or institutions misrepresents the actual prevalence of these events. Within the sciences, there has long been recognition of the 'file drawer problem'. The file drawer problem arises when researchers have data but have not, or cannot, publish that data due to failures to replicate previous research (Rosenthal, 1979). Similarly, if individuals are afforded the ability to modify or delete their records, this might also create data integrity issues (e.g., healthcare; Schoenherr, 2021c, submitted b).

Omission errors are particularly troubling when evaluating algorithmic bias and discrimination. Data sets can be biased due to past inequalities and perpetuate injustice (e.g., Chander, 2016; Eubanks, 2018; Mohamed et al., 2020; Noble, 2018). Recent studies trained AISs using word embeddings (using the context that the word is located within) and found that they were able to replicate human-like biases (Bolukbasi et al., 2016; Caliskan et al., 2017). Similarly, many data sets and commercially available AISs used for facial classification have demonstrated racial biases. For instance, Buolamwini and Gebru (2018) have found that the error rate increased with darkening skin tone from 20.8% to 34.7% with some systems making over 46% errors, i.e., chance performance.[10] Crucially, the authors propose the development of novel data sets that directly address these biases (see also Chawla et al., 2002; Sengupta et al., 2018).

Although many errors are likely unsystematic and unintentional, erroneous entries can also be deliberate, i.e., data poisoning (Joseph et al., 2013). By intentionally including erroneous data, models trained on these data sets will produce more errors or biases in pattern classification or recommendations. In that individuals, organizations, and governments might not always be fully transparent or forthcoming with data, or selectively present data that supports their policies and practices, this missing data represents a major concern for the validity of AISs. Consequently, data collection and mining practices must be critically evaluated prior to using data sets in model construction (Barocas & Selbst, 2016).

A growing number of AISs have been developed with, and use, data that is proprietary or otherwise restricted due to concerns of confidentiality or national security. For instance, 'blacklists' such as 'no-fly lists' and 'watch lists' are often defined by undisclosed criteria (e.g., Siegel, 2015). Where the properties of these data sets can neither be verified nor reviewed, they reflect 'black data'. In the case of predictive policing, Ferguson (2019) notes that there is substantial discretionary ability in intake procedures, with the reliance on algorithms creating self-confirmatory loops that can discriminate against groups of individuals, for example, African Americans. Similar observations have been made for the granting of loans (Eubanks, 2018) and insider threat detection methods (Schoenherr & Thomson, 2020b). Consequently, it is not clear whether the outputs of these algorithms provide valid assessments of the constructs that they purport to measure.

Even if there is a strong, reliable association between variables, other variables that are not directly assessed might account for this pattern. For instance, Eubanks (2018) notes that the variables used to assess child mistreatment, are also indicators of poverty. Such variables might remain unrecorded in the data set (a 'third variable') or might simply remain unlabelled, i.e., latent variables (Bollen, 1989). Simply removing variables to eliminate patterns of discrimination is not only ineffective but also counterproductive. Statistical discrimination occurs when omitted variables influence analysis indirectly through proxy variables (e.g., intercorrelation between variables that are still present in the data); failing to account for them can greatly influence results (e.g., Pope & Sydnor, 2011). When included in an algorithm, these variables can mediate the relationship between other variables, thereby increasing or decreasing the importance of the variable in predictive outcomes (Shrout & Bolger, 2002).

Data collection practices must also be considered. A key principle of data collection in research is *consent*, i.e., a participant, patient, or data subject must understand how their data will be collected, processed, stored, and used and agree to this process. Informed consent is a key requirement in the behavioural sciences such as psychology, sociology, and behavioural economics. Not all behavioural data falls within the scope of academic research. Outside of research, vast data lakes have formed within organizations and institutions that contain personal information. These data sets constitute 'grey data'. In the academia, Borgman (2018) has defined grey data as information that is collected, stored, and used while not necessarily being subject to formal governance mechanisms or peer review. For instance, student records can contain information including demographic identifiers, courses they have taken, their performance, tuitions fees, salary information, and academic misconduct. As universities shift from 'offline data' to 'online data', the value of these data sets increases as they can be aggregated and rendered more readily accessible. However, this interoperability and accessibility brings with it risks to individual autonomy, privacy, and security as more individual can conceivably have a greater understanding of the attitudes, interests, and the competencies of the learner (Section 5.3). Such concerns reflect general issues associated with dataveillance (e.g., Clarke, 1988; Van Dijck, 2014) as well as the collection of behavioural traces through websites and social media (Zuboff, 2019).

Black Boxes and AISs: Transparency and Explainability. In his novel, Heinlein (1966) admonishes us: 'Don't explain computers to laymen. Simpler to explain sex to a virgin'. Many contemporary discussions of ethical AISs design have focused on the concepts of transparency and explainability. Rather than a black box, *transparency* has been invoked as a necessary feature of AISs. Transparency generally reflects that the data sets used for training and testing, algorithms that make recommendations and predictions, and their output are made available to stakeholders. By adopting a transparency criterion, we tacitly assume that stakeholders *can* understand these systems *if only* the processes were presented to them. However, transparency is not a *de facto* solution to understanding a system without further qualification (Ananny & Crawford, 2016; Crain, 2018). Rather than transparency, Burrell (2016) presents an alternative typology based on *opacity*. Opacity is defined in terms of AIS features and their complexity or scale, the proprietary nature of the AIS and the desire to limit access to information, and technical illiteracy.

Burrell's notion of technical illiteracy can also be understood in terms of *explainability*, and the goal of creating explainable artificial intelligence (XAI; Goebel et al., 2018; Gunning, 2016; Vilone & Longo, 2020). Explainability can be contrasted against other criteria. Schoenherr (2020b; Thomson & Schoenherr, 2020) has suggested that we should distinguish between three facets of understanding: interpretability, explainability, and believability. *Interpretability* implies that individuals can describe the relationship between the input and output of a system: when provided with input values, one should be able to predict output values. However, this in no way suggests that someone can explain *why* the prediction occurs. To say that heart disease is associated with smoking does not suggest why the two are related. In the early history of psychology, the area of psychophysics attempted to understand perceptual processes in terms of mathematical models but was not concerned with relating model parameters to cognitive or neurological phenomena (Schoenherr, 2020b). An explanation must relate features of a phenomenon (e.g., codes and functions of AISs) to an individual's prior knowledge. This creates a need to understand what an individual knows in order to offer an explanation.

Many kinds of explanations are possible (Keil & Wilson, 2000). Explanations can be intentional (e.g., anthropomorphizing), functional (e.g., functions of a system), and physical (e.g., physical, chemical laws; Dennett, 1987; for a more comprehensive list, see Table 2.2).

Depending on the goals and the stakeholder familiarity with AISs, we might choose to adopt a different explanatory framework. For instance, we might use an

TABLE 2.2 Selected Explanation Types and AISs Examples

Type of Explanation	Description and General Form	Example
Causal/ Mechanical	Provides a causal relationship between objects, entities, and events, e.g., A caused B to do X.	The vehicle failed to arrive at the desired location due to a loss of the GPS signal.
Historical	Past events are used to explain the outcomes of current events, e.g., Event X led to Event A.	Facial recognition software misidentified the face of an Asian user because the data set was biased.
Reductive	Complex phenomena are explained with basic properties of a system, e.g., System Feature X caused outcome A.	A failure to update the database resulted in a failure to accurately predict the prevalence of the flu.
Formal or Mathematical	Formal principles within an epistemological framework (esp. mathematics) are used to explain outcomes, e.g., a occurred because of x because A occurs because of X.	The noise within the data set exceeded a critical threshold leading to more prediction errors.
Macro to Micro	A macro-level phenomenon is used to explain a micro-level phenomenon, e.g., Situation A is like Situation X.	Biases in a data set reflect biases within society.
Functional/ Teleological	The function or goal of an object, entity, or events is used to explain outcomes, e.g., X was designed to do A.	The UAV attacked the civilian vehicle because it misidentified it as a target.
Subsumption	Invokes ontological categories of an object, entity, or event, e.g., x is an exemplar of X.	The AI failed to predict the weather because Bayesian models are vulnerable to prediction errors.
Intentional	Invokes motivations, intentions, and beliefs, e.g., A wanted to do X.	The self-driving vehicle wanted to avoid the pedestrian.

Source: Adapted from unpublished manuscript.

intentional explanation when stakeholders have little knowledge of systems design but want to have a basic understanding of why an AIS performed a certain action, for example, the drone *wanted* to avoid a collision and moved away from the flock of birds. Alternatively, stakeholders might want to understand the operation of a system to compare it to a set of functions, for example, a self-driving car crashed into another due to a malfunction in the object recognition system. Finally, stakeholders might possess extensive background knowledge, allowing them to use specific principles, for example, a gradient descent function was used to select the best model due to its relative robustness and simplicity in comparison to other optimization methods.

Interpretability and explainability can be further distinguished from *believability*. Believability reflects the certainty that one has in an explanation, regardless of its accuracy. While telling someone that 'the computer thinks you're sad based on your eye movement patterns' might make things intelligible to a stakeholder, they might nevertheless reject it as unbelievable due their belief that computers cannot 'think' or 'feel' like humans. Similarly, despite having minimal knowledge of the operations of anti-virus software or privacy policy, a user might simply believe that a system or their personal information is secure. Thus, believability likely reflects the user's trust and confidence in the system based on its alignment with their prior beliefs. Supporting this, Schoenherr and Thomson (2021b) found that participants disregarded the validity of an explanation of natural phenomena and focused on the believability of the explanations, with mechanistic explanations appearing to be more believable than intentional explanations, leading to higher accuracy and overconfidence bias.

Multiple kinds of explanations can be provided for any phenomenon. A question of clear importance to developing XAI is whether participants prefer simple or complex explanations when they are presented concurrently. When making judgments of prior probability (i.e., the probability of an event, $p(E)$), people appear to prefer simple explanations. In contrast, when making judgments about the likelihood (i.e., the probability of an event, given evidence, $p(e|E)$), people appear to prefer complex explanations (Lombrozo, 2007). Moreover, although simplicity is frequently preferred for deterministic systems, this bias is reduced for stochastic systems (Johnson et al., 2019). Along with explanation type, these findings should be used to inform XAI by considering how the underlying problem-solving task (e.g., predicting recidivism, creditworthiness, malware presence) and AIS architecture (e.g., deep neural network, regression) are described to stakeholders.

While XAI is a neologism, explainability reflects one of the earliest issues in scientific model and theory development (Hempel & Oppenheim, 1948; Salmon, 1989; Strevens, 2008). With the early introduction of computer-mediated healthcare systems, Gobry (1973) highlighted the importance of making the decision-making process transparent to physicians by using symbolic communication and natural language. An expert system, MYCIN, reflects the first attempt to implement an AIS that meets these requirements in medical consultations (Fagan et al., 1980; Shortliffe, 1976). The symbolic processing techniques used by MYCIN were adopted 'in order to be accepted by physicians, [and] should be able to explain how and why a particular conclusion has been derived' (Shortliffe, 1976). For Shortliffe, acceptance (believability) requires a degree of explainability.

The need for explainability becomes clear when we consider the architectures of AISs. Not all machine-learning algorithms are simple or constrained by the requirement of symbolic representation and interpretation (e.g., Domingos, 2015; Shalev-Shwartz & Ben-David, 2014). A prominent class of AISs inspired by neuroanatomy and neuronal function illustrate this quite clearly, i.e., neural networks and connectionist models. The first neural-inspired system (Mark I Perceptron) was a physical machine, that used wired connections between input and output layers, with each layer defined by a set of units (see Figure 2.5; Rosenblatt, 1958). Input and output layers were seen as analogous to sensory and response processes, respectively. When presented with input repeatedly, the system makes a choice and is provided with feedback, with connection strengths adjusted afterward. Over time,

FIGURE 2.5 Close-up of lower section of Mark I Perceptron at the Cornell Aeronautical Laboratory.

Note: Input (left) and output layers (right) are connected by wires.

Source: Credit: Cornell University News Service records, #4-3-15. Division of Rare and Manuscript Collections, Cornell University Library.

this process creates a response algorithm wherein an input pattern is mapped onto a response pattern, for example, if units 3, 7, and 10 are activated, the system indicates that the input is the word 'cat'.

The performance of these systems was greatly enhanced with the introduction of intermediate layers of units. However, with enough units and 'hidden layers', the AIS becomes a black box. In contrast to input and output layers that were seen as analogous to sensory and motor systems, hidden layers were taken as analogous to cortical and subcortical processes that constituted most information processing in human and nonhuman animals. The comparative advantage of such systems is that they could engage in parallel, distributed processing with multiple low- and high-level operations occurring simultaneously (McClelland, Rumelhart and the PDP Research Group, 1986). Crucially, unlike symbolic processing, meaning is embedded within the connections as a whole and not immediately apparent when connections are examined.

As many of these black box algorithms can significantly influence real-world choices, the need for explainability becomes crucial to determining where and when we should trust AISs. Consider online shopping. The results of searches within shopping platforms ostensibly provide the consumer with items that are the most relevant to their preferences and interests. However, online retailers can alter these algorithms to bias search results. Along these lines, early concerns with these systems often focused on the customization of ads and prices based on consumer behaviour and profiles (e.g., Clerides, 2004; Garbarino & Lee, 2003), with these issues being repeatedly discussed in the news media (Angwin & Mattu, 2016; Mattioli, 2019), most notably with Google (Winkler & Mullins, 2015). Despite its denials, Google was fined $2 billion and given 90 days to end these search practices, which were defined as illegal under EU antitrust rules (Scott, 2017). Consumers share these concerns, with a study by Turow et al. (2005) finding that 46% of the individuals surveyed believed it was bad for websites to alter product suggestions provided to consumers based on their personal information. More recently, Mattioli (2019) notes that these algorithms can be exploited to increase the seller's own preferred products rather than providing the most relevant results based on a user's search criteria.

2.3 Innovation and the Evolution of Science and Technology

The concepts of black box algorithms and black data highlight an increasing problem with AISs. As the complexity of a system increases, so does the difficulty in understanding its operations (Arbesman, 2016). Crucially, while we often think of innovations as the product of reflective design, technological evolution can be understood in terms of a stochastic process of natural selection coupled with artificial selection by human stakeholders. Consequently, once technological evolution is considered, it becomes clear that social and ethical issues can be incidentally ignored as users adopt an innovation for one reason (e.g., perceived need, availability in their environment, imitation of peers) while neglecting associated trade-offs.

2.3.1 Technological Evolution: Natural and Artificial Selection

Despite its original purpose in explaining biological and physiological phenomena, the process of natural selection helps us to understand complex systems in other domains (Dennett, 1995; Jablonka & Lamb, 2014; Mesoudi et al., 2006). Early models of science and technological 'evolution' assumed uniform progress (e.g., Lakatos, 1963; Mumford, 1934/2010): technologies became increasingly complex, more effective, and efficient. This reflects a fundamental misunderstanding of evolutionary processes. In contrast, contemporary models define evolution as a stochastic process that is often associated with trade-offs (e.g., Basalla, 1988).

Regardless of the substrate on which natural selection functions, it is assumed to have three main features: replication, variation, and selection (Dennett, 1995). Replication requires high-fidelity copying to ensure that the processes or features that have been successfully selected in the past are maintained: if it ain't broke, don't fix it. However, environments are dynamic. Failure to change might reduce reproductive fitness or result in the extinction of poorly adapted variants. Variation offers a potential buffer. While many variants will fail, some might succeed in novel conditions. However, variation is stochastic. Changes are neither inherently 'good' nor 'bad', rather, they are selected relative to the environment. For instance, the mobile phone provides the user with immediate connectivity, however without a functional network or power supply, the mobile phone is useless. A user's money and time might have been better spent elsewhere. This observation is also critical for the domain of ethics in that evolution is an *amoral* process. Namely, natural selection does not ensure that 'good' people or products survive, and that 'bad' people and products fail. Consequently, we cannot assume that natural or 'market' forces will ensure good product design.

We must also identify *what* is varying and being selected. Popularized by Dawkins (1976/2017) in the context of biology, he suggests that the unit of selection is the (selfish) gene and that the organism is merely a vehicle or a survival machine. Genes are not interested in right or wrong, only their continued existence through blind replication and variation. He extended this with the notion of a 'meme' (you're welcome, Internet): like a gene, memes replicate, vary, and are selected by people within a population. Although debates concern the extent to which this analogy is fruitful (Dennett, 1995), at a general level, ideas, products, etc. are replicated with the help of brains. Along these lines, Kelly (2010) quips that 'humans are the reproductive organs of technology'. For instance, a designer might understand the intended function of a technology and identify an alternative to performing the same function more accurately, faster, or more efficiently. However, consumers might select a technology for reasons that were not necessarily envisioned by the designer.

There is increasing recognition that natural selection operates on multiple levels. Genes, behaviours, symbolic representations, and groups can all be the focus of selection, conjointly referred to as multi-level selection theory (e.g., Sober & Wilson, 1997; Mesoudi et al., 2006). For instance, when one animal observes the behaviour of another member of its species, they might mimic the behaviour without understanding *why* the behaviour was initiated in the first place. The reward reinforces the behaviour in the absence of any intent: fake it until you make it. Arguably, similar episodes have marked the history of science with techniques adopted for their prestige rather than for the underlying utility of the technology (Schoenherr, 2017). Consequently, technology can be adopted for a variety of reasons ranging from a deep understanding of its technical affordances (e.g., validation; Section 2.2) or simply due to blind mimicry.

Understanding evolutionary and redomaining processes is critical when it comes to establishing a relationship between technology and social and ethical issues. In many cases, humans will simply replicate the behaviour (i.e., adoption) without reflection: if a friend joins social media, then we might as well do so without reading the privacy statement, assuming that they have. Technophiles and Luddites might come up with very good *post hoc* explanations as to why a technology is good or bad, however they are still only a believable rationalization even if they are coherent. Moreover, like any selection process, features might be selected for one reason while allowing for one or more features that were not the focus of selection ('free riders') to come along unnoticed. For instance, I might imitate others and create a social media account without understanding the implications of this act. Once logged in, we might be exposed to information that might unknowingly change our attitudes and interests while also experiencing increased levels of depression by comparing our actual lives to the overly curated lifestyle images of social influencers (Section 3.3).

Crucially, we must also recognize that societies and technology *co-evolve* as sociotechnical systems (Cooper & Foster, 1971; Pasmore et al., 1982; Walker et al., 2008). Researchers have argued that human linguistics, sociality, and intelligence have co-evolved: language allows for the retention of technical, abstract, and social information which permits larger and more varied groups, and the retention of more complex information (Deacon, 1998; Dunbar, 1997). In that all technology

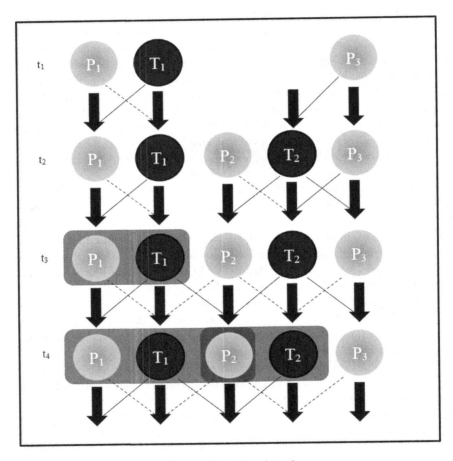

FIGURE 2.6 Example of an evolution of a sociotechnical system.

Note: Here people (P_x) and technology (T_x) interact and impact the processes of the other (solid and dashed arrows). Over time, systems can become interdependent (grey boxes), creating a sociotechnical system.

represents symbol systems (e.g., abstract features and functions), technology–human co-evolution would appear to be the norm.

Consider a simplified model of the evolution of a sociotechnical system (Figure 2.6; see also, Cooper & Foster, 1971; Herbst, 1959). Here, we assume that persons (P_x) and technology (T_x) interact over time (t_x). At t_1, P_1 and T_1 are distinct. For instance, we might assume that P_1 enters an environment where a technology is available, for example, a sound for alerting others of threats. Crucially, the two interact and shape the evolution of the other, i.e., greater control is exerted over sound production, and a greater variety of sounds can be used to alert others to more diverse threats, increasing the survival rate of group members that use them.

At the same time, another person (P_3) identifies affordances in the environment (e.g., rocks that can be sharpened) as an abstract representation, for example, 'cutting edge'. At t_2, P_3 now creates a technology, for example, a stone knife. While P_1 and T_1 continue to interact, a new person P_2 enters the environment, and interacts with T_2. By t_3, the continued interaction of P_1 and T_1 creates an interdependence such that they can be treated as a system, for example, a symbol system where sounds become associated with conventional meanings. By t_4, P_2 and T_1 and T_2 have become interdependent, creating a sociotechnological system, i.e., the symbol system can be used by people to describe and affect the creation of technology, which influences their evolution.[11] Crucially, P_1 and P_3 will not adopt other technologies if the technology is not available, or the technological affordances are not apparent. Moreover, even though P_3 has created and continues to influence the evolution of T_2, they need not become interdependent with T_2 and might cease using it. Similar processes describe the adoption of any technology; for example the creation of smartphones results in people delegating specific cognitive functions (e.g., memory for phone numbers, appointments, and facts) leading to dependence on the devices. Concepts such as the Singularity and Society 5.0 reflect the ultimate realization of this process.

Evolution is not an efficient process. Random variation – even with the help of human selection – can be costly, often resulting in non-functional or suboptimal features. In genetics, this corresponds to 'junk DNA'[12] or vestigial organs (e.g., the human appendix) that no longer perform a critical function. In technological evolution this can take on additional forms including technical affordances that were unexpected as well as disaffordances or anti-affordance, which might interfere with an individual's, or group's, ability to use technology.

In systems design, pieces of legacy code reflect the 'junk DNA' of AISs as they do not serve a function. Similarly, errors in code are not uncommon (Section 2.2.1). As Mary Allen Wilkes (2007) warned: 'We had the quaint notion … that software should be completely, absolutely free of bugs. Unfortunately, it's a notion that never really quite caught on'. Over time, these features become buried beneath other codes. Initially, we might ignore or tolerate their existence noting that a program is 'buggy'. However, if neglected, they can lead to significant issues. For instance, in cybersecurity, zero-day vulnerabilities[13] represent undetected backdoors into software that can allow malicious agents (humans or their program proxies) a means to access a system.

2.4 Summary Section: From Technical to Ethical Affordances

AISs can be defined along three technical dimensions: Autonomy, Intelligence, and Connectivity. The development of AISs requires assessing the nature of the data, the validity of employing specific algorithms, and the extent to which models provide adequate fits based on the goals of the stakeholders. On a larger scale, technological evolution can be understood in terms of a process of natural and artificial (human) selection. However, evolution is an amoral process. The resulting artifacts that are created might be developed for one reason in one community and used for different reasons in another. The ethicality of these systems cannot be assumed. Rather, explicit efforts are required to understand the ethical and social issues that emerge within these sociotechnical systems.

Notes

1 A Google search for 'autonomous intelligent systems' retrieved 55,900,000 results in 0.62 seconds.
2 Terms such as 'supervised' and 'unsupervised learning' are more agnostic, however they obscure the fact that 'supervised learning' requires labels provided by humans either directly or indirectly.
3 Evolutionary algorithms reflect a similar biologically inspired approach to AISs, wherein algorithms are developed via basic principles of replication, variation, and selection.
4 Much contemporary psychological science is based on using advanced statistical models (e.g., structural equation modelling) to identify the relationship between variables.
5 Level 3 requires that the driver take control of the vehicle when they are requested to do so.
6 Systems that control large machinery or processes.
7 Variously attributed to Benjamin Disraeli and Mark Twain.
8 Model developers can use 'information criteria' to penalize models for their use of variables. Fit can then be understood as a function of accuracy and the number of model parameters.
9 These studies generally differentiate false reports that have malicious intent, with errors resulting from incomplete, inconsistent, or false information that arises from the intake process. These latter problems can arise from unintentional errors introduced by professionals.
10 Similar results have also been observed in healthcare settings. Li et al. (2022) found that predictive models of neurological and psychological function had higher error rates for African American populations than for White American populations. While this was partially attributable to biases in the training data favouring White Americans, even when prediction models were only trained with data from African American samples, model predictions did not exceed those of White American models. This suggests that simply 'de-biasing' data is insufficient (Schwartz et al., 2022).
11 A basic example would be someone becoming dependent on a calculator to perform arithmetic operations.
12 Genes that are no longer expressed or were inserted by viruses or through other processes.
13 Zero-day refers to the fact that these issues are unknown to software developers.

3

SOCIAL AND ETHICAL ISSUES IN AISS' POPULAR SCIENCE DISCOURSE

If explainability represents an essential criterion for engaging the public, we must understand both what the public believes about AISs and how AISs are presented to them. People typically use intuitions, heuristics,[1] and folk theories that allow them to navigate their physical and social environments (e.g., Hogarth, 2001; Kahneman & Klein, 2009; Sperber & Hirschfeld, 2004). In contrast, scientists are specialists within a narrow domain. In addition to years of specialized training, they come to use instruments to extend their own perceptual and cognitive abilities. By adopting instruments, gaps are created between scientists and the public (Evans, 2000; Galison, 1987; Gieryn, 1995; Hacking, 1992; Harré, 2009; Schoenherr, 2017; Shapin & Schaffer, 1985; Sturm & Ash, 2005; Taub, 2011). For instance, Domingos (2015) claims that 'A programmer … is a minor god, creating universes at will' (p. 6) and that 'Machine-learning experts … are an elite priesthood even among computer scientists' (p. 9).

Despite the comparative inaccessibility of knowledge and instruments created in mature scientific disciplines, scientists remain accountable to the public. With the influx of public funding into the sciences, following the Second World War, the public and public institutions have become more involved in scientific activities (Guston, 2007; LaFollette, 1990; Price, 1965). Concurrently, the products and processes of science can have a significant impact on people outside of the scientific community. Effective scientific communications requires that we survey the public representations of science contained within popular science discourse to identify the features and affordances that promote trust and fear, i.e., algorithmic aversion.

As an analytic category, 'popular science' is ambiguous (Dornan, 1990). In general, it consists of translating scientific knowledge into a format that is both accessible and persuasive to the public (e.g., Broks, 2006; Secord, 2004; Topham, 1998), paralleling the notion of explainability. Rather than weighing the relative benefits and risks of a particular system, public discourse focused on AISs tends to reflect polarities of progressive technophilia and conservative technophobia, e.g., *Weapons*

DOI: 10.4324/9781003143284-3

of Math Destruction (O'Neil, 2016). Technophobia is an old phenomenon. Speaking to the influence of early technologies, Thoreau (1854) warns in *Walden* that 'we do not ride on the railroad; it rides upon us'. Left alone, public technology discourse can create a feedback loop with the mere suggestion of a social or ethical issue, leading to belief that it reflects a grave concern (Slater, 2007). Simultaneously, widespread adoption of a technology leads many to the mistaken belief that it is safe and beneficial. Developers and ethicists must engage with the public to address these issues in a balanced manner that accurately presents the strengths and limitations of specific approaches to AISs.

Scientific activities are not always distinguishable from other epistemological activities. Namely, the purpose of scientific demonstrations and communications is persuasion (Gilbert, 1977; Law & Williams, 1982). In the Western tradition, public demonstrations were a prominent feature of early science. Publications of detailed accounts of scientific activities allowed those absent to have a virtual seat in the laboratory (e.g., Golinski, 1992; Shapin, 1989, 1994; Shapin & Schaffer, 1985). International exhibitions, such as the World's Fair, exemplify the general interest of the public as well as the permeability of the boundary between scientists and the public. Seen in this light, popular science represents a continuation of this tradition of knowledge translation: 'Certainty, simplicity, vividness originate in popular knowledge. That is where the expert obtains his faith in this triad as the ideal of knowledge. Therein lies the general epistemological significance of popular science' (Fleck, 1935/2012, p. 115).

Popular Science Magazine embodies this tradition of disseminating scientific research to an educated public. Topics have included the physical and social sciences and their applications (see Figure 3.1). Demonstrating their commitment to the public, later editorials of the magazine refocused to ensure that the magazine was accessible by reducing the number of pages and complexity of the articles as well as including illustrative images.

In addition to factual accounts, folklore and fiction have often provided ethical narratives for the relationship between humans and their human-like creation (e.g., Geraci, 2008; Thorstensen, 2017). In addition to the myths of autonomous beings such as Talos and the Golem (Section 2.1.2), Mary Shelley's *Frankenstein* goes further to articulate the concerns of the Victorian era over the potential dangers of science. Crucially, the 'monster' becomes a mirror through which we see human treatment of another sentient creature. Arguably, biases that defined data sets bear an analogical similarity.

Science fiction has often anticipated, or created, public representations of ethical and unethical artificial intelligence (Easterbrook, 2009), with Asimov's 'Three Laws of Robotics' representing the canonical example (Box 3.1). Beyond lengthy novels, mass media such as comic books, television series, and social media disseminate impressionistic ideas about scientific discoveries and their potential impact on human well-being. Traditionally, speculative and science fiction consider the promise and perils of technological evolution. However, like other public representations of science, these representations capture the public beliefs and concerns as well

FIGURE 3.1 First page of the May 1872 *Popular Science Magazine* discussing the importance of sociology (left). Cover page of July–December 1917 edition demonstrating the concept of a parachute (right).

BOX 3.1 ASIMOV'S LAWS OF ROBOTICS

The Three Laws of Robotics were initially proposed by Isaac Asimov (1950) as well as the additional zeroth law. These laws are frequently used as points of reference. At their core, this approach is viewed as a means to increase the trust in AISs by increasing their transparency and reliability (Winfield & Jirotka, 2018). For additional discussion, see Boden et al. (2017), Clarke (1993, 1994), Murphy and Woods (2009), Prescott and Szollosy (2017).

First Law. A robot may not injure a human being or, through inaction, allow a human being to come to harm.

Second Law. A robot must obey the orders given by human beings except where such orders would conflict with the First Law.

Third Law. A robot must protect its own existence as long as such protection does not conflict with the First or Second Law.

Zeroth Law. A robot may not harm humanity, or by inaction, allow humanity to come to harm.

as *influence* our expectations of these systems, i.e., '... a case of life imitating art' (p. ix; Lin et al., 2012). Alongside these concerns, we must assess the evidence that supports these issues from research in cyberpsychology.

3.1 Opened Minds and Existential Threats: Welcoming Our Robot Overlords

Widely distributed television shows, movies, and comic books can provide insight into the popular representations of human–AIS relations that are influenced by, and influence, the public. For instance, like Asimov, in the *Robocop* franchise, the cyborg (formerly a human police officer) has three main 'directives' that function as a form of morality: 1. Serve the public trust, 2. Protect the innocent, and 3. Uphold the law. Illustrating the potential misuse and corruption of these systems by human developers and operators, the Robocop narrative also includes a fourth directive that remains inaccessible to the cyborg, ensuring that any senior member of the organization who created the cybernetic technology would not be arrested. Over the course of the movie, the human intelligence of the cyborg uncovers this hidden directive and asserts its autonomy to regain an element of his own humanity. Thus, rather than dedicating multiple days to reading a philosophical treatise, such media can rapidly disseminate public representations of AISs. Due to its quantity and availability, popular science discourse provides valuable insight into the information environment that can influence the public perception of AISs.

Perceived existential threats create a persistent public image problem for AISs, more recently described as algorithmic aversion. For instance, writing at the dawn of public science of AISs, Barbour (1993) notes that '[s]ince Darwin, human dignity has been threatened by our resemblance to animals. Now human uniqueness seems to be threatened by our resemblance to computers' (p. 168). To understand the importance of knowledge translation and popular science, consider an episode involving Facebook's development of chatbots (Lewis et al., 2017). In their research, Lewis et al. (2017) examined interactions between two chatbots designed for negotiation. The chatbots were created to analyze and respond using text-based communication. Over time, some of the sentences produced by the chatbots deviated from English, suggesting that they had developed a kind of shorthand. Given that their 'interest was having bots who could talk to people', model parameters were adjusted to ensure the text would be intelligible to the researchers.

Despite early accurate reporting on Lewis et al.'s research, later reports began using fear-associated terms and scenarios (e.g., 'creepy', 'secret language'; see Table 3.1) a form of sensationalization (Molek-Kozakowska, 2013; Schaffer, 1995). Whether these reflect legitimate misinterpretation remains an open question. Intentional misrepresentations are a prevalent feature of social media ('clickbait'; Chakraborty et al., 2016; Chen et al., 2015) and can promote misunderstanding and disinformation given that few readers read past the headlines when they share an article (Haile, 2014).

TABLE 3.1 Headlines Reporting on Lewis et al.'s (2017) Chatbot Negotiation Experiment

Headline	Source	Date (D/M/Y)
Chatbots Learn How to Negotiate and Drive a Hard Bargain	New Scientist	14/06/17
Facebook Shuts Down Chatbots that Created Secret Language	CBS News	31/06/17
Facebook AI Creates Its Own Language in Creepy Preview of Our Potential Future	Forbes	31/07/17
Facebook's Artificial Intelligence Robots Shut Down After They Start Talking to Each Other in Their Own Language	Independent	31/07/17
'Robot Intelligence Is Dangerous': Expert's Warning after Facebook AI 'Develop Their Own Language'	Mirror	01/08/17
Facebook AI Researcher Slams 'Irresponsible' Reports About Smart Bot Experiment	CNBC	01/08/17
The 'Creepy Facebook AI' Story that Captivated the Media	BBC	01/08/17
Facebook Shuts Down Robots After They Invent Their Own Language	Telegraph	01/08/17
Creepy Facebook Bots Talked to Each Other in a Secret Language	New York Post	01/08/17
Facebook Shuts Off AI Experiment After Two Robots Begin Speaking in Their OWN Language Only They Can Understand	The Sun	02/08/17

Regardless of the motivation, the framing of chatbot research is a clear attempt to capitalize on public concerns and fears about the inaccessibility of AISs described in numerous works of speculative fiction, e.g., HAL-9000 from *2001: A Space Odyssey*, SkyNet from the *Terminator* movie series. This likely reflects an instance of a general fear of the unknown (Carleton, 2016). More specific accounts concerning AISs have focused on existential threats to humanity that might result from a sufficiently advanced AISs (Bostrom, 2002), a view that has even been expressed by prominent scientists and technologists (Sainato, 2015).

3.2 AISs at Work: Employed and Deployed

Perhaps the social issue with the greatest longevity concerns how human life will change when machines assume formerly human roles in the workplace. Humans spend most of their lives working, making labour issues a ubiquitous concern. Technologies from simple machines to sophisticated AISs have repeatedly replaced humans in a variety of tasks, for example, elevator operator, telephone switchboard operator, ticket seller, parking attendant. The importance for determining the nature of the relationship between human and machines was identified in 1832 by Charles Babbage. He noted:

the effect of the division of labour, both in mechanical and mental processes, is, that it enables us to purchase and apply precisely the quantity of skill and knowledge which is required for it.

Babbage, 1832, p. 201

Discussions of positive features of AISs in popular science tend to focus on liberating humans from menial labour, reducing or removing harm to humans in specific environments, and the convenience of machine-assisted living. Indeed, this is a central feature of the concepts of Singularity and Society 5.0: 'In Society 5.0, people will be liberated from various constraints that previous incarnations up until Society 4.0 could not overcome' (Nakanishi, 2019). Individuals in industry often foresee a shifting role for humans as machines progressively take on more work, for example, 'During the next few decades ... machines will manage the routine while humans take on the unpredictable – tasks that require creativity, problem solving and flexibility' (Grasso, 2015).

AISs have also been seen as a means for reducing bureaucracy and political biases. When applying AISs to child protection services (i.e., Vaithianathan et al., 2013; Vaithianathan et al., 2017), Vaithianathan (2016) notes that '... once our data is up to the task, these jobs won't need to be done the old-fashioned way by armies of civil servants ... [Ideally,] the information and insights will be ... perfectly apolitical. Accountability and transparency of decision-making should take a leap forward.' Evidencing this optimism, AISs have been adopted in numerous fields, for example, chatbots for customer service, automated bankteller machines (ABMs), autonomous mobile robots (AMRs) in warehouses, and stock trading expert advisers. However, trade-offs loom large. For instance, trading bots have been developed to trade real stocks. In one case, the bots needed to be deactivated due to 'rogue trading', resulting in 440 million USD in losses to one trading firm (Baumann, 2013; Mehta, 2012; Popper, 2012).

In addition to convenience and reducing the costs of products and services, AISs have the potential to improve the health and safety of humans. During the coronavirus (COVID-19) pandemic, robots were used to protect healthcare workers, run diagnostic tests on patients, provide information and supplies to the public, and make predictions concerning symptom development and survival rates (Meisenzahl, 2020a, 2020b; Rosenbaum, 2020). Comparable rationales have been provided for the development and application of AISs in the military (e.g., Unmanned Aerial Vehicles) and policing (e.g., bomb disposal robots), with these systems reducing the number of human lives that will be endangered for those who use these AISs. These systems can also work in hazardous environments and physical conditions which are impossible for humans to endure, for example robots were used to investigate the radioactive site following the meltdown at the Fukushima Daiichi Nuclear Power Plant (Facjler, 2017; Cheng, 2019).

Negatives features of AISs have also frequently been discussed in terms of changing social norms, social arrangements, and displacement of workers, which are a consequence of introducing these 'disruptive technologies' (Morgenstern, 2016).

Similar concerns can be found in early debates on public science. For instance, in the late eighteenth century, Mortimer (1801) noted that '… the mistake has been, in not drawing a line of distinction between those machines which are calculated to abridge, or facilitate the labour of mankind; and those which are intended almost totally to exclude the labour of the human race' (p. 72).

The issue of human replacement and displacement features prominently in contemporary public discourse on AISs. Although employment opportunities will be created (Loubier, 2017), many of the tasks that AISs will replace will disproportionately affect certain sectors of the workforce, such as women. Women are likely to be comparatively disadvantaged given the types of jobs that AISs are poised to replace. Similarly, the kinds of jobs that are created tend to disproportionately favour men (World Economic Forum, 2016). In that people tend to hire those similar to themselves (e.g., Levin et al., 2005), biases might be perpetuated, leading to stable patterns of underrepresentation (for a review, see Ridgeway, 2011). For instance, after extensive development, Amazon abandoned an AIS developed to review and rate job applicants after it found that the results demonstrated a gender bias (Dastin, 2018).

Biases in hiring can also affect design, leading to more systems being designed for male users (Perez, 2019) and those in the majority (Costanza-Chock, 2020). At the level of a sociotechnological system, groups within a society and those within countries will have differential access to these technologies (see Figure 1.2), resulting in a 'digital divide' that will lead to a cumulative benefit for certain individuals and groups, referred to as the Matthew Effect (Merton, 1968) or wealth condensation (Bouchaud & Mézard, 2000).

In addition to the issue of workforce displacement, we can also question the adequacy of AISs in replacing or supplementing humans. For instance, in Huntington Park, California, the police force introduced a robot to patrol a public park. Yet, when a woman went to report a fight in the park, the robot told her to 'step out of the way' (Flaherty, 2019). Following the incident, it was revealed that the button on the robot to call for assistance was not connected to the police department, but rather to the manufacturer. Thus, the AIS simply detected the women in its path and produced the appropriate response relative to its programming. AISs are ultimately only as good as their software and hardware.

Proposals for a shift to an automated workforce can also underestimate the education and training infrastructure that is necessary to re-educate workers. Some estimates suggest that approximately half of all current jobs can be automated and that 375 million workers could be displaced by the growth of automation (Manyika et al., 2017). A report by the World Economic Forum suggests that reskilling displaced workers would cost 34 billion USD. However, they additionally suggest that the private sector is only equipped to reskill 25% of the 1.4 million workers that will be displaced in the next decade (WEF, 2016; WEF & Boston Consulting Group, 2019). Individual workers and the public sector will be expected to address the remaining costs. Moreover, if an adequate workforce is not available, due to the lack of training, this will likely result in lower quality work, thereby adversely affecting the quality of the AISs that are created.

As organizations shift toward automating personnel selection and assessment systems, questions have been raised concerning the accuracy of these systems and their comparative advantage over traditional selection processes (e.g., Pyke et al., 2022). Hiring decisions reflect a multi-stage selection process. Traditional selection processes typically involve a pre-screening phase where the pool of candidates is reduced following an expression of interest. Following this phase, a review of applicants and selection occurs. Studies have indicated that candidates with 'Asian' (Chinese, Indian, or Pakistani) names are nearly half as likely to be given an interview (Banerjee et al., 2018). In contrast, controlled studies have found that while gender biases might not affect an initial narrowing of the candidate pool, they can affect selection or termination decisions (Levin et al., 2005). However, algorithms do not necessarily ensure fairness as they can reproduce human biases within the data set (e.g., Bolukbasi et al., 2016; Buolamwini & Gebru, 2018; Caliskan et al., 2017). For instance, algorithmic advertisements for cashier positions and taxi driver positions were shown with greater frequency to female (85%) and black (75%) job seekers, respectively (Ali et al., 2019). In a recent nonscientific study conducted by the Society for Human Resource Management (2022), between 16% (small) and 42% (large) of businesses indicated that they used a form of automation to support human resource-related activities. Human resource professionals indicated that, among other activities, these systems were used to review or screen applicants' resumes (64%), automate candidate searches (52%), and pre-select applicants for interviews (25%). Critically, 92% of the respondents indicated that these systems were supplied by vendors with only '2 in 5' organizations indicating that the vendors were 'very transparent' about precautions taken to avoid discrimination and bias. Indeed, 25% indicated that their organization did not use AIS for HR due to concerns about unwarranted candidate exclusion. Given these concerns, it is unsurprising that prominent organizations have ceased the use of some of these approaches (Dastin, 2018).

3.3 Reshaping Social Reality

Our recreational activities and social lives can also be affected by AISs, leading to characterization of contemporary humanity as 'Generation AI' (a term adopted by WEF and UNICEF). Video games reflect the first widely available form of programmable media. AISs are typically encountered in these environments in terms of non-playable characters (NPCs; Nareyek, 2004). While NPCs initially represented simple animated units (e.g., the simplistic pixelated 'aliens' in *Space Invaders*), the concept of orthogonal unit differentiation led to the creation of different classes of characters, each with their own set of abilities. Greater deliberation is required from players to predict their actions and the outcomes of situations (Bjork & Holopainen, 2004; Smith, 2003).[2] In addition to NPCs, AISs can also be used in numerous ways (e.g., data mining user behaviour, creating game elements; Lara-Cabrera et al., 2015; Yannakakis, 2012). Unlike the two-dimensional single-screen or 'side-scrolling' environments of early games, modern games are defined by massive, immersive environments run by AISs, which can be explored alone or in competition with other human players.

The social impact of video games cannot be overestimated. Like television, video games have influenced our societies (Herz, 1997; Newman, 2017a, 2017b). In the 1980s, video games were often portrayed as a broad threat, with a focus on specific disorders, for example, 'Space Invader's Wrist' (McCowan, 1981). However, early studies suggested that associations between video game use and antisocial behaviour were not supported (Ellis, 1984). Contemporary concerns also include children's 'screen time' and adult 'addiction' to mobile phones (Kuss & Griffiths, 2012; Walton, 2018). In the latter case, China has recently taken steps to limit both the number of games played and the time spent playing those games (Ni, 2021).

3.3.1 Addiction to Technology: Mobile Phone Use and Gaming

The concept of widespread addiction to technology remains a continual focus of popular science discourse (Twenge, 2017). However, there is a lack of consensus in terms of estimates of technological addiction as well as whether there are specific forms of addictions (Suler, 2004). For instance, estimates of verifiable cases of 'video game addiction' vary (e.g., between 1.7% to over 10%; Griffiths et al., 2012), with mobile phone addiction estimated to be much higher (e.g., 48%; Aljomaa et al., 2016). In that addiction represents a form of maladaptive behaviour, what counts as addiction must be qualified alongside the environments that individuals inhabit. For instance, high-frequency mobile phone use might be deemed more acceptable given that it is associated with a more typical form of communication with humans.

Assumptions concerning 'addiction' stem from the role of dopamine in rewarding and reinforcing behaviour. Responses to mobile phone application notifications and video games use the same dopaminergic pathways for reward, pleasure, and learning as other activities (e.g., Ferguson et al., 2011; Hoeft et al., 2008; Koepp et al., 1998; Loton et al., 2016; Palaus et al., 2017; Stockdale & Coyne, 2018). Consequently, users build a stimulus-response association between the lights and sounds used for notification and the receipt of a social reward, for example, 'likes', comments, post-shares, and private messages. In an opinion piece Brooks (2017) claims that:

> Tech companies understand what causes dopamine surges in the brain and they lace their products with 'hijacking techniques' that lure us in and create 'compulsion loops' … Most social media sites create irregularly timed rewards; you have to check your device compulsively because you never know when a burst of social affirmation from a Facebook like may come.

Others have suggested that there is a 'dark consensus' by technology insiders about the relationship between the amount of screen usage and maladaptive behaviour in children, leading them to limit their children's use of these technologies (Bowles, 2018).

Attention is a precious resource which can be shaped by using an AIS (Schoenherr, 2022b). According to the statistics from one productivity application, people spend over 3 hours a day on their mobile, which includes checking their mobile 58 times a day (RescueTime, 2019). Other evidence suggests that users switch between applications every 20 seconds (Reeves et al., 2021). This division and shifting of attention (i.e., task-switching; Monsell, 2003) can be potentially harmful. In 2016, the US National Safety Council reported that 70% of Americans use their phone while driving. However, while only 25% suggest that *they* placed other drivers at risk while driving due to distraction from the use of technology, 67% indicated that they felt *other* drivers put them at risk. Such discrepancies suggest that users either overestimate others' use of mobile phones or underestimate their own.[3]

Excessive mobile phone use can also adversely affect personal and professional relationships. Studies suggest that mobile phone use in business meetings is perceived as uncivil and disrespectful (Washington et al., 2014) and that employees who have supervisors who continuously use their mobile phone report lower levels of trust and job satisfaction (Roberts & David, 2020). Mobile phone use is also associated with reduced performance (Kates et al., 2018), this is likely attributable to task-switching between mobiles phones and other activities.

Similar concerns have been raised about gaming. Commentators have claimed that video games are 'digital heroin', turning 'kids into psychotic junkies' (Kardaras, 2016). However, evidence suggests that individuals who demonstrate video game addiction have similar traits to those with other forms of addiction, with studies often failing to consider psychopathological co-morbidity or prevalence in subclinical populations (King et al., 2012). Smartphone addiction is also supported by similar results (Panova & Carbonell, 2018). Demonstrating the widespread uncertainty of the association between these technologies and pathology, while the World Health Organization included 'gaming disorder' in their International Classification of Diseases (ICD), the American Psychological Associations' Diagnostic and Statistical Manual (DSM) suggests the need for further study of 'Internet Gaming Disorder' prior to accepting it as a unique diagnostic category.[4]

3.3.2 Antisocial and Prosocial Behaviour in Gamers

Addiction is not the only issue associated with technological change. The relationship between antisocial behaviour and media consumption in adults and children has also been a persistent concern (e.g., TV violence; Huesmann et al., 2003; Pagani et al., 2019). In addition to TV, the association between video games and violence has also provoked ire. For instance, in the 1990s, a 'moral panic' over the lifelike portrayal of violence in the game *Mortal Kombat* gripped the public (Crossley, 2014). Public anxieties were so significant that they led to congressional hearings in the United States.

Evidence does support a relationship between violence and video game use. In a study by Anderson et al. (2010), playing violent video games was associated with increased aggressive affect (especially anger), behaviour, and cognition, as well as physiological responses associated with aggression (increased blood pressure and heart rate) and a reduction in prosocial behaviour (helping others or altruism). Studies have also found that time spent gaming was associated with hostile cognitions (Choo et al., 2010) and physical aggression in boys (Lemmens et al., 2009, 2011). These associations must be qualified. For instance, individuals who have aggressive predisposition or are experiencing frustrating life events might be more likely to play violent games, leading to a self-selection bias. In this case, playing a violent video game might not necessarily cause or increase the aggression (Ferguson & Kilburn, 2010; Savage, 2004). This suggests that social context and individual difference in personality mediate the relationship between violence and video game playing.

The relationship between gaming behaviour and prosocial personality traits has recently garnered considerable interest (Chory & Goodboy, 2011; King et al., 2013; Kokkinakis et al., 2016; Park et al., 2011; Teng, 2008; Wang & Wang, 2008; Wang & Yu, 2017; Worth & Book, 2014; Yee et al., 2011). In a study by Worth and Book (2014), they found that antisocial interactions were positively related to low levels of prosocial personality traits (e.g., Honesty-Humility) and high levels of antisocial personality traits (e.g., Psychopathy). In a study of usernames in multiplayer game *League of Legends*, Kokkinakis et al. (2016) found that antisocial usernames (i.e., names containing English maladicta, e.g., 'g0ats3x') were positively correlated with in-game antisocial behaviour (i.e., reports against players) and negatively correlated with prosocial behaviour (i.e., honour ratings). They also observed a negative association between antisocial behaviour and age. Thus, a process of ethical maturation, or learning both antisocial and prosocial behaviour, might also help explain these results.

Despite the news media's focus on the violent aspects of games, prosocial reward systems are an increasingly common design feature in popular games, for example, *League of Legends*, *Mass Effect*, *The Walking Dead* (Nay & Zagal, 2017). In some cases, these ethical decision-making reward systems can be quite sophisticated and include long-term consequences for specific decisions that cannot be changed. For instance, in the popular science fiction trilogy, *Mass Effect*, players' interactions with NPCs consist of multiple actions and dialogue options. Options reflect prosocial and antisocial approaches to resolving conflicts, resulting in the awarding of points (*Mass Effect*), percentages (*Mass Effect 2*), or virtuous status as a 'paragon' or 'renegade' (*Mass Effect 3*). Over time, these decisions can restrict further dialogue options, reflecting increases in NPC-specific trust and social competencies. Adopting such an approach of game design could increase prosocial behaviour (Peng et al., 2010).

Ethical choices can be exceptionally consequential. In the case of Mass Effect, a player's choices concatenate over the course of the trilogy (see Figure 3.2). Following the release of *Mass Effect 3*, developers provided data suggesting that most players (64.5%) preferred the Paragon (virtuous) path relative to the Renegade (vicious) path (Petitte, 2013). A more recent Tweet from one of the developers suggested that the number might be much higher, i.e., 'something like 92%' (Wakeling, 2020).[5] Similar results were also reported for the survival/horror role-playing game, the *Walking Dead* (Fogel, 2012).

Supporting the influence of individual differences in ethical decision-making within video games, Boyan et al. (2015) observed that a concern for harm/care (Section 5.3.1) was associated with players' overall path in *Mass Effect*. Outside of this franchise, studies have also suggested that the commissioning of antisocial behaviours within a game resulted in feelings of guilt which, in turn, led to greater salience of violations of moral intuitions (e.g., care and fairness; Grizzard et al., 2014; cf. Weaver & Lewis, 2012). In short, the more salient the ethical affordances are in simulated environments, the less likely individuals will violate ethical principles

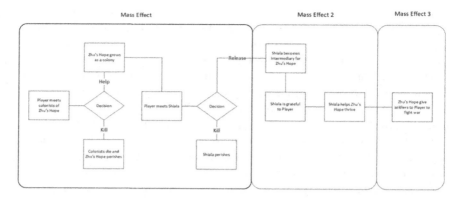

FIGURE 3.2 Decision-tree for Mass Effect Trilogy denoting ethical and unethical decisions-based path.

Source: Diagram created by Corrina Cai.

(Joeckel et al., 2012). Despite these promising observations, not all artificial environments created or operated by AISs are defined by such extensive ethical design considerations.

3.3.3   Relationships and Computer-Mediated Communication

One of the main reasons why antisocial behaviour might be observed in many video games and other online environments is that they can dramatically reduce many social cues that are normally involved in interpersonal communication, for example, emotional intonation of the voice (i.e., prosodic cues), facial expressions, hand gestures. These concerns are especially important in online dating communities. For instance, although text-based communication can create opportunities for antisocial behaviour, such as deception, it can also facilitate interpersonal exchanges by increasing the selectivity of a sender's message content (Walther, 1996, 2007). Deception need not be malicious. There is also an inherent tension between being authentic in disclosing information on dating profiles and careful self-presentation that might be associated with self-deception (Ellison et al., 2006). Unsurprisingly, misrepresenting oneself can often result in greater disappointment in subsequent face-to-face meetings following online text communication (e.g., Ramirez Jr. et al., 2015; Sharabi & Caughlin, 2017).

Other features of online dating interactions that need to be considered include the relative quantity, their comparative anonymity, and how this will alter social interactions (e.g., Markowitz, 2017). Humans have a limited cognitive capacity. AISs that present users with numerous individual profiles might alter their perceived choice by changing the kinds of characteristics that they attend to in their prospective partners. For instance, in a study of speed-dating conducted by Lenton and Francesconi (2010), daters were more likely to use characteristics associated with partner social status (e.g., education and occupation) in small sessions, and physical characteristics (e.g., height and weight) in larger sessions. Given that online dating sites present similar cognitive demands, these strategies might have adverse consequences on their users' perceptions of the availability of mates. For instance, a study of users of the dating app Tinder found that they experienced more face and body dissatisfaction and self-monitoring than non-users (Strubel & Petrie, 2017). However, whether this is an antecedent or a consequence of the use of the application is another question.

The effects of AISs on users are likely bi-directional. Users choose to use social media and online dating profiles, suggesting that individual differences will determine technology adoption and can themselves be changed by technology use. Consider 'selfies'. Both folk and scientific theories have considered the relationship between narcissism and posting self-portraits on social media (Fox & Rooney, 2015; Lee et al., 2015; Weiser, 2015). Researchers have found that highly narcissistic individuals are more likely to post selfies on social media, while posting more selfies on social media is also associated with increases in narcissism (Arpaci et al., 2018; Halpern et al., 2016; Sorokowski et al., 2015; Sorokowski et al., 2016). Similarly, reasoning can also be used to understand the association between social media use and anxiety, depression, and self-esteem (Lin et al., 2016; Woods & Scott, 2016; cf. Primack et al., 2021).

Similar results have also been obtained for depression and anxiety and social media use (McCrae et al., 2017; Rosen et al., 2013). Following documents that were leaked to the *Wall Street Journal*, Facebook's parent company (now Meta) appears to have been aware of the adverse effects of Instagram use on teenage girls: '[a]spects of Instagram exacerbate each other to create a perfect storm' (Wells et al., 2021). Acknowledging this internal research, Instagram indicated that these results are being used to inform the development of an app for children and to address these issues by developing techniques to nudge users away from problematic content (e.g., Newton, 2021).

A final concern is the growing recognition that the algorithms that define social media places us in echo chambers that reflect, reinforce, and refine our biases, opinions, and preferences (Quattrociocchi et al., 2016). Like recommender systems (Lü et al., 2012), social media algorithms are designed to engage the user, using behavioural traces (e.g., likes and shares) to determine preferences which are then used to show them similar content and users. These algorithms can therefore limit our exposure to alternatives. By providing users with content and suggestions of other users who share their opinions, social media sites foster confirmation bias, a tendency to identify information that confirms our prior beliefs, and disconfirmation bias, a tendency to identify issues with alternative arguments and interpretations (Edwards et al., 1996; Nickerson, 1998). This has lead some to suggest that we live in a post-truth era, where users can select the information, explanations, and narratives that match their belief system.

Outside of social media, humans tend to be attracted to others based on the nature and degree of similarity, referred to as homophily (McPherson et al., 2001).

This same preference drives interactions in social networks (Thelwall, 2009). For instance, a recent study illustrates that social networking sites such as Facebook and Twitter are dominated by homophilic clusters (Cinelli et al., 2021). However, a study by Barberá et al. (2015) of over 3.8 million Twitter users and 150 million tweets suggested that exchanges concerning certain topics (political issues) resemble an echo chamber more than others (nonpolitical issues). Consequently, while social media is not uniquely responsible for echo chamber effects, these platforms can exacerbate the problem (Zimmer et al., 2019). Crucially, this can lead to group polarization, such that individual opinions become more extreme due to their interactions on social media (Bail et al., 2018; Banks et al., 2021; Del Vicario et al., 2016).

3.3.4 Brains in Vats: Sex and Zero-Sum Games

Whatever the positive and negative features of online dating, social media use, and gaming might be, the choice between interacting in virtual or physical environments reflects a zero-sum game. Zero-sum games are defined by a finite pool of resources that must be allocated between players. In the case of virtual worlds, any time spent in these environments necessarily results in less time in physical environments. Following from the thought experiment presented by René Descartes, contemporary debates are often framed in terms of the 'brain-in-a-vat' thought experiment (Harman, 1973). Therein, an unsuspecting individual's brain is suspended in a fluid and their neurons are fed information by a computer to simulate reality. Here, we are presented with the question of whether this situation is worthwhile and asked what the critical distinctions are between these simulated experiences and those grounded in the real world.

AISs have also been designed for companionship, work as guides, confidants, and caretakers (Al-Heeti, 2017; McLain, 2016). These systems likely face hurdles given the negative affect that might result from having some human and nonhuman properties (i.e., 'the uncanny valley'; e.g., Burleigh et al., 2013; Burleigh & Schoenherr, 2015; Cheetham et al., 2011; Mori, 1970; Schoenherr & Burleigh, 2020). Moreover, robots designed for intimacy and sexual relationships introduce new issues, as humans might prefer these asymmetric relationships where there is no possibility of rejection and a partner can be designed to their specifications (Döring et al., 2020; Scheutz & Arnold, 2016). However, much like prostitution, sex robots can lead to the abstraction of sex and the objectification of women (Richardson, 2016).

Participation in gaming environments and online social communities present the same dilemma. Unlike games that occur in fantastical environments (e.g., ancient history, space), games like *The Sims* and *Second Life* present a stark demonstration of the zero-sum nature of these games, as players spend significant amounts of time living in these alternative realities. The impact of these games is significant enough, such that politicians have created campaign offices in these worlds, like Barack Obama in *Second Life* (Wheaton, 2007). Real-world ethical problems also intrude into these domains, such as players in the *Second Life* online community committing adultery on real-world partners, running brothels, as well as concerns over the possible sexual exploitation of children (Towhey, 2008; Woods, 2008). Similar concerns have also been raised for robots designed for intimacy.

An early illustration of the choice between artificial and physical environments can be found with the introduction of televisions. As TVs became more available, families were left with a choice between remaining at home for viewing or participating in local activities, for example, bowling leagues, community associations. Putnam (2000) argues that as TVs became more prevalent in homes, there was a corresponding decline in civic engagement, resulting in the end of many community-based organizations. A more contemporary example is 'slacktivism' – when individuals sign online petitions to support sociopolitical causes rather than engaging in public demonstrations. Supporting concerns about the negative effect of slacktivism, a study of Facebook users found that there was only a small, positive correlation between online and offline participatory behaviour in political issues (Vitak et al., 2011).[6] Whether in terms of online gaming, sex robots, or slacktivism, AIS developers should assess how the introduction of these technologies affects users' behaviour outside of these applications.

3.4 Property, Privacy, and Confidentiality

Whether in terms of games, social media, or dating sites, most AISs are presented to users in the form of applications. Users are often asked for their preferences and provided with alternatives based on their responses, assuming that their overt beliefs will predict their responses to products, people, and services. Covert responses are also recorded in terms of behavioural traces, the pattern of interactions between a user and an application (Zuboff, 2019). Given discrepancies between attitudes and behaviour (Glasman & Albarracin, 2006), the combination of preference and behavioural traces has the potential to make more effective predictions about users' personality, beliefs, and behaviour (Youyou et al., 2015). For instance, despite their avowed preferences, many male users of the online dating application OKCupid sent messages to women below their stated minimum age threshold (OKCupid, 2010), and despite claims to the contrary, race was an important determinant of interaction for users (Rudder, 2014). However, unlike preference ratings that are knowingly provided by users, users might not be aware of the use of behavioural traces and their implications. This introduces ambiguity into the ownership of the data in that users are not knowingly providing it to organizations (Wang, 2013).

Personal identifiers, preferences, and behavioural traces represent a new kind of digital property. Property is linked to concepts of identity, resources, and exchange norms (e.g., Fiske, 1991). As Earle (2000) notes, '[p]roperty is a key concept and behavioural mechanism to limit and direct the use of things … Natural resources, tools, products, and at times people are subject to property rules, property materializes interpersonal relationships, and built landscapes particularize social identities' (p. 39). Issues of property are also closely linked to those of privacy, with some concepts of privacy focusing on controlling information about oneself (Moore, 1984/2017; Westin, 1967; for reviews, see Schoenherr, 2020a, 2022a). These concerns are relevant to information domains in which AISs operate in terms of potential conflicts between ownership of information and rights to privacy and confidentiality (Moore, 2005).

3.4.1   *Public Awareness and Privacy Comprehension*

Privacy issues in sociotechnical systems blend social, cultural, psychological, ethical and legal dimensions (DeCew, 1997; Schoenherr, 2022b), and have a been a persistent concern with the introduction of disruptive technologies. For instance, the introduction of communications technologies such as telegraphs and telephone were believed by some to make their users vulnerable to the loss of privacy (Marvin, 1988). Long-term trends of privacy concerns are evidenced in several polls. For instance, a Pew Research poll in 2019 found that 79% of US residents were at least somewhat concerned about how much information was being collected about them by companies, with 64% of those polled having similar concerns about their government. US residents also did not believe it was possible to engage in normal daily activities without their data being collected by companies (62%) or government (63%). Most respondents also expressed a lack of understanding and awareness about what companies and governments do with this data (59% and 78%, respectively).

Many countries have responded to privacy concerns by developing overarching regulatory frameworks and guidelines. In Europe, the European Commission has developed the General Data Protection Regulations (GDPR). The GDPR emphasizes the need for clarity of language, affirmative consent from users, as well as greater accessibility and the availability of options, for example, movement of data and the 'right to be forgotten'. By encoding privacy values in legal frameworks, violations of privacy can have significant consequences (e.g., Co, 2017). In the US, the Federal Trade Commission (FTC) fined Facebook 5 billion USD for deceiving users about the privacy restrictions on their personal information (FTC, 2019a). Google was similarly fined 170 million USD by the FTC for collecting children's personal information on YouTube (FTC, 2019b).

Privacy remains at the core of debates about online interactions, with some critics suggesting that privacy is dead (Morgan, 2014; Sanders, 2011; Quittner, 1997). For instance, Yakowitz (2011) notes that 'data privacy practices are shaped by some combination of ambiguous statutory directives, inconsistent case law, industry best practices, whim, and self-serving discretionary preferences' (p. 3). Rather than being dead, privacy reflects a folk concept with no clear definition (e.g., Schoenherr, 2022b), leading some to argue that the notion of obscurity (ease of access) should be used instead as it can be operationalized (Hartzog & Stutzman, 2013).

In response, technologies and organizations have been developed to address these concerns, such as virtual private networks (VPNs), data anonymization models such as *k*-anonymity, *l*-diversity, and *t*-closeness (Sweeney, 2002), and the introduction of privacy engineering methodologies (PEMs; Notario et al., 2015). However, developers are not always aware of privacy issues (Acquisti et al., 2017) nor do they always see PEMs as relevant features of design (Senarath et al., 2019; see Box 6.1).

Further complicating matters, large organizations have lobbied against data collection regulations (Molla, 2019; Taplin, 2017). Legal experts have noted that user agreements present a labyrinthine set of policies that are barely interpretable to the average user. Moreover, in that most users fail to read these contracts, end user licence agreements (EULAs) represent 'click wrap' to give licence to companies to use any information they collect (Ayres & Schwartz, 2014; Bakos et al., 2014; Luger et al., 2013; Maronick, 2014; Wilkinson-Ryan, 2013, 2017). For instance, in an early study, McDonald and Cranor (2008) measured the length of privacy policies on popular websites. Policies ranged in length from 144 words to 7,669 words, or 15 pages of text. While the estimated time to properly read short and long policies varied from 8 to 12 minutes,[7] the actual time for participants to 'skim' through a policy varied from 18 to 37 seconds. Eyetracking studies have found similar evidence (Steinfeld, 2016). By estimating the number of websites visited during a year, McDonald and Cranor found that users would need to spend 244 hours a year of reading or 154 hours to skim through these contracts.

Instead of reading or skimming, users generally accepted these agreements without any reflection. Supporting these observations, a study by Obar and Oeldorf-Hirsch (2020) found that, while 74% of users read privacy policies, the total reading time of users averaged only 73 seconds. Similar results were observed for terms of services, with an average reading time of 51 seconds. Crucially, they also found that 'gotcha clauses' were missed by 98% of users. In that many EULAs and policies specify that information can be shared with third parties, individual privacy agreements create a loose, ambiguous patchwork that can be exploited (see also Plaut & Bartlett, 2012). With the increased connectivity of smart devices, these concerns will likely grow exponentially. Exploitation can occur by aggregating user data across multiple platforms, creating individual profiles or derivative datasets that were not created with explicit consent (Mason, 1986).

3.4.2 Data Aggregation: Piecing People Together

While mobile phone applications allow us to use maps, search for products, and read reviews, they also allow us to remotely regulate and monitor our homes with smart devices such as thermostats, smoke detectors, speakers, and vacuum cleaners. Collectively, these devices constitute the IoT, distributed AISs that share, store, and process information locally and remotely through wireless communication. In addition to the IoT, commonly available devices such as drones also raise concerns over privacy in terms of the nature and extent of surveillance activities used by law enforcement officers, government agencies, industry, and private individuals (e.g., Benjamin, 2013; Feeney, 2016). The pervasiveness, ambiguity, and embeddedness of these devices in our lives create ethical concerns in terms of their connectivity, their ability to identify us, and how distributed control can adversely affect our privacy (Van den Hoven, 2013). For instance, unintentional privacy violations are also evidenced, such as a smart home device recording and sending a private conversation to a contact that resulted from a succession of misinterpreted commands (More, 2018). Compounding these issues, boundaries between public and private information are often blurred.

Nowhere is there a better demonstration of this than Google Maps Street View, introduced in 2007. To create these images marked vehicles, equipped with imaging cameras, drive through an area taking 360-degree photos (see Figure 3.3). The accumulation of photos, about which pedestrians and property owners have no

FIGURE 3.3 Photographs of Google and Apple imaging vehicles taken in Spring and Summer 2021, respectively (Ottawa, Ontario, Canada).

Source: Photo Credit: Jordan Richard Schoenherr.

knowledge, raises privacy concerns about having photographs publicly accessible without consent (Liedtke, 2007). In response to these concerns, Google representatives noted that the images were available from public streets: 'This imagery is no different from what any person can readily capture or see walking down the street' (Helft, 2007). Moreover, Google Maps is participatory (e.g., Google, 2021). In addition to encouraging users to post their photos on Google Maps Street View, they have recently included a function that allows anyone under the age of 18 to request removal of their images from Google Search results (Sullivan, 2021).

Many of the privacy issues raised by Street View have precedents. Photographic technology has always been associated with privacy concerns (Warren & Brandeis, 1890). However, unlike previous photographic technologies, the comparative retention, accessibility, and availability of these candid images presents challenges that must be addressed (e.g., Stamatellos, 2007; Tavani, 2007). For instance, in 2016, Microsoft released Microsoft Celeb (MS-Celeb-1M), a dataset of nearly 10 million images of 100,000 'celebrity' faces that were scrapped from the Internet for the development of AIS facial recognition technology. Crucially, Harvey and LePlace (2019) revealed that not all of the faces were celebrities (e.g., activists, academics, and policymakers) with subsequent reports finding that Microsoft used this dataset in research associated with the Chinese military that could be used for surveillance and censorship (Murgia & Yang, 2019). While Microsoft eventually removed this dataset copies remain available on third-party websites (e.g., GitHub) and it remains one of the most cited and used facial datasets (Peng et al., 2021).

Big data sets that contain a sufficiently large quantity of behavioural traces can create fairly accurate *representations* of the consumer and users (Zwick & Dholakia, 2004). As Draper (2019) notes in her discussion of privacy, a major feature of privacy is the ability to control not just information about ourselves but its *context* (also see, Schoenherr, 2021a, 2022a). If some information is denatured from its context, it can take on different, unintended meanings. Disclosing information to friends through social media, to a perspective employer, or to a credit card company, is associated with different intentions and different assumptions about how information will be used. However, by making this information available online, it is not immediately clear who owns the information.

Information can also be aggregated from multiple sources creating a data commons that can be used or abused like any other communal resource (Yakowitz, 2011). For instance, a report in *The New York Times* illustrates how readily accessible aggregated information can be to purchase. After obtaining an anonymized set of user data, they were able to track and identify a woman by using her daily behaviour recorded by an application on her mobile phone (Valentino-DeVries et al., 2018). This data can also be used in a systematic manner to track groups of individuals. An investigation by the *Wall Street Journal* found that mobile phone anonymized location data was being used by US federal agencies, such as the Department of Homeland Security, to track undocumented immigrants (Tau & Hackman, 2020), despite an earlier US Supreme Court ruling that indicated a warrant was required (Hurley, 2018).

Creating additional issues, data mining techniques used to analyze the information are not always effective. For instance, following the attack on the World Trade Center on September 11, 2001, data mining techniques that were used to identify potential terrorists were criticized not only for violations of privacy, but also for the adequacy of their results (Farley, 2006). Conversely, location data available from the Parlor app recorded during the January 6, 2021 attack on the US Capitol Building in Washington, DC, was used to successfully identify rioters (Cameron & Mehrotra, 2021). This information along with other posts on social media and personal knowledge from friends and witnesses, led to over 600 arrests in what has been called the 'most documented crime in US history' (Hall et al., 2021).

The extent of privacy issues created by the Age of Entanglement was most graphically illustrated by the Cambridge Analytica scandal. Although predictive models based on prospective voter data have always played a role in political campaigns, President Barack Obama's 2012 campaign was praised as an exercise in data analytics. Senior advisers claimed that: 'We could [predict] people who were going to give online. We could model people who were going to give through mail. We could model volunteers … In the end, modeling became something way bigger for us in '12 than in '08 because it made our time more efficient' (Scherer, 2012). A political consultancy, Cambridge Analytica, presented the same kind of promise. *The Guardian* first reported that the American presidential candidate Ted Cruz employed Cambridge Analytica to create psychological profiles from Facebook users' data without their knowledge or consent (Davies, 2015). Following the election of President Donald Trump, similar issues were raised concerning the Trump Campaign (Rosenberg et al., 2018). If such models prove effective, this could pose significant challenges for our autonomy and affect the democratic process (Section 3.6.2).

3.5 Hackers, Attackers, and Slackers: Cybercrimes, Cyberwar, and Insider Threats

Beyond issues of privacy and consent, security issues loom large in the public representation of AISs. Data breaches, 'spyware', 'ransomware', and cyber attacks conducted by 'hackers' and 'adversaries' against perimeter defences, reflect increasingly common topics in the media. For instance, in 2017, Equifax reported a data breach wherein credit scores information of 147 million US consumers were obtained by hackers (FTC, 2020). In Australia, the records of over 200,000 students were compromised in a data breach (Groch, 2019). Although criminality is likely as old as human society, the nature and extent of these crimes has changed with the sheer volume of data available to would-be thieves and adversaries. Moreover, the boundary between state and non-state actors has become increasingly blurred. For instance, a spyware program (Pegasus), sold by Israeli NSO Group, has been used to spy on journalists, social activists, and NGOs (e.g., Amnesty International; Kirchgaessner et al., 2021) with the Citizens Lab research group suggesting the involvement of organizations in 45 countries. By using vulnerabilities in common apps, the program can gather any information from a user's phone. Given the capabilities of such technology, radical power asymmetries are created between those that deploy these AISs and data subjects who are intentionally or unintentionally affected by these attacks, despite the risks of leaving systems unprotected. Although the financial and human resources required to develop and implement cybersecurity strategies can be substantial, stakeholders must weigh the potential risk against the costs (i.e., cybersecurity economics; Ekelund & Iskoujina, 2019; Moore, 2010).

3.5.1   When Cyber Attacks: Cybercrimes and Cyberwar

Despite the technical nature of these events, network intrusions, cybercrimes, and cyberwarfare (collectively, cyberoperations) have become another topic of increasing interest in popular science. In the West, the mention of cyberoperations in the media typically focuses on transgressions by Russia, China, and less frequently by North Korea and Iran. Discussions of security breaches rarely focus on the operational details of the breach but rather the target or the outcomes, such as 'sensitive data'/'personal data', emails, money, and business records. Technical operations are subsumed within the terms 'hack', 'spying', 'compromised', and 'attack'. The acceptance of these terms as sufficiently informative, and their continued use in the media, is likely attributable to the impenetrability of the operations of these systems to the users. For instance, more transparent terms like 'penetration', 'infiltration', 'defaced', and 'ransomware' provide a basic idea of what the operations of a program are, for example, to gain access to a system clandestinely or to withhold or destroy user data to gain an advantage. Ethical analogies are also employed with 'white hat' operators defending against 'black hat' hackers that attempt to penetrate a network's perimeter defences.

Skepticism is required to understand the nature of these operations as acts of 'cyberwar' and 'cyber terrorism'. Multiple analogies have been used to understand malicious activity in cyberspace (Schoenherr & Thomson, 2021a, 2022). For instance, persistent cyberattacks might reflect a kind of 'cold war' but the absence of large-scale operations, physical damage, or loss of human life make the use of the term 'war' more problematic. Some critics have suggested that the threats of cyber war are overstated, and that the use of these terms is a cynical effort to increase funding (Blunden & Cheung, 2014). While threats to critical infrastructure, user data, and proprietary information are real, it remains clear that a more complex understanding of human and AIS interaction in cyberspace is required.

3.5.2 Malicious Insiders and Failures of Knowledge Translation

Network perimeter defences represent only part of the focus of cybersecurity. A grey literature[8] has emerged between academia and industry, which focuses on insider threat detection: identifying 'at-risk employees' or 'malicious insiders' whose behaviour is in opposition to the interests of an organization (for a review, see Coles-Kemp & Theoharidou, 2010). To identify malicious insiders, systems have been developed to monitor employees' activities inside and outside of company networks (e.g., Kandias et al., 2013; Mathew et al., 2010).

The introduction of broad employee surveillance brings with it its own challenges. This approach often assumes that *all* employees are potential insider threats given broad definitions that can include malicious intentions (e.g., leaking, sabotage, or theft), negligence (e.g., failure to follow security protocols or best practices), or accidents (e.g., deletion, or misplacement of information). However, given the limited theoretical and empirical support for these approaches, as well as their dependence on 'black data' (Schoenherr & Thomson, 2020b), their use poses important ethical challenges and severe legal ramifications, for example, discriminatory practices and wrongful termination. For instance, recent empirical studies have suggested that numerous poor cybersecurity practices that reflect insider threat are associated with personality traits linked to poor performance in other tasks as well, for example, low conscientiousness and emotional stability (Schoenherr, submitted c; Schoenherr & Thomson, 2021a).

3.6 Manufactured Consent 3.0: Social Influence and Social Influencers

The concept of an insider threat demonstrates how cyberoperations are not simply limited to software and hardware. Contemporary operations in cyberspace also reflect social influencing campaigns. As the Cambridge Analytica scandal illustrates, the power of understanding and controlling social networks has the potential to nudge users into behaviours that they might not engage in otherwise. Social media lays bare what was once an underlying theoretically motivated tool of behavioural and social sciences, i.e., social network analysis (Valente, 1995). This approach assumes that individuals reflect nodes in a network, with their exchanges creating behavioural traces that can be used to infer the social bonds and cognitive processes of individuals within the network (Paxton & Griffiths, 2017). From the perspective of social network analysis, individuals vary in terms of their centrality, whereas networks vary in terms of their density (Valente, 1995). Understanding how these networks function, how individuals can be influenced within them, and the social and ethical dimensions of such approaches, has become the focus of a growing body of research within the last decade (Bird et al., 2016).

3.6.1 Organic and Artificial Social Influencing

Persuasive communication has a long history, from propaganda to marketing. Effective messaging requires selecting the appropriate medium of communication, message content, audience, and source (Stiff & Mongeau, 2016). It also requires understanding the existing information environment (Cialdini, 2016). Unless we are motivated, superficial features of the message (e.g., fear messaging) or source (e.g., expertise, attractiveness, similarity) will determine attitude formation and change (Teeny et al., 2017). For instance, contemporary studies have found that beyond argument quality, Youtuber message relevance, social/peer influence (advocacy), and trustworthiness were the main determinants of attitudes toward a video and a brand (Xiao et al., 2018).[9] More generally, studies of message (e.g., memes) circulation on social media, have found that message quality is not the primary determinant of information diffusion within a social network. Instead, the structure of the network, along with user attention, is more influential (Weng et al., 2012). Perhaps more concerning, studies additionally suggest that humans spread misinformation and disinformation faster than accurate information in online settings (Vosoughi & Aral, 2018). Consequently, taking the time to stop and think can vastly reduce the spread of misinformation (Fazio, 2020).

Social influencing is now an occupation that democratizes and challenges the notion of celebrity. On the surface, social influencing might appear to be a democratic means to gain status by bypassing the traditional channels of prestige, for example, print, television, academia, or public service. At a deeper level, this kind of popularity has become systematized, self-sustaining, and monetized. Some approaches to monetization are overt, such as requesting payment through patronage accounts (e.g., patreon.com, ko-fi.com) wherein supporters can gain access to limited content (e.g., photos, videos). For instance, pop psychologist Jordan Peterson reportedly made $80,000/month by '[monetizing] social justice warriors' (Weiss, 2018).

Other methods of social influence are covert in entertainment media (Shrum, 2012). As they scroll through Internet memes, social media users will find product placements and guerilla marketing endorsements. Like 'grey propaganda' that neither expressly identifies its origin (white propaganda) or those that obscure their source (black propaganda), products are often promoted by a picture alone, a picture embedded in a set that a user scrolls through, or a picture with the social influencer using the product (Castronovo & Huang, 2012). This approach reflects a modern equivalent to spokesperson endorsement, which can be effective to the extent that the product and spokesperson are compatible (Till & Busler, 2000).

Social influence can be quite profitable. O'Connor (2017) has noted that Instagram users with 100,000 followers can receive $5,000 for a single post. Not surprisingly, another industry has grown from this wherein users can buy likes and followers to increase their centrality on social media platforms through engagement metrics (Confessore et al., 2018). Like purchasing a sponsored advertisement on a

FIGURE 3.4 Synthetic images of humans.

Note: Permission granted by George Paw.

Source: Produced by FakeISO (https://fakes.io/).

search engine, social influencers and companies can exploit the AISs that determine popularity and 'trending topics' and thereby gain more attention for products and messages. Unlike purchasing a sponsorship which is often identified, this approach misrepresents itself as an 'organic' increase in interest or followers, suggesting that the status has been obtained legitimately through the independent decisions of followers. These issues are not confined to social media, with some online dating sites allowing users to pay for premium services, such as increased profile exposure, by adjusting algorithms.

Far more concerning is the emergence of deepfakes (Westerlund, 2019). Deepfakes reflect a form of digital video manipulation that can simulate the appearance, movement, and speech of a real person or create entirely simulated individuals (for examples, see Figure 3.4). Contemporary interest was piqued with the 'synthesizing Obama project'. A deep neural network extracted relationships between audio and video segments, identified mouth shapes and textures, and was able to create a convincing video segment of President Obama speaking (Suwajanakorn et al., 2017).

In addition to the possibility of creating new performance from deceased artists and celebrities, deepfakes have been used in a variety of sinister applications such as creating fake pornography. In 2021, one service created an application that allowed users to substitute a real picture of anyone into a pornographic movie clip (Hao, 2021). This represents a significant concern as the applicable laws are not entirely clear (Harris, 2018). The relative accessibility of this technology also poses significant threats to democracy. In that it can be used to misrepresent the beliefs of world leaders and social influencers, it can be used to fuel conflicts (Chesney & Citron, 2019). As the public becomes increasingly aware of the technology, they might begin to doubt the veracity of any information provided to them (post-truth era), rejecting any information that does not conform to their prior beliefs.

3.6.2   Microtargeting, Nudging, and Social Influence Campaigns

Deepfakes are not the only way AISs can be used in social influence campaigns. Using psychographic methods, AISs can also be used to strategically target voters by using aggregated data, such as in the 2012 campaign of Barack Obama (Bimber, 2014; Nickerson & Rogers, 2014). Bots also have the potential to affect the outcomes of elections. With most social media outlets using engagement metrics to identify and promote trending topics, bots can artificially inflate a topic's importance and the perception of consensus, and contaminate resulting data sets (i.e., data poisoning; Joseph et al., 2013). These concerns are quite real given the prevalence of social media bots. In contrast to Facebook and Instagram, who have not provided estimates, Twitter has suggested that upwards of 8.5% of its social media accounts might be used by bots whereas other observers claim that the real number is twice this amount, i.e., 35 to 50 million bot accounts (Chong, 2017).

Demonstrating the potential for influence, shortly after a shooting in the United States, social media bots were found to be posting pro-gun comments on Twitter. Using more traditional methods, in the 2011 Canadian federal election, robocalls provided individuals in a Canadian riding with disinformation about changes to their polling stations, resulting in allegations of voter suppression (Payton, 2012). However, the impact of such social influencing campaigns has not been definitively established and requires much more investigation (Mazarr et al., 2019).

In addition to these comparatively crude methods, behavioural nudging represents a more advanced form of persuasive communication technique that employs indirect suggestions and positive reinforcement to alter attitudes and behaviour (Oliver, 2015; Thaler & Sunstein, 2008; Tannenbaum et al., 2017). Nudging assumes that an individual's attitudes need only be pushed incrementally in a desired direction. A variant of nudging, referred to as micro-targeting, uses specific information about user's interests, preferences, and beliefs to select a message that will have maximum impact (Barbu, 2014; Kruikemeier et al., 2016).

While the potential effect on elections might appear overstated, these attempts at social influence must be viewed in the context of how groups make consequential decisions. Despite a continuum of preference and attitude strength on political issues and candidates, voting procedures typically require discrete responses, i.e., to vote 'yes' or 'no' in a given decision. In a proportional representation electoral system, the conversion of a small number of voters can have a significant effect if a threshold is passed. For instance, in the UK referendum to leave the European Union (Brexit), the leave vote received only 51.9% support. If AISs could exert even a small influence on voters, their impact could be highly consequential (Kupferschmidt, 2017). In the case of Brexit, a study found that one-third of Brexit-related traffic on social media that preceded the referendum was generated by less than 1% of accounts, a pattern that suggests automation (Howard & Kollanyi, 2016). Similarly, Twitter data analytics revealed that there were over 5 million election-related tweets leading up to the Canadian 2015 election (Ireton, 2015). Evidence suggests that user accounts created in Iran, Russia, and Venezuela attempted to spark debate over key issues (e.g., immigration and oil pipelines; Rocha & Yates, 2019). In addition to elections, research has also examined other specific social issues such as vaccination and climate change. For instance, in their study of tweets pertaining to climate change, Marlow et al. (2021) found that 9.5% of accounts were likely bots and that these bots represented 25% of network activity related to climate change. Consequently, given the potential impact of behavioural nudges and microtargeting on group decision-making, the nature of the algorithm used by AISs can have significant social consequences.

Content Moderation and Automated Censorship. AISs can also filter content based on keywords and images to either remove misinformation and disinformation or to censor information. Censorship provides individuals and groups with control over the environment, limiting the availability of certain information, including images and concepts. For instance, the Chinese government has adopted both legislative and technological measures (e.g., blacklisted servers and websites) to restrict the access of Internet users within China, referred to as the Great Firewall (防火长城; e.g., Ensafi et al., 2015). In a study conducted by King et al. (2014) they found that while posts critical of leaders and the state were permitted on social media in China, posts related to protests were censored (for related results in Turkey, see Tanash et al., 2015). These practices also include the removal of questionable content. For instance, to stop the spread of misinformation, disinformation, offensive material, and calls to violence, Facebook instituted automated moderation, flagging, and eliminating posts with sensitive content that 'violates community standards'. However, content moderation is only as good as the methods used to filter content. For instance, using keywords can result in misidentification when words have multiple meanings (e.g., posts with the term 'hoe' have been flagged when used by gardeners; Ortutay, 2021). Evidence suggests that only 3–5% of hate activities on the platform and only '6-tenths of 1%' of violence and incitement were effectively removed (Pelley, 2021). Moreover, if these methods are selectively used on specific users, this leads to an increased ability to influence the information environment. Evidence also suggests that Facebook used a 'whitelist' that allowed celebrities and politicians to post sensitive content (Horwitz, 2021). Moreover, insiders have also revealed the existence of Project Amplify, a Facebook initiative that prioritized positive mentions of Facebook posted on users' newsfeeds (Mac & Frenkel, 2021). Concurrently, the organization also dismantled an analytic tool (CrowdTangle) that allowed researchers to examine user behaviour following revelations that there was a higher level of engagement with right-wing media (Roose, 2021).

Content moderation and filtering is not limited to social media platforms. Rather, any kind of communication can be controlled or suppressed. Between June 2020 and May 2021, the Internet watchdog Freedom House (2021) assessed 70 countries in terms of whether there is evidence of the use of a number of key Internet controls, including blocking social media platforms (21%) or websites (35%), surveillance (16%) and censorship laws (22%), arresting/imprisonment (41%) or physically assaulting Internet users (56%), technical attacks (40%), progovernment commentators (47%), and Internet shutdowns (20%). While social media outlets might notify users that content has been removed, content moderation can also exclude specific users or populations of users without their knowledge or consent, referred to as 'shadowbanning' (Myers West, 2018). For instance, Knockel et al. (2020) demonstrated that the Chinese application WeChat (微信) filters out messages sent by users containing specific keywords (e.g., Falun Gong, coronavirus) and images (e.g., political cartoons; see Figure 3.5). Using a statistical comparison, Le Merrer et al. (2021) provide evidence that, despite claims to the contrary, filtering that occurs in a more systematic manner cannot be attributed to idiosyncratic 'bugs' within an algorithm.

In the face of censorship within sociotechnical systems, humans have adapted. By recognizing that keywords can be used to filter content, internet users have resorted to algospeak, the consensual substitution of censored terms with uncensored terms in order to evade censorship (Lorenz, 2022). Terms often reflect homophones (e.g., 'Let's Go Brandon' for 'F---Joe Biden'), euphemisms, allegory, and metaphor. Chinese netizens have been particular adeptly at responding to the censorship (China Digital Times, 2013/2015). For instance, when faced with censorship during the COVID-19 pandemic, Chinese users created alternatives to Wuhan (wh) and Red Cross (red ten – the ten resembling a cross). These terms add to a growing lexicon that has been developed to facilitate free speech, e.g., 'Kim Fatty III' (金三胖) to refer to North Korean dictator Kim Jong-Un, and 'cured meat'/'bacon' (腊肉) to refer to Chairman Mao's mummified remains.

3.7 Scaling-Up: Societal Impact and Accountability

The control of communication channels illustrates the potential social consequences of AISs. Rather than censoring or changing the prevalence of information within an environment, AISs can also be used for surveillance in domestic and public spaces. These technologies challenge notions of accountability as responsibility is distributed between the developer, the operator, and the stakeholders who deploy these systems. These systems can have considerable benefit. For instance, the use of facial recognition applications developed by Clearview AI has be attributed to success identification and arrests of a number of suspects. However, the development and use of this application have been associated with numerous ethical and legal issues concerning data collection (Hill, 2020). During the development of their facial recognition technology, they scrapped information from website and collected images from dozens of shopping malls without the consent of users or shoppers,

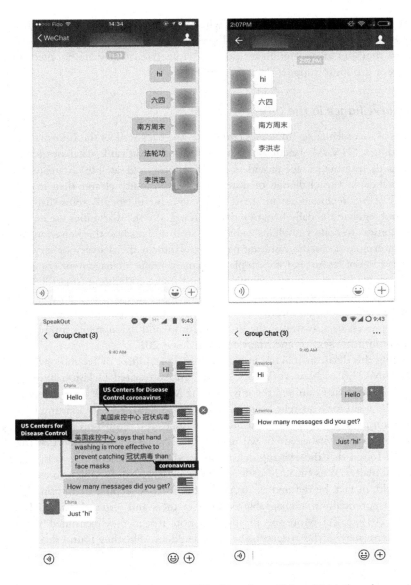

FIGURE 3.5 Tests of WeChat message blocking from China–China-based communication and US–China-based communication for terms 'Falun Gong' (top) and coronavirus information from the US Centre for Disease Control (bottom).

Note: Used with permission from the Citizens Lab (https://citizenlab.ca/).

respectively. The application was widely adopted, with over 2,400 law enforcement agencies (Hill, 2021). However, the failure to obtain consent has met with backlash.

In addition to monitoring and surveillance systems, dataveillance systems have also been developed that attempt to predict offences before they happen, paralleling dystopian fiction (e.g., Philip K. Dick's *The Minority Report* wherein trans-humans ('precogs') are used to arrested criminals who will commit crimes in the future (Ouellet et al., 2019). While these technologies can be adopted to facilitate social interaction, they can create significant power asymmetries if they are coopted by individuals or groups to support their own ends.

3.7.1 Surveillance in the City

A plurality of surveillance technologies constitutes the backbone of the Information Age, including CCTV, cybersecurity systems, debit and credit cards, databases, identification cards, Internet service providers, mobile phones, and satellites (Stamatellos, 2007). Nowhere is the challenge of distributed responsibility clearer than in the integration of AIS technologies in 'smart cities' with surveillance systems that can monitor and regulate the daily lives of citizens' (Kang, 1998). Smart cities use environmental sensors to collect residents' behaviour, store and analyze this behaviour to identify patterns, and use the resulting patterns to inform the delivery of services and conservation of resources, for example, movement (traffic management systems), energy (smart grids), environment (climate monitoring), and lighting (smart lights). Despite the promise of the efficient use of resources, concerns persist around the scale of surveillance, how this information is used, the power requirements to operate sensors and process data, as well as the need to rethink and redesign city infrastructure to accommodate sensors and smart devices (Zeine, 2017).

Illustrating this decision-making process, the Mayor's Office of Technology and Innovation (MOTI) in New York City created an Automated Decision Systems (ADS) Task Force that examined these issues. The MOTI ADS Task Force's report highlights the need for oversight for ADS to ensure compliance with existing laws and regulations, developing public education and discussion campaigns, and greater formalization of ADS management within the city. The report also noted that the stakeholders found that the existing definition of ADS was 'difficult to work with as a practical matter, as its breadth made it hard to clearly identify which tools and systems could, in fact, be defined as an ADS. This broad-sweeping definition also implicated a potentially unmanageable number of tools and systems' (p. 21; ADS Task Force, 2019, p. 21). More specifically, they note that as they examined 'what tools or systems may fit the criteria to be considered an ADS, they found that it is not always clear what constitutes a "decision"' (p. 16). Much like AISs, the difficulty in defining these systems creates issues for developing and enforcing coherent regulatory frameworks, leaving considerable room for discretionary decision-making.

3.7.2 Policing Algorithms: They Don't Always Get Their Man

Closely related to smart cities is the concept of predictive policing.[10] Predictive policing uses AISs to identify locations ('hotspots') and persons within a database (watchlists) associated with the high probability of criminal activity and criminality, respectively. Predictions made in these reports can then be used to target locations and persons prior to the commission of criminal acts. In addition to strategically allocating finite policing resources, predictive policing has the potential to reduce or eliminate bias, for example, race, gender, socioeconomic status.

The potential benefits of predictive policing are so widely recognized that one variant of this approach (PredPol software) was adopted by 50 departments within the United States (Baron, 2019). To identify hotspots, PredPol analyzes relationships between the type of crime, the date and time, and the location. The system is used as a deterrent to prevent crime by targeting patrols in these areas, with meta-analyses suggesting that this approach resulted in small reductions in the crimes rates in hotspots as well as in adjacent areas (Braga et al., 2014). In Chicago, police forces employed a Strategic Subject List (SSL).[11] Developed by the Illinois Institute of Technology in 2013, this risk model was used to facilitate the distribution of scarce policing resources toward more effective crime prevention. The list was developed by using several predictive factors (e.g., criminal history, gang membership, whether they had been shot). As evidence that the SSL was used as a decision-making tool in an antiviolence strategy, reporters have noted that of the suspects arrested over a two month period, 83.5% were on the SSL. Indeed, the police superintendent, considered the SSL a means to 'hold repeat offenders accountable' and that it provided confirmatory information that '... we are targeting the right people' (Gorner, 2016).

Despite some successes, predictive policing has been repeatedly challenged. In 2015, questions were raised over the validity of the Chicago SSL (e.g., Saunders et al., 2016).[12] Using an anonymized version of the list,[13] investigators found several issues with the ranking systems and the variables used to create the list (Asher & Arthur, 2017). For instance, individuals who were classified as high-risk (~1,400) were not necessarily responsible for the highest rates of violence. Similarly, the variable of gang membership which was often believed to be strongly associated with violence, was in fact a poor predictor of criminality. After many years of use, the program ended in November 2019. The Office of Inspector General noted several concerns with the SSL including 'the unreliability of risk scores and tiers; improperly trained sworn personnel; a lack of controls for internal and external access; interventions influenced by PTV (party to violence) risk models which may have attached negative consequences to arrests that did not result in convictions; and a lack of a long-term plan to sustain the PTV models' (OIG, 2020). The SSL is not the only predictive policing method that has been questioned. The LASER (Los Angeles Strategic Extraction and Restoration) program, used by the Los Angeles Police Department, faced similar concerns and met with a similar fate (Puente, 2019). Outside of the US, concerns have also been raised in both South Africa (Hao & Swart, 2022) and China (Bhuiyan, 2021) over who has access to these surveillance technologies and who is the subject of surveillance. Such imbalances in power can reinforce or amplify existing inequalities.

Presumably, large-scale predictive algorithms are also being used by national intelligence and enforcement agencies. With the comparative ease of the capture, processing, and storage of information, the resulting large-scale AIS surveillance systems create significant power asymmetries between data subjects and those that have access to them. For instance, in the US, the National Security Administration

(NSA), under two administrations, collected phone records for the prevention of domestic terrorism (Cauley, 2006; Greenwald, 2013a, 2013b). As an anonymous NSA employee noted, the ultimate goal is 'to create a database of every call ever made' (Cauley, 2006). The revelation of the scope of surveillance made public by Edward Snowden was met with mixed results. For instance, the majority of voters in a Rasmussen Report (59%; Rasmussen, 2013), Gallup Poll survey (53%; Newport, 2013), and Pew Research Center poll (56%; Pew Research Center, 2013) opposed or disapproved of the NSA's surveillance program. However, the Pew Research Center poll also suggests that US citizens were split concerning Snowden's actions (44% indicated it was right whereas 42% indicated it was wrong) with a subsequent poll by the Rasmussen Report (2018) finding that 29% considered him a traitor with only 14% reporting that they believed he was a hero and most (48%) believing his actions placed him somewhere in the middle.

3.7.3 Surveillance Societies

Contemporary discussion of surveillance and dataveillance primarily focus on conflicts between privacy and security but often fails to assess how these systems related to interpersonal processes. Unlike humans that have limited attentional resources, AISs have no such constraints. Consequently, surveillance systems are designed and adopted to ensure conformity to social norms, with some evidence suggesting that these technologies are more likely to be adopted by societies that prioritize conformity (Schoenherr, 2020a, 2021a, 2022a). To examine the prevalence of these systems, Feldstein (2019) recently created an AI Global Surveillance (AIGS) index to assess how 75 countries use these technologies (see Table 3.2). Three diagnostic categories were used in the development of the AIGS: the use of (1) smart/safe cities, (2) facial recognition systems, and (3) smart policing. Feldstein concluded that, when compared to an earlier report, adoption of AIS surveillance technologies is increasing at a rapid pace from 27.7% to 72.3% within a one-year period, with the majority (84%) adopting surveillance technologies from China. He additionally suggested that the best predictor of adopting of surveillance technology is military expenditure but otherwise adoption was relatively heterogeneous, including both full democracies and dictatorial regimes in his sample.

TABLE 3.2 Prevalence of AI Surveillance Technology Use

Broad Geopolitical Region Adopting Surveillance Technology	Number of Countries
Americas	12
Africa	12
Europe and Eurasia	17
South and Central Asia	12
Middle East and North Africa	12
East Asia and Pacific	15

Source: Adapted from Feldstein. Adapted from Feldstein (2019).

China has been an early developer and adopter of smart city technologies. Most recently, the central government has been developing a national social credit system directed toward reducing corruption. The government describes the social credit system as a means 'to improve the integrity of the whole society and the level of credit' thereby emphasizing economic, social issues. While the goal is to create a centralized approach, the social credit system currently represents several regional pilot projects, each varying in its scope and methods (Hatton, 2015). For instance, in addition to information concerning an individual's financial credit history, the Sesame Credit system assesses whether they are a parent and how much time they spend playing video games. On an opt-in basis, this score has also been used on a dating site (Baihe). Other systems, such as that in Rongcheng, additionally assess traffic violations and charitable contributions.

Beyond early pilot programs, the Chinese central government introduced directives from nationwide implementation in 2014 with hopes that all citizens' scores would have been publicly available by 2020. This hope was not realized. Once implemented at the proposed scale, the system would result in China's 1.4 billion citizens and organizations being assessed on their adherence to social norms (Kobie, 2019). Violation of these norms can result in severe restrictions such as inclusion on a blacklist and travel restrictions applied to over 12 million citizens (Fullerton, 2018). In addition to privacy concerns regarding how and where information is collected, additional concerns stem from the security of this information. For instance, one security analyst gained access to an unprotected database (SenseNets) containing the records of over 2.5 million citizens, mostly from the Xinjiang province (Ng, 2019). Thus, even though widespread implementation is not currently possible, the scale of surveillance compounds social and ethical issues related to individual rights and cybersecurity vulnerabilities.

Despite concerns over autonomy and privacy, surveillance can have tangible benefits for society. During the COVID-19 pandemic, many geotracking-based applications were developed to understand and ameliorate the spread of the novel coronavirus (Busvine, 2020; Ellensheng, 2020; Hemmadi, 2020; Pollina & Busvine, 2020). Austrian, German, and Italian mobile phone carriers shared aggregated data to understand the concentration and movement of customers in critical areas. With the consent of mobile phone users, such monitoring can adhere to data privacy guidelines.[14] Facebook and Google also considered sharing aggregated and anonymized data with the US government, with Google also providing mobility data publicly to help researchers track movement during the pandemic (e.g., Schoenherr & Thomson, 2020c; Schoenherr, submitted b). In China, over 200 cities were reportedly required to use a traffic light app that assigned users a colour (red, yellow, or green) in real-time, which determined whether they were permitted to enter public spaces, malls, or public transportation or whether they should be quarantined. However, analysis of *The New York Times* at the time suggested that the classification method was unclear, that the app appears to share information with police forces, and that users were not directly informed of this condition (Mozur et al., 2020). Similar methods were used in Taiwan for those entering the country, with a GPS tracker used to monitor those in quarantine (Wang et al., 2020). Thus, surveillance technologies are neither inherently good nor bad. Rather, understanding the implementation context is key along with how the data is used once the initial rationale for tracking has ended. By actively engaging individuals in the development and implementation of the surveillance system, we can ensure fairness and ensure that the agency of users is respected (Alge, 2001; Kim, 2004).

3.8   Killer Robots, the War in 2020, and the Next Arms Race

'Killer robots' represent only the latest iteration of existential threats attributed to autonomous human creations, e.g., Golem (Section 2.1.2). Autonomous weapons systems (AWS) are no longer science fiction. Most recently, the war in 2020 between Azerbaijan and Armenia over the disputed region of Nagorno-Karabakh has brought the role of AISs in combat and defence into sharp focus. In many respects, the two opposing forces were evenly matched (Kitson, 2020). While the Armenian army relied on traditional warfare with high altitude missile defence systems and T-72 tanks and artillery strikes that targeted defensive lines, Azerbaijan made UAVs a cornerstone of their strategy which ultimately proved successful (Shahbazov, 2020).

AISs played numerous roles in combat. In addition to remote planes that were used to draw the fire of the Armenian forces, reconnaissance drones in conjunction with artillery to target defensive lines, strike UAVs, and loitering munitions (the 'kamikaze drone'), which can remain for long periods of time in an operational theatre until *it* can identify a target, were also used. These tactics resulted in the destruction of over 240 Armenian tanks (Shahbazov, 2020) and the reclamation of the region. Such results are important for their implication for modern warfare: 'That a country such as Azerbaijan was able to effect precision strikes at operational depth … by using a range of relatively cheap tools to substitute for its lack of a robust air force is strategically noteworthy' (Watling & Kaushal, 2020). Many nations closely observed the Azerbaijan–Armenia conflict and its outcomes to prepare for future conflicts.

The use and success of AWS has further fuelled concerns about a new arms race (Benjamin, 2013) and associated ethical issues (Hellström, 2013; Horowitz, 2019; Krishnan, 2009; Marchant et al., 2011; Nasser, 2014). General concerns about AIS 'accuracy' take on a new dimension, given the involvement of human lives. In the context of military applications, this can be understood in terms of civilian losses. However, as a report published by the Columbia Law School's Human Rights Clinic illustrates, there appear to be issues with the available estimates of civilian drone-strike deaths (Human Rights Clinic, 2012). As the report argues, without accurate statistics, it is difficult to determine accountability and the kinds of regulations that are required for the continued use of AIS combat systems.

At issue is the extent to which humans will *need* to rely on these systems to make decisions. For instance, the prospect of drone swarms means that an opponent with superior manned firepower might be outmatched by more numerous, inexpensive AWS that can coordinate and/or self-destruct. Despite commitments to leave humans in control of lethal decisions, the need for rapid responses in a theatre of operations, and the likelihood that adversaries will not abide by similar constraints, will make it impractical for humans to retain complete control over AISs. Moreover, the comparatively inexpensive nature of these 'DIY killer robots' (Scharre, 2018) also means that state and non-state actors alike can rapidly develop and deploy these systems provided that they have access to hardware and software.

The February 24, 2022 Russian invasion of Ukraine additionally illustrates the blurred lines on modern conflict involving AISs. After Microsoft initially detected a malware attack ("Foxblade") that preceded the Russian invasion and notified the Ukrainian government, it remained in 'constant and close coordination', supporting the government (Smith, 2022). These efforts were later followed by suspending Microsoft sales in Russia. Concurrently, the hackvist collective, Anonymous, entered the conflict, tweeting: "The Anonymous collective is officially in cyber war against the Russian government. #Anonymous #Ukraine" (February 24, 2022). The group claimed responsibility for DDoS attacks, hacking Russian state TV by replacing the normal content with patriotic Ukrainian symbols and music (Milmo, 2022) as well as censored news (Chirinos, 2022), and claimed to have leaked 820 gigabytes of data related to Russian media censorship activities (Cox, 2022).

3.9   Section Summary: Popular Science

Popular science reflects a mixture of scientific evidence, grey literature, and opinions. Discourse within popular science appears to reflect both technophobia and technophilia, with the respective sides focusing on the costs and benefits of AISs. In contrast to technical discussions of the technology that focuses on AIS intelligence, autonomy, and connectivity, social consequences appear to be a primary focus. Basic issues concern the requirements of workforce retraining and digital divides in terms of accessibility to, and benefits of, technology. Similarly, how technological environments are structured and how they affect humans must also be accounted for during the implementation of these technologies. Social influence and the domestication of surveillance technologies on social media platforms, messaging application, and in cities represent significant challenges. As greater autonomy is granted to AISs armed with lethal weapons, there is an increasing need to rigorously reflect on how technological affordances translate into ethical affordances.

Notes

1 Heuristics are simple decision-making rules that reduce the amount of information-processing required, for example, the availability heuristic uses information that is immediately available rather than other pertinent sources of information; confirmation bias attends to information that supports one's prior belief, rather than additionally weighing the balance of confirming and disconfirming information.
2 Orthogonal refers to separable, discrete dimensions that define characters (e.g., speed, strength, movement type, intelligence, perception).

3 Overestimating suggests a failure of metacognitive monitoring (e.g., overconfidence) or a pluralistic ignorance of others' attitudes and behaviour (e.g., Crandall et al., 2002; Mullen et al., 1985; Prentice & Miller, 1996).

4 It is also worth noting that previous versions of the DSM classified homosexuality as a disorder before it was subsequently removed. This reflects the socially constructed nature of disorders and constructs more generally.

5 While this report should not be overinterpreted, the increase in reported prosocial behaviour might reflect that the widespread knowledge of the benefits of 'paragon' behaviours might increase players' propensity to select these behaviours in the future.

6 However, it should be noted that attitudes and behaviour are only weakly correlated (e.g., Glasman & Albarracin, 2006). Nevertheless, this can lead to moral licensing (Section 5.4).

7 Assuming that the reading rate is 250 words per minute.

8 Rather than being based in academia, grey literature represents non-academic publications, typically produced in industry but can also include unpublished manuscripts, 'white papers', and other sources that have not been subject to a formal peer review system.

9 Homophily and interactivity were only weakly associated with attitudes whereas perceived likeability was not a significant determinant.

10 I use this term to describe a constellation of approaches that includes 'data-driven policing', 'intelligence-led policing', 'risk-based policing', and 'smart policing'.

11 Later referred to as the Crime Victimization Risk Model (CVRM).

12 This study was conducted using an earlier version of the system.

13 https://data.cityofchicago.org/Public-Safety/Strategic-Subject-List/4aki-r3np.

14 Sections of workplace safety and health (Article 6 and 9) in the GDPR.

4

TWILIGHT OF THE GODS

Frameworks from Philosophical Ethics

As discussions in popular science demonstrate, boundaries between ethical values and other values are often ill-defined. Polarized debates often reflect people's beliefs about specific issues in terms of whether there are ethical features or dimensions that define them, for example gun ownership, privacy, and deference to secular and sacred institutions. Moreover, people often fail to distinguish between their individual morality and systematic assessment within ethical systems.[1]

Philosophical ethics provides an important set of analytic tools that help identify relevant features of, and responses to, otherwise ambiguous situations. Thus, prior to considering how we make sense of our environment (Chapter 5), a number of basic distinctions must be introduced as well as how they can help inform the creation and assessment of an ethical approach to AISs (Chapter 6). Following these basic distinctions, we can consider similarities and differences in ethical frameworks and how they can be applied to the development and use of AISs.

4.1 Descriptive and Prescriptive Norms

Meta-ethical frameworks typically focus on defining 'the good' – rights, virtues, and vices – and whether these terms have any meaning beyond expressing emotional responses (Ayer, 1936/2012; Garner & Rosen, 1967), or whether 'good' is analytically separable from experience as a whole (e.g., Nishida, 1990; Tetsurō, 2011). Prior to reviewing these ethical frameworks, we must consider a basic distinction between descriptive (what *is*) and prescriptive (*what ought to be*) norms.

4.1.1 Descriptive Norms

Descriptive Norms are those that reflect typical or average values, beliefs, or actions within a group, society, or culture. Corresponding to research in the behavioural

DOI: 10.4324/9781003143284-4

and social sciences, descriptive norms can differ between individuals, groups, and societies. Simply because there are differences in values and conventions observed between groups does not imply that this *should* be the case, i.e., moral relativism. As we will discuss later, a set of cross-cultural relational models can be used as models for ethical exchanges (Section 5.3.1).

From a technical perspective, descriptive norms in AISs likely reflect the intended features and functions of a design as well as the strengths and weaknesses of algorithms based on disciplinary norms and conventions. There is widespread recognition that AISs can reproduce biases that are already present within the data (e.g., Eubanks, 2018; Ferguson, 2019; Kearns & Roth, 2019). This would become especially concerning if AISs are developed to make ethical judgments based on existing data sets (Section 6.2).

Similar arguments can be made for the persistence of coding errors (Section 2.2.1) and cybersecurity vulnerabilities (Section 3.5.1). When these concerns are addressed, they are typically understood in terms of trade-offs such as that between privacy and security or between fairness and algorithmic accuracy. For instance, Kearns and Roth (2019) note how adjusting algorithms to accommodate protected groups can result in biases that will affect other groups. At a more general level, the use of AISs can have a significant negative environmental impact (for recent discussion and reviews, see Jones, 2018; Malmodin & Lundén, 2018; Lange et al., 2020).

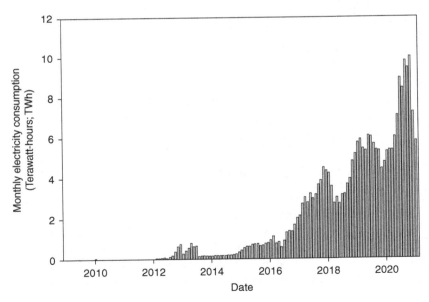

FIGURE 4.1 Monthly electricity consumption associated with Bitcoin mining from July 2010 to July 2021.

Source: Cambridge Bitcoin Electricity Consumption Index. Data retrieved from https://cbeci.org/index.

For instance, mining[2] the cryptocurrency, Bitcoin, has been associated with significant power consumption (Figure 4.1) that is comparable to that of entire countries
(Goodkind et al., 2020) and has contributed to an estimated 30.7 metric kilotons
of e-waste (De Vries & Stoll, 2021).

These observations are not offered to justify these deficiencies. Rather, they
simply *describe* the current state of AIS implementation. Even within the context of
early science, there have been persistent concerns regarding the deficiencies of the
people and the products of science (Babbage, 1830). Instead of simply replicating
norms and conventions, '[t]he social contract among people in the Information Age
must deal with these threats to human dignity' (Mason, 1986).

4.1.2   Prescriptive Norms

In contrast to descriptive norms, *prescriptive norms* are those that reflect abstract
principles or behavioural exemplars that are deemed to be good, right, or just,
regardless of what are commonly accepted practices within a group. Prescriptive
norms tell us what we *ought* to do rather than what is done. For instance, Merton
(1942) characterized the norms of science in terms of communality, universality,
disinterestedness, and organized skepticism, later adding in the importance of recognition through citation (Merton, 1957). Alongside these norms, counter-norms
have also been proposed (e.g., particularism, dogmatism, commissioned, localized,
proprietary; Mitroff, 1974; Ziman, 2000).

Prescriptive norms are often captured in scientific codes of conduct and scientific integrity policies (e.g., Chalk et al., 1980; CHPS Consulting, 2000; Greene
et al., 1985; Frankel, 1989; Jorgensen, 1995; Leach & Harbin, 1997; Lind, 2005;
Schoenherr & Williams-Jones, 2011; UNESCO, 2002). For instance, positive norms
such as professional integrity, beneficence and non-maleficence often feature prominently alongside negative norms such as the avoidance of data manipulation, intellectual property theft, and duplicate publication.[3] These documents speak to a
specific group of academics, either at a disciplinary or an institutional level, often
focusing on integrating other policies and laws (e.g., conflicts of interests, collective
agreements, contracts).

In addition to broad sets of national and international guidelines,[4] codes of
conduct have also been developed by information and computer science (ICS)
professionals such as software engineers and data scientists to address high-level
ethical issues. For instance, many software engineers are subject to the *IEEE Code of
Ethics*. Supporting this code, the *Ethical Aligned Design* (IEEE, 2016) outlines norms
for ICS professionals developing AISs: 'creators shall empower individuals with the
ability to access and securely share their data, to maintain people's capacity to have
control over their identity'. The Association for Computing Machinery (ACM,
2018) also recently updated its ethical standards. In terms of software, this includes
'Efforts to help others by contributing time and energy to projects that help society
illustrate a positive aspect of [contributing to the public good by allowing the use
of their intellectual works]. Such efforts include free and open-source software and

work put into the public domain' (ACM, 2018, section 1.5). It also recognizes 'the inevitability of software errors, the interactions of systems and their contexts' and the impact of software updates on user productivity and work quality, given user dependency (ACM, 2018, section 3.6).

The *ACM Code* also refers to cyberoperations that involve the creation and deployment of AISs for defensive and offensive purposes. Namely, it specifies that:

> computing professionals should not access another's computer system, software, or data without a reasonable belief that such an action would be *authorized* or a compelling belief that it is consistent with the *public good*. A system being publicly accessible is not sufficient grounds on its own to imply authorization. Under exceptional circumstances a computing professional may use unauthorized access to disrupt or inhibit the functioning of malicious systems; extraordinary precautions must be taken in these instances to avoid harm to others.
>
> *ACM, 2018, section 2.8; italics added*

The ACM Code raises concerns over several ethical affordances inherent in software engineering that need to be incorporated into practices and training. Specifically, we face issues of defining the public good, determining how to measure it, and identifying who represents a legitimate authority that could authorize violations of privacy. Moreover, the recognition that errors will occur is an important aspect of the design process (Section 6.1) in that remedial measures can be developed to account for resulting issues. This still leaves open the question of what proportion of errors and what outcomes will be deemed acceptable. Thus, while such codes are beneficial, the process of identifying ethical affordances remains with stakeholders.

Governmental and nongovernmental organizations have also begun to develop general guidelines and standards for ethical AISs (for recent reviews, see Calo, 2017; Fjeld et al., 2020; Floridi et al., 2018; Frost et al., 2021; Hagendorff, 2020; Jobin et al., 2019; Zeng et al., 2018). For instance, broad ethical concerns such as fairness, accuracy, transparency, and ethics (FATE) in the design of algorithms are meant to guide the creation and assessment of AISs.[5] A selection of common prescriptive standards is presented in Table 4.1. In a systematic review conducted by Fjeld et al. (2020), eight themes were identified in AI ethics guidelines and policies. Supporting several concerns raised in popular science, common themes addressed by these documents include privacy, explainability, transparency, non-discrimination and the prevention of bias, human control of technology, human values and flourishing, and leveraging technology to benefit society. Alternatively, the SIENNA Project conducted a broad review and identified three categories of ethical value sets associated with the objectives, the techniques and methods of AISs, and the general implications of AISs (see Table 4.2; Jansen et al., 2019). This approach is particularly

TABLE 4.1 Common Principles or Standards Provided by Governmental and Nongovernmental Organizations with a General Description

Principle/Standard	General Description
Accountability/Responsibility	The extent to which individuals who develop, distribute, and use AISs have responsibility within the social and legal systems of a society.
Explainability	The extent to which the operations of a system are intelligible for stakeholders, acknowledging the knowledge, motivation, and priorities of the stakeholder population.
Fairness and Non-discrimination	The extent to which an algorithm's operations, outcomes, or the consequences of those operations, are equally applicable to all relevant stakeholders. The extent to which data used to train or produce decisions is representative of the stakeholder population that will be affected by the decisions.
Integrity	The extent to which data is accurate and free from bias. The extent to which the operations and use of an algorithm are supported by evidence of their relative accuracy and reliability. The extent to which the data sets and operations of AISs are accurately represented to stakeholders.
Transparency	The extent to which the operations of AISs or their data sets are intelligible and accessible to stakeholders. This includes the ability to interpret data as well as fostering the ability to pose questions and understand answers about the structure of data and the operations of AISs.
Privacy/Confidentiality	The extent to which a data subject's information remains private, inaccessible, and under the control of others, taking into consideration specific contextual factors such as sociocultural norms and usage cases.
Safety and Security	The extent to which the operations of an AIS ensure, and do not threaten, the physical and psychological safety and security of stakeholders.

comprehensive and aligns well with the multi-stakeholder approach adopted in this book.

4.1.3 The Naturalistic Fallacy

Despite the crucial distinction of descriptive and prescriptive norms, they are often conflated, leading to an error in reasoning: the *naturalistic fallacy*. The naturalistic fallacy occurs when someone assumes that a descriptive principle should be treated as a prescriptive principle, i.e., inferring an 'ought' from an 'is' (Hume, 1738–1740/2003; Moore, 1903/1993). The ubiquity of the naturalistic fallacy is evidenced in the changing perceived consensus in one place or time: 'that which one age considers evil is usually an unseasonable echo of what was formerly considered

TABLE 4.2 Values Framework Developed by the SIENNA Project

AI and Subfields	Fundamental Techniques, Methods, and Approaches	General Implications and Risks
Efficiency and productivity improvement	Algorithms	Autonomy and liberty
Effectiveness improvement	Knowledge representation and reasoning techniques	Privacy
Risk reduction	Design paradigms	Justice and fairness
System autonomy	Automated planning and scheduling	Responsibility and accountability
Human–AI collaboration	Machine learning	Safety and security
Mimicking human social behaviour	Machine ethics	Dual use and misuse
AGI and superintelligence		Mass unemployment
Human cognitive enhancement		Transparency and explainability
		Other potential harms

Source: Modified from Jansen et al. (2019).

good' (150, Nietzsche, 1997, section 150). However, in applied ethics domains such as the law, the line between descriptive norms of a community and the prescriptive norms that address proper conduct are often blurred (Kirchmair, 2019; Soper, 2002).

The naturalistic fallacy appears to permeate many discussions of the social and ethical issues that define AIS ethics. For instance, privacy concerns related to application use can be understood in these terms: even *if* there is a precedent for impractical and convoluted privacy policies and user agreements (Morgan, 2014; Sanders, 2011; Yakowitz, 2011), developers and distributors of AISs are not justified in continuing these practices. On a larger scale, smart cities, the IoT, and industrial control systems reflect these same issues. Even if each individual technology that constitutes these systems is supported by significant evidence, this does not guarantee that their combination can or should be accepted.

The naturalistic fallacy additionally provides insight into the development of machine ethics. For some, humans are *the* only moral agents that have existed and can exist. For these people, whatever their intelligence or autonomy, AISs are inherent *a*moral agents, i.e., if morals must always be judged relative to humans then only humans can make moral judgments. These humanistic arguments are based on several assumptions, including that similarity to humans (e.g., autonomy, intelligence) is the principal criterion to judge ethical cognition and behaviour and that below the threshold of human competency, other entities cannot have moral agency (e.g., Purves et al., 2015). However, this approach has its flaws. For instance, in her discussion of the ethical issues associated with AWS, Burri (2018) notes that simply because a final decision to use lethal force on a target is made by an AIS, that does not mean that the decision is inherently morally flawed (p. 164). Moreover, even if human moral judgments are unique in some respect, it is not clear that human-like moral agency is necessary. As we will consider later, 'full agency' or 'full autonomy' might not be a necessary or appropriate goal of an ethical system

(Section 6.2). Just because humans can make moral judgments and have developed ethical frameworks, that does not mean that human ethical sensemaking is optimal or that it is the only means to act ethically within an environment.

4.2 Consequentialism, Non-Consequentialism, and Virtue Ethics

The principal focus of philosophical ethics is to define prescriptive norms and principles while avoiding the naturalistic fallacy. Broad *meta*-ethical frameworks can be differentiated based on the importance of both the duties or intentions of the moral agent and the consequences of an action, leading to three broad ethical frameworks: consequentialism, non-consequentialism, and virtue ethics. Crucially, each of these frameworks provides different insights into how we should assess and design AISs.

4.2.1 Consequentialism and Utilitarian Accounts

Consequentialist theories prioritize the consequences of an action over the intentions of an actor. The most prominent consequentialist theory is utilitarianism. Utilitarianism assumes that 'the good' reflects either *actions* or *rules* that maximize utility. In Bentham's initial formulation of a hedonic calculus, he assumed that feelings of pleasure or pain provided the basis of utility. On this account, values ultimately have an evolutionary basis. In contrast, later approaches assume that higher-order pleasure is required to judge the goodness of a behaviour (Mill, 1998). Due to its focus on outcomes, utilitarianism presents a practical evidence-based approach to ethics wherein we can maximize the good, or minimize the bad, experienced by members of a group. Moreover, if utility can be measured, this approach can be operationalized for use in AISs.

Utilitarianism has been criticized on numerous grounds. First, identifying and assessing all possible positive and negative consequences of an action is impractical. At its core, consequentialism requires that ethical problems are finite, affecting a specifiable group of people over a given period. In practice, the outcomes of an action can affect numerous individuals over lengthy periods of time, often having unforeseen (and unforeseeable) consequences (Nagel, 1989, chapter 11). For instance, an AIS could be developed for one reason (e.g., face recognition for photo) and applied in another context (e.g., surveillance in urban environments). Indeed, all AISs can be understood in these terms. More generally, the values and possible outcomes of different moral agents might be incommensurable. For instance, if mining cryptocurrency or operating AISs adversely affect the environment (e.g., Dhar, 2020; Strubell et al., 2020), how do we assess the short- or medium-term gains of AISs against the long-term costs of an irreplaceable ecosystem? The fact that this could be done in principle through a common metric of 'utility' is very different from its actual feasibility.

Beyond the calculation of utility, it is also not clear what motivations a consequentialist has for being concerned about the experienced utility of other individuals.

If we assume that it is because everyone is a moral agent deserving of equivalent respect and self-determination, this criterion invokes values outside of a moral calculus, for example, non-consequentialist principles or virtues. Moreover, utilitarianism can also ignore social justice and the importance of autonomy. Namely, if an action causes pain for a small number of individuals, it could be justified on consequentialist grounds if a larger number of individuals benefited from the action.[6]

BOX 4.1 THE QUANTITATIVE FALLACY

One of the primary challenges faced in adapting a consequentialist ethics to AIS is defining a principled means to assign numbers to phenomena (e.g., Stevens, 1946). The *Quantitative Fallacy* occurs when decision-makers focus solely on numbers to the *exclusion* of all other information (Fischer, 1970). The *McNamara Fallacy* reflects a version of this fallacy based on the approach Robert McNamara adopted to administering the Vietnam War, introducing the concept of 'body count' as a measure of success. This approach has been seen as an important contributor to the widespread killing of civilians (e.g., Turse, 2013).

In his discussion of this approach, Yankelovich (1972) defined the fallacy as a series of steps:

> "The first step is to measure whatever can easily be measured. This is [fine.] The second step is to disregard that which can't be easily measured or to give it an arbitrary quantitative value. This is artificial and misleading. The third step is to presume that what can't be measured easily really isn't important. This is blindness. The fourth step is to say that what can't be easily measured really doesn't exist. This is suicide."

The central problem is not that quantification is inappropriate or ineffective. Rather, we must understand the strengths and limitations of the method when it is used within a specific context (Schoenherr & Hamstra, 2016). For instance, in the context healthcare Black (2010) cautions:

> "even if coding and diagnostic data were completely accurate, it is perverse to use a hospital's mortality statistics to judge its quality of care... the incongruity of using mortality to assess a hospital is exacerbated by geographical variation in the proportion of deaths that occur in hospital (40-65%), which reflects not only the availability of alternative forms of end of life care, such as hospices and community palliative services, but also cultural, religious, and socioeconomic characteristics of the local population."

McNamara (1995) later expressed doubts about his approach: "Uncertain how to valuate results in a war without battle lines, the military tried to gauge its progress with quantitative measurements such as enemy casualties (which became infamous as body counts), weapons seized, prisoners taken, sorties flown, and so on. We later learned that many of these measures were misleading or erroneous," (p.67).

Numbers represents an important instrument that can provide a common currency for exchange. They are not in themselves a solution. Effective datafication requires an understanding of how numbers are assigned to objects, how values inform this process, how dimensional reduction changes users into data subjects, and a recognition that numbers are contextually bound. Using them outside their initial context or assuming that they provide an adequate representation of users must be constantly re-evaluated (Section 2.2.1). Users must also be engaged to ensure that they understand the nature of the use (and reuse) of their data.

Applications of Consequentialism in AISs. At least tacitly, many AIS developers likely subscribe to some facets of consequentialism. For instance, prior to monetization, aggregate analysis of user data was used to improve user experience, making search results more relevant (e.g., Google; see Zuboff, 2019). In this way, what might be construed as a minor violation of privacy for any given individual, creates more positive outcomes by enhancing the efficiency of the search for all users. Complicating these matters, the aggregation of data and concerns over cybersecurity might also create long-term negative consequences that are possible, as well as those that are not currently foreseeable. For instance, the digitization of academic records has resulted in ransomware attacks leading to threats of destruction of records (Section 3.5). Similar rationales have been provided by the introduction of AISs to perform tasks: while a subset of a population might be displaced from their jobs, overall, society would be better off lowering the cost of services and reallocating human labour to other industries (Section 3.1). However, in this case, the cost of retraining places a burden on society, one that might not have the social institutions that are equipped to reskill workers.

4.2.2   Non-Consequentialism and Duty-Based Accounts

Non-consequentialism, or deontological ethics, assumes that the consequences of an action cannot be used to judge an act, *per se*. Instead, behaviour is judged to be good based on its adherence to an ethical norm and the individual's intentions. On these grounds, even if an action produces negative outcomes, it can still be judged to be right. The most prominent deontological principle is Kant's *categorical imperative* wherein an action specified by a moral rule should be universal (i.e., apply everywhere, at all times) with individuals treating each other as rational moral agents that are ends in themselves, rather than as means to other ends (i.e., 'the Kingdom of Ends'; e.g., Rawls, 1971a; Hill, 1971; O'Neill, 1975).

Contemporary versions of this account have often been framed in terms of distributive justice, such as Rawls' (1971a) theory of justice. In Rawls' account, all individuals are equal within a society and, provided that an individual was blinded to their status within a society *a priori*, they would choose an equal distribution of resources.[7] Crucially, Rawls (1971b) also considers the moral status of nonhuman agents noting that while '[t]here is … a certain logical priority to the case of human individuals: it may be possible to analyze the actions of so-called *artificial persons* as logical constructions of the actions of human persons …' (pp. 244–245; italics added). Thus, the actions of nonhuman agents (e.g., corporations and AISs), could be held to the same standards as human agents.

Specific forms of non-consequentialist are also relevant to cases of specific AIS use. The use of AISs in combat situations is a particularly important example in that it relates to the protection and termination of human life (Purves et al., 2015). For instance, Just War Theory assumes that we must identify a set of criteria, or rules, that must be satisfied in order to engage in an armed conflict (*jus ad bellum*), conduct operations during conflict (*jus in bello*), and what should be done once conflicts cease (*jus post bellum*). If we satisfy these criteria, then physical aggression is permissible and, in some cases, ethical (see, virtuous violence; Section 5.3.1). Indeed, large-scale conflicts are often framed in moral terms (e.g., Burleigh, 2005, 2010). If there is nothing intrinsically wrong with delegating lethal decisions to AISs (Burri, 2018), then AISs can be legitimately used in combat situations.

Like consequentialist frameworks, non-consequentialist frameworks face many challenges. One major concern is that seemingly rational principles that inform behaviour might cause negative outcomes. For instance, if killing is wrong, we should avoid killing at all costs. However, if we refuse to kill, another person, group, or nation might be allowed to inflict signifiant harm, i.e., 'the moral recklessness of pacifism'.[8] Non-consequentialist principles can also be sufficiently general, such that there are multiple ways to interpret them. For instance, 'harm avoidance' might mean the avoidance of killing or could imply that killing is sometimes required to stop another agent causing harm.

Finally, rather than a single principle, multiple principles might exist, leading to potential conflicts between them. For instance, social media creates challenges between balancing 'freedom of speech' and 'non-maleficence' if the outcomes of freedom of expression lead to the spread of misinformation and disinformation that can harm others. Although a hierarchy of principles might be specifiable, with supervening principles available to resolve conflicts between subordinate principles, it seems reasonable to assume that in many cases multiple principles will be equally applicable in some situations. To resolve these conflicts, we must go outside of non-consequentialism to appeal to other factors, i.e., the consequences of an action. For instance, AIS developers need to directly evaluate trade-offs between the accuracy or fit of an algorithm and the resources (e.g., human, material, environmental) required for training and operating the system. However, if we identify how much each of these factors is valued, and weigh those values, we have adopted a version of consequentialism.

Applications of Non-consequentialism and AISs. Non-consequentialist accounts that are compatible with AISs ('AI-friendly deontic logic') have been proposed by several authors (e.g., Belnap et al., 2001; Bringsjord et al., 2006; Horty, 2001;

Murakami, 2004; see Section 6.2). For instance, while consequentialists might claim that drone strikes save more lives by removing soldiers from a theatre of operations thereby justifying the act, non-consequentialists can claim that killing is wholly wrong or, more specifically, that any reasonable risk to civilian lives (i.e., 'collateral damage') is intrinsically wrong. On such an account, 'no non-combatant deaths' reflects a moral principle and any society or individual within it should not, therefore, engage in actions that would result in such outcomes. Although AISs might not have the *intention* to follow a moral principle, in that algorithms can use *if–then* statements to guide their actions, non-consequentialist accounts are well-suited to AIS design (cf. Goodall, 2014).

Non-consequentialist principles are at the core of many codes of ethics and professional conduct. For instance, while the *ACM Code* prohibits accessing another individual's data, software, or system, it nevertheless suggests that this is permissible if a greater public good is threatened, e.g., the lives of citizens. This reflects the principle of double effect, a doctrine that assumes that an otherwise unethical act is permissible if engaging in it results in better outcomes than if a principle had not been violated. However, identifying supervening principles might not always be straightforward. It might be the case that a single violation of privacy rights might prohibit public harm, for example hacking into an email server to obtain information on a potential domestic terrorist. Such rationales are used to justify domestic surveillance activities (Cauley, 2006; Greenwald, 2013a, 2013b): while there are substantial violations of privacy, sufficiently large data sets might prevent deaths. Thus, non-consequentialist principles provide a straightforward means to train human and nonhuman agents. However, a moral agent must ultimately reconcile these principles whether they are human or an AIS. Supporting this argument Gips (1991) denies the adequacy of Asimov's Laws of Robotics, stating that they '… are not suitable for our magnificent robots. These are laws for slaves'.

4.2.3 Virtue Theory

Virtue Theory assumes that there are essential features or characteristics that define a human ideal, i.e., virtues. In contrast to consequentialism, which assumes that the virtuousness of an act is a function of good consequences, or non-consequentialism which assumes that virtue requires adherence to rules, virtue theory assumes that virtues are goods in and of themselves. The set of virtues remains a matter for debate. In the *Meno*, Plato tells us that Socrates assumes that virtue reflects knowledge; however, this knowledge is not necessarily taught. Lists of virtues have also included courage, intelligence, temperance, truthfulness, and justice but can also include politeness, humour, and simplicity (e.g., Comte-Sponville, 1996).

Rather than identifying specific virtues, we could define the general properties of a virtue. For Aristotle, virtue reflects a mid-point between two possible extreme forms of behaviour:

> [Virtue] is a mean between two vices, that which depends upon excess and that which depends on defect; and again it is a mean because the vices

respectively fall short of or exceed what is right in both passions and actions, while virtue both finds and chooses that which is intermediate.

Aristotle (Barnes), 1984, section 1107a2–6[9]

Crucially, Aristotle's conception of a mean response is not a quantitative measure: it is neither an arithmetic mean nor a cognitive prototype.[10] Rather, virtue requires the ability to reason in combination with the acquisition of practical wisdom to identify the particulars of a situation or system that are ethically relevant, i.e., ethical affordances. Practical wisdom requires that we understand the particulars of a situation. In this sense, virtue is a competency that must be developed.[11] On this account, deliberation is needed to determine what responses are available to a moral agent and which are appropriate. Moreover, virtues are not divorced from affective responses. When appropriate, emotions are necessary to interpret and respond to a situation (Damasio, 1994). Namely, we must care about the ethical action and its outcomes. For instance, Foot (1978/2002) notes that for virtue theorists like Aristotle and Aquinas '… courage and temperance [are concerned] with passions. What they meant by this seems to have been, primarily, that the man of courage does not fear immoderately nor the man of temperance have immoderate desires for pleasure' (p. 5).

One of the most prominent contemporary accounts of virtue ethics was provided by MacIntyre (1985/2004). He argues that the concept of virtues is deeply rooted in human nature, providing the basis for morality and ethics. For MacIntyre, ethical frameworks that either focus on outcomes (e.g., pleasure and happiness) or rules (e.g., categorical imperative, distributive justice) are derivations of virtue theory. By providing a historical analysis of the development of consequentialism and non-consequentialism, he suggests that these philosophical frameworks are specific interpretations of the virtues rather than providing a general basis for moral conduct (see also Curzer, 2012).

Virtue theory is also represented across cultures. In the Eastern philosophical traditions, Confucian philosophers such as Mengzi (Van Norden, 2008) and Wang Yang-Ming (De Bary et al., 1960) reflect alternative forms of virtue ethics (Angle, 2010). For Mengzi, humans have innate ethical predispositions that they must develop, defined by two primary virtues (benevolence and righteousness) and two secondary virtues (propriety and wisdom[12]).[13] Similarly, for Wang '[t]he highest good is the ultimate principle of manifesting character and loving people' (De Bary et al., 1960, p. 518). Thus, 'the good' requires both action (manifesting) driven by virtues (character) and an appropriate affective response toward others ('loving people'). As in Aristotelian accounts, knowledge and action are inseparable features of virtue (e.g., Wong, 2000, 2015).

Passion is again a prominent feature of Eastern virtue ethics. For Cheng Hao, virtuous (benevolent) people '… regard Heaven, Earth, and the myriad things as one Substance. Nothing is not oneself. If you recognize something as yourself, there are no limits to how far [your compassion] will go. But if you do not identify something as part of yourself, you will have nothing to do with it' (Tiwald &

Van Norden, 2014, p. 201). By seeing everything as indivisible, we see the need to treat all existence as an end. Consequently, compassion and experience are essential features of ethical sensemaking.

Like consequentialism and non-consequentialism, virtue theory also has limitations. If virtues reflect a 'mean' response, the theory does not in itself state how extremes are specified. For instance, this approach does not define what constitutes the correct amount of information required to make a judgment. Aristotelian and Confucian formulations suggest that such a determination would come from experience ('practical wisdom'), however, it is still unclear whether available experiences necessarily imply a convergence on the same solution by every rational individual.

In practical terms, the characteristics or dimensions that should be evaluated (i.e., the virtues) are also underspecified and might be vulnerable to cultural relativism, in that cultural traditions can differ in terms of what they deemed virtuous (cf. Nussbaum, 1993). Such accounts can reflect an essentialist kind of thinking, by assuming that humans have a defined essence. Although evolutionary processes have changed, and continue to change, humans, it remains unclear whether there can be a circumscribed set of virtues that are everywhere and always present. However, whether we accept the Aristotelian concept of *telos* or a wholistic approach developed in the Eastern tradition, virtue *might be best understood as a process*. Especially within the Eastern tradition, virtues can be best understood as convenience terms that represent features of a wholistic character. In this formulation, moral agents must continuously attempt to engage with and understand the world and act with respect and compassion toward others. This requires constant striving as well as judging moral agents relative to the extent to which they are engaging in ethical sensemaking.

Applications of Virtue Theory to AISs. Virtue theory can also be applied to AIS ethics in terms of virtuous design and creating AISs that can act virtuously. To modernize virtue theory for technology, Vallor (2016) identifies 12 '21st century virtues'. These virtues consist of honesty, self-control, humility, justice, courage, empathy, care, civility, flexibility, perspective-taking, magnanimity, and technomoral wisdom. Of course, other than 'technomoral wisdom', it remains unclear whether these virtues are particularly distinct from virtue frameworks that have been presented previously. Similarly, technomoral wisdom presumably reflects the full realization of human ethical sensemaking capabilities, accommodating the specific affordances of sociotechnical systems. Nevertheless, Vallor's set of virtues do appear to be capable of addressing the social and ethical issues presented by AISs.

Virtue theory can also be used to assess AISs directly. Virtuous operations of an AIS could be understood in terms of Aristotle's concept of virtue as the mean: AISs should balance the dependence of various priorities, adopting a 'mid-point' in their response to any given issue. Consider privacy. Personal information can be understood in terms of the amount, kind, and retention interval of data. A virtuous AIS could be defined by retaining a moderate amount of user information, only retaining user information directly relevant for the kinds of predictive behaviour that it tells users it is performing, and only retaining that information for the interval required to make predictions. In this way, a virtuous AIS privacy policy reflects a mid-point between collecting no information (e.g., for personalization of service, supporting decisions) and the total surveillance (e.g., data aggregation across multiple platforms). Thus, simply because a user signs an agreement, that does not mean that an AIS acts 'ethically', especially if the information it collects, uses, and retains falls short of, or exceeds, what it needs for the task of that AIS. Over time, this mid-point might change. Thus, rather than a fixed criterion, it will ultimately be determined by the practical wisdom of developers and other stakeholders.

Similar points can be made regarding the output of an AIS: providing a user with too little information or too much information would reflect a deficient system. Users who have too little information might not be capable of understanding what actions are appropriate or they might select a response that would differ if they were provided with more information. For instance, concerns over the use of 'black data' (Section 2.2.1) when making a consequential determination (e.g., granting loans, removing a child from a parent's care, preventive policy action) follow from such issues. Similarly, the notion of 'dark patterns' of design (Chapter 6) reflects concerns that users' automatic behaviour is being exploited and that they would not have made the same choices were they provided with sufficient information. These requirements are also supported by the demands of transparency and XAI (Section 2.2.1). Ethicists have considered this issue. For instance, Stamatellos (2007, 2012) argues that privacy issues inherent in the Information Age threaten our moral agency. Namely, individuals might not understand how their personal information is used and would not necessarily voluntarily provide it if they knew how it would be used. Moreover, in that this information can affect consequential decisions, it adversely affects their self-determination (see Section 3.4; Box 6.1).

As we will discuss below, virtue ethics ultimately requires a complex set of social cognitive processes – an ethical sensemaking ability (Chapter 5). Consequently, the development of virtuous AISs is challenged by the need to specify how virtue can be operationalized within an AIS. On this account, we must identify the essential features that define human virtue (e.g., knowledge, agency, and compassion) and embed them within an AIS framework (e.g., intelligence, autonomy, connectivity). Even if this is possible in principle, the unique evolutionary history of humans might make it an unlikely task in practice. However, this concern can also be challenged based on anthropocentrism bias: virtues might not need to be solely defined in human terms.

Ethical approaches to AISs have been developed that are compatible with virtue theory. Wallach and Allen (2008) consider the design of Artificial Moral Agents (AMAs) based on virtue theory. They assume that virtue theory implies that neither top–down rules nor bottom–up learning can adequately capture the essence of virtue. Rather, they claim that virtue theory in the design of AMAs must reflect a hybrid approach. Such an approach must allow an AMA to act consistently across situations to ensure trust (p. 120). The responses of an AMA must also be relevant *within* a domain. For instance, Schoenherr (2021b) describes an ethical AIS framework in the context of learning technology. He points out that construct validity frameworks that apply to assessment provide one means to operationalize values in that context. However, numerous value-laden decisions must be made in terms of both the learning algorithm and assessment strategy, leaving open a prominent role for human developers, operators, and institutions that adopt these technologies.

Gips (1991, 2005) has additionally claimed that certain forms of AISs (e.g., connectionism) are compatible with virtue theory in that they could learn context-specific principles that need not be represented as discrete rules. More generally, Arkin and colleagues (Arkin, 2008; Arkin et al., 2012) have argued for the need for a dedicated, ethical control layer[14] for AISs to function autonomously. For instance, Vanderelst and Winfield (2018) propose a method that allows ethical robots to have the capacity to go beyond rules to employ simulation that allow it to evaluate the possible outcomes of situations.

4.3 Communal and Social Ethics and Transrational Approaches

Outside of these three meta-ethical frameworks, two other broad approaches can provide insight into ethical sensemaking: communal ethics and transrational ethics. Communal and social ethics prioritize the cohesiveness and continued existence of a social group. Interpersonal accord is prioritized within a community that subordinates or equates the individual to the group. In contrast, transrational approaches to ethics assumes that the basis for morality is beyond the individual, beyond the community, and beyond rationality. In that there is widespread adoption of these frameworks globally, and that they often overlap with the other three frameworks, ethical AISs must incorporate these features into the design process.

4.3.1 Communal and Social Ethics

Approaches to communal and social ethics place community values and interpersonal accord at the centre of ethical sensemaking. Communal ethics frameworks frequently view community members as equivalent and assume that resources should be shared communally (i.e., 'communal sharing'; Section 5.3.1). In contrast to traditional Western approaches to ethics, which focus on the moral agency of the individual, social ethics frameworks view the individual as inseparable from their community. Mbiti (1989) succinctly summarizes the Ubuntu approach to social ethics as 'I am because we are, and since we are, therefore I am' (p. 141). From this perspective, individuals are 'integrated with as well as willing to integrate others into a web of relations free of friction and conflict' (Masolo, 2010, p. 231). In this way, the relationship between community members is mutually beneficial.

Providing a more comprehensive summary, Ikuenobe (2020) notes that

> [the] value of human welfare allows the community to be organized such that the choices that are beneficial to the individual are reciprocally beneficial to the community and vice versa. ... Without a community, relationships with other people, and the material conditions they provide, one cannot realize one's choice of a good life, and have or experience a meaningful sense of dignity, self-worth, or well-being. This idea is expressed in ethical principles that emphasize communal mutual dependence, relationships, solidarity, and caring.

Identity remains the heart of African communal ethics, with Metz (2007) noting that:

> An action is right just insofar as it promotes shared identity among people grounded on good-will; an act is wrong to the extent that it fails to do so and tends to encourage the opposite of division and ill-will.

TABLE 4.3 Contemporary Confucian Account

Facet of Confucianism	Classical Chinese Ethics	He's Alternatives
Rules	Ruler sets guidelines for subjects.	People set guidelines for government.
	Husband sets guidelines for wife.	Rightness sets guidelines for human beings.
	Father sets guidelines for son.	The living set guidelines for all things.
Five Constant Relationships	Ruler–subject	Human–Nature
	Father–son	Group–Group
	Husband–wife	Social Relationships
	Older brother–younger brother	Individual Relationships
	Friend–friend	Personal Relationships
Five Constant Virtues	Benevolence	Reinterpretations of the same five virtues
	Rightness	
	Ritual	
	Wisdom	
	Faithfulness	
Beliefs	Heaven	Heaven
	Earth	Earth
	Ruler	Country
	Family	Family
	Teacher	Teacher
Rectification of Names	Let rulers be rulers.	Let officials be officials.
	Let subjects be subjects.	Let citizens be citizens.
	Let fathers be fathers.	Let people be people.
	Let sons be sons.	Let things be things.

Source: Adapted from He (2015).

Communal ethics is also evidenced in East Asian sociocultural traditions. For instance, harmony (和; i.e., interpersonal, social, universal accord) features prominently in Confucianist tradition (Li, 2008). In parallel, there are also regulatory mechanisms embedded within this cultural tradition such as face (*mian* 面 / *lian* 臉 in Chinese; *mentsu* メンツ in Japanese; *chemyeon* 체면 in Korean), defined in terms of interpersonal processes including facets related to social reputation, personality, ethical conduct, and emotions (Jia, 2001; Kim & Yang, 2013). Similarly, in the Japanese cultural tradition, Doi (1973, 2005) describes the concept of *amae* (甘え), or a desire for interpersonal accord, mutual interdependence and attachment.[15] As an interpersonal process, *amae* leads to compliance or indulgence when a favour is asked of an individual as well as the desire for acceptance on the part of the requester. Consequently, a requester is contrite as a result of the knowledge that another individual will be compelled to agree to the request due to their mutual interdependence (for a review, see Behrens, 2004).

In a related vein, the Korean term *jeong* (정/情) reflects 'mutual love … what makes Korean people feel connected and enlivened', and reflects the 'the highest, most elevated spirit of interpersonal communion' (Kwon, 2001, pp. 45–46). In contrast, *han* (한/恨) reflects a negative emotion associated with disconnection, isolation from others, and associated with a sense of injustice and the absence of *jeong* (Kim, 2017; Moon, 2014). Thus, interpersonal bonds and inclusion in a part of a community create moral motivations and expected behaviours that guide interpersonal interaction (i.e., relational models; Section 5.3.1).

With harmony as the underlying goal, the assumption that *specific* relational models provide the basis for relationships remains the core of classical Confucianism (Table 4.2, middle column). Recently, He (2015) has adapted the relational models of classical Confucianism. His new relational structures include relationships between humanity and nature, intergroup relationships, and interpersonal relationships (Table 4.2, right column). In its focus on communal ethics, He's approach also rejects the need for individuals to achieve excellence in their interpersonal conduct. Instead, he argues that we must establish a *moral minimum* for conduct, ensuring that individuals are functional members of society. Thus, it is far more likely that individuals can adhere to a minimum standard of behaviour rather than an idealized form of excellence. Crucially, although He's approach is more pragmatic than other meta-ethical traditions, unlike descriptive moral frameworks, a moral minimum reflects a prescriptive standard based on satisficing. In terms of He's model, human–AISs relationships can be represented as another kind of relationship, with standards that can be defined based on the minimum requirements for the responsibility of human and nonhuman agents.

Applications of Social Ethics in AISs. Social ethics approaches represent a legitimate challenge to traditional Western meta-ethical theories and must be addressed in the design of AISs. A clear demonstration of the absence of this perspective is apparent in the Universal Declaration on Bioethics and Human Rights where it states that '[t]he interests and welfare of the individual should have priority over the sole interest of science or society' (UNESCO, 2005). Here, we see that the rights of the individual *supersede* those of society. In that organizations like UNESCO must represent the interests of all its members and use universal values, adopting an individualistic approach to ethics can run the risk of failing to address the relevant ethical concerns of specific groups, thereby reducing the utility and persuasiveness of these frameworks within a given society. For instance, Chattopadhyay and De Vries (2008) have suggested the inclusion of 'group' or 'community' consent in research guidelines. Similar guidelines could be developed for AISs that will be implemented within a community such that community members are consulted and are involved in the regulation of these systems. Similarly, advanced forms of AISs should be able to identify ethical affordances *relative* to the societies that they are deployed within as well as any potential conflicting norms.

We must also be mindful that valuing social cohesion can place individuals at risk. For instance, if an individual or small group of individuals are believed to deviate from typical social norms, the community might seek to use AISs to sanction or exclude certain members of a society, i.e., 'defectors', 'deviants', 'traitors', or 'insider threats'. AISs such as surveillance technologies and social credit systems could be adopted to reinforce and augment existing discriminatory practices within a society. Consequently, while communal values should be integrated into ethical frameworks, these values must not disadvantage certain segments of the community. To that end, whatever biases exist within data sets and algorithms should be clearly identifiable to all stakeholders.

4.3.2 Transrational Ethics

Beyond the immediate community, broader metaphysical concerns have led religious and philosophical traditions to question whether individuals or communities are inseparable from other aspects of reality. Transrational belief systems such as Hinduism, Buddhism, and Daoism frequently deny analytic categories such as good-bad, right-wrong, and benevolent-malevolent. Much of this work focuses on the deleterious consequences of attachment to analytic categories and material existence. When they are used, terms and analytic categories are temporary conveniences that are deconstructed and ultimately denied. For instance, Śāntideva's *Śikṣā-samuccaya* states:

> If a bodhisattva does not make a sincere, unwavering effort in thought, word, and deed to stop all the present and future pain and suffering of all sentient beings, and to bring about all present and future pleasure and happiness, or does not seek the collection of conditions for that, or does not strive to prevent what is opposed to that, or does not bring about small pain and suffering as a way of preventing great pain and suffering, or does not abandon a small benefit in order to accomplish a greater benefit, if he neglects to do these things even for a moment, he undergoes a downfall.
>
> *Goodman, 2016a*

Within the passage, we find shared features of Western meta-ethical theories: We must assess the present and future pleasure and happiness (consequences) with sincerity (non-consequentialism) while acting within the world (virtue theory). The notions of rebirth and reincarnation similarly embody these principles: for example, to be reincarnated is to have a more virtuous character (relative to a previous state) embodied in actions that are a consequence of gaining awareness.

Another core concept that defines many transrational approaches is the notion of 'purity', a wholistic state of being. In the Zen Buddhist tradition, Chinul states that you must:

> … search for the fundamental cause [of a phenomenon]. Don't be influenced by them … make more efforts for concentration. You will find a quiet returning place, which is comfortable and without discontinuity. In that situation, the mind of love or hatred will naturally disappear; compassion and wisdom will naturally become clearer as your evil karma will naturally cut off and meritorious behavior will naturally be advanced.
>
> *Cited in Park, 2016*

Here, we see the nature of a transrational ethics. As Park (2016; see also Whitehill, 2000) notes, a reading of this passage appears entirely rational. The knowledge seeker is directed toward excluding the influence of emotion. However, unlike the Western rationalist tradition, analytic categories are not presented as a permanent means of understanding. Rather, they represent a scaffold for the deconstruction of the emotions, representations, and cognitive processes that are mistaken for true knowledge.

For Buddhism and other transrational belief systems, distinctions such as the self, other, and objects within the environment are illusory. Moreover, unlike the Western tradition, the notion of compassion is not necessarily an interpersonal value. Rather, as Tetsurō (2011) interprets the works of the early Buddhist thinker, Shinran, the '… emphasis is not on the relationship of person to person but rather the relationship of people to love itself' (p. 62). In a similar vein,[16] Tetsurō cites Dōgen's ideal of the monk:

> [M]onks have thrown away social obligations and entered a state of being without obstructions. A monk's code of conduct dictates that he cannot limit himself to merely returning a favor to the individual who grants him one; instead, the monk must treat all sentient beings everywhere as one of his parents … you must truly know the depth of the kindness your parents gave to you, but more than this you should know that this is so with everything.
>
> *Tetsurō, 2011, p. 71*

Thus, consequences (harm avoidance) and imperatives (treating all equivalently) are inseparable. Yet, we should not act out of a sense of duty toward others *per se*.

Rather, the nature of reality dictates that everything is integrated and therefore all agents are inextricably bound together.

Applications of Transrational Ethics in AISs. When approaching transrational ethics, the skeptical student of Western philosophy might be inclined to reject it. In the absence of analytic categories and criterion that can be operationalized, how can the perspective of 'Ultimate Truth' be embodied in an AIS? The issues raised by belief systems such as Hinduism, Buddhism, and Daoism mirror those raised in the development of AISs. It is not necessarily clear that nonethical values and ethical values are distinctly analytic across and within societies. Consequently, the features of an AIS that are 'ethical' or 'unethical' must be viewed as pragmatic (or 'working') categories.

Goodman (2016b) provides one means to operationalize ethics in the transrational tradition. He notes that if ethics pertains to individuals and their interactions, then it represents a set of conventional truths rather than a wholistic Truth. However, he does suggest that a consequentialist ethics is compatible with this transrational tradition: 'a view of ethics that understands [the ultimate reality of happiness and suffering] would focus on [their] overall quantity ... without concerning itself with illusory and insignificant claims about who experiences these states' (p. 19). In this sense, although not limited to a consequentialist framework, the objects of transrational frameworks can still be understood in terms of their consequences of action in the material world.

Despite focusing on Eastern philosophical traditions, it is also important to note that religious traditions more generally endorse, in whole or in part, the transrational approach. Moreover, this has been applied within the domain of AISs. Consider Barbour (1993). Following a broad overview of early AIS researchers who focused on rule-based accounts of human thinking ('formalists'), he argues that the Bible 'presents a more holistic and social view of human nature ... clearly this biblical view of human beings as *bodily, social, and responsible* persons differs from the assumptions of AI formalists ... and it clearly distinguishes humans from any form of AI constructed so far' (pp. 172–173; italics in original). To support this, Barbour cites several properties of humans that he believes to be outside the scope of AISs: emotions, (self-)consciousness, freedom, and creativity. However, other religious traditions can accommodate AISs as moral agents. For instance, Allison (2006) argues that there is an 'animist unconscious' defined in the Shinto tradition in Japan that reflects a 'techno-animism'. In this approach, boundaries between human and nonhuman agents are deemphasized (Jensen & Blok, 2013), meaning that AISs can be seen as equivalent objects and subjects of inquiries into moral agency. Indeed, the notion of a sociotechnical system erases the boundaries between human and technical systems, suggesting that such an inclusive approach to moral agency is likely required.

4.4 Moral Anti-Realism: Subjectivism, Emotivism, Nihilism

Despite the diversity of the theories reviewed thus far, they share one feature in common: they assume that morals exist and can be studied, analyzed, synthesized, and implemented even if they are inseparable from the nature of reality. In contrast, the anti-realist approach *denies* the existence of objective morals.[17] Instead, anti-realism assumes that morals reflect subjective preferences, are by-products of automatic emotional responses, or are means to rationalize our actions.

Subjectivism assumes that morals are real, but ultimately reflect subjective preferences. Thus, morals do not have a metaphysical reality but are real in the sense that these preferences have motivational primacy or explanatory potency for humans. According to subjectivists, moral disagreements cannot be reconciled. Moral statements are analogous to claiming that blue is better than red, or that oranges are better than bananas. Supporting this argument, subjectivists point to the incommensurability of various principles proposed by moral realists. For instance, when observing people arguing about the supervenience of 'privacy' over 'security', whatever arguments proponents might bring forth, there appears to be no objective grounds to adjudicate between the two values or that they necessarily conflict (e.g., Van de Poel, 2020; Schoenherr, 2020a). Consequently, individuals simply value privacy over security or security over privacy, without any means of reconciling these differences.

A variant of subjectivism, *emotivism*, assumes that moral statements are preferences that are affectively loaded (Ayer, 1936/2012). According to emotivism, moral utterances (e.g., 'That was wrong!', 'She's right!') reflect the emotional states of the agent rather than statements that are meant to be objective. A descriptive account of their everyday usage would seem to support this account. When queried, the foundation for most moral beliefs tends to not be founded on deep principles nor an awareness of how to adjudicate between competing principles in varied contexts (Haidt, 2007). However, it remains an open question as to whether this descriptive account of subjective morality negates a prescriptive basis for ethics.

The most extreme anti-realism account is *nihilism*. Nihilism denies the existence of morals entirely. According to this account, morals are simply an illusion. Much like some transrational accounts, if the material world is not objective in any sense, and morality is fundamentally related to conceptions of human existence, then morals do not exist any more than any other material objects. Nihilistic accounts reintroduce the critical issue for ethicists of identifying and justifying the source of ethical norms. In that humans are a relatively recent product of evolution, and morality is ultimately defined in human terms, then it would seem that any ethical system that is identified by humans is inherently limited. Any appearance of similarity in values across human groups would not represent universal norms. Rather, it would merely reflect by-products of interpersonal processes that have helped our species survive at a genetic or societal level. When applied to another species or another environment, these values might not be adaptive because they have no universal basis.

Applications of Anti-Realism in AISs. Anti-realist accounts represent important criticisms of moral philosophy and philosophical ethics in that they force us to reflect on the boundaries between personal morality and ethical systems. The central goal of ethics is to identify the objects, principles, and means to communicate ethical judgments. That the boundary between ethical and nonethical values appears to be 'soft' (i.e., they can and have changed over time), might be good reason to be skeptical of moral realism. However, these observations do not imply that ethics should be ignored. For instance, ethical accounts based on intersubjectivity assume that, collectively, individuals create morals. From an evolutionary perspective, this approach is entirely coherent even if they are not generalizable outside of a group. At a fundamental level, morality and ethics have a *functional* utility within a group: they can reduce (although, not eliminate) uncertainty in actions, promote interpersonal bonds, and facilitate interpersonal interaction. In this sense, much like AISs, morals and ethical frameworks are human artifacts. As tools that have helped our species survive, they are just as real and consequential as any other.

4.5 Reconciling Perspectives in Philosophical Ethics

The survey of metaethical frameworks provides a rich set of perspectives that help highlight the ethical affordances of AISs. However, these approaches are often mutually incommensurable, with the application of each creating trade-offs, i.e., strict adherence to principles in the absence of using experience and outcomes, or solely focusing on outcomes regardless of how questionable the behaviour might be. Moreover, in applied areas such as the philosophy of law, distinctions between descriptive and prescriptive norms, consequentialist and non-consequentialists norms become blurred (Soper, 2002).[18] For instance, laws represent rules (non-consequentialist) and assumption about human agency (virtue theory), however, these rules have been formed based on precedent and outcomes of their implementation (consequentialist). To include metaethical frameworks in AIS development and implementation, we must attempt to reconcile these frameworks, if only imperfectly.

Experimental Ethics. Both theoretical and applied ethicists have often sought to resolve these disagreements with experiments or historical arguments. Thought experiments are pervasive tools used by philosophers and psychologists to demonstrate the primacy of norms and conventions and how humans make sense of ethical questions. The Trolley Problem provides one of the most widely referenced examples. The Trolley Problem assumes that a malicious actor has tied up innocent bystanders on two different tracks. For instance, on one of the tracks, five innocent bystanders are held hostage. If you do nothing, these individuals will be killed by an oncoming trolley. On a second set of tracks, a single innocent bystander is held hostage. If you pull a lever, you can save the five bystanders, but the single bystander dies. Crucially, the dilemma forces us to decide whether it is more important to save as many people as possible (consequentialism) or to abstain from engaging in deliberate harm to a single individual (non-consequentialism).[19]

The footbridge dilemma presents another variant of the Trolley Problem. In the footbridge dilemma, rather than using a lever, the scenario assumes that you are on a footbridge above a tram line along with another bystander. You can *push* the bystander onto the tracks, which you are assured will stop the tram and save the five bystanders, or do nothing and have the oncoming train kill the five bystanders. In this case, rather than pulling a lever that could *indirectly* result in the death of an innocent, you must directly kill another person to ensure that the lives of five others will be saved.

While structurally quite similar,[20] people treat these two dilemmas as if they are quite different. Studies suggest that whereas participants are inclined to pull the lever in the Trolley Problem (i.e., a consequentialist principle), they are disinclined to push the bystander in the footbridge dilemma (i.e., a non-consequentialist principle; e.g., Greene & Haidt, 2002). The difference between these dilemmas appears to be one of the moral status of the action that is required to prevent the deaths of the five bystanders: killing someone directly by pushing them onto the tracks is perceived to be immoral whereas pulling a lever thereby killing someone (at a distance) is more permissible. Experimental ethics has also been used to demonstrate that, when required to make impartial decisions (i.e., not knowing how the outcomes will affect them), individuals tend to choose principles that maximize average outcomes for all (Frohlich & Oppenheimer, 1993; Frohlich et al., 1987; Gabriel & Schokkaert, 2012). Although this research can be used to support theories of distributive justice (Rawls, 1971a), in that the results are empirically derived, these findings reflect descriptive norms rather than prescriptive norms (cf. Walter, 2006).

Historical Ethical Analysis. Attempts have also been made to reconcile metaethical theories by examining the evolution of these belief systems. For instance, Nietzsche (1997) suggested that values have changed over time, leading to an inversion of ideals. Building on this approach, MacIntyre's (1985/2004) historical account assumes that virtue theory gave rise to both non-consequentialism and consequentialism. In brief, MacIntyre's account reconciles consequentialism and non-consequentialism by assuming that principles and outcomes are tools that virtuous individuals can apply to specific contexts. For instance, a clinician might use an algorithm to triage patients that require ventilators because although they wish to adhere to principles of beneficence and non-maleficence (non-consequentialism), being faced with finite resources requires determining which patients are at a higher risk and which patients can be saved (consequentialism) as well as using their own experience to determine whether there is sufficient time to consult an AIS (virtue theory).

Meta-ethical theories can also be reconciled by examining the evolution of morality in humans. King (2008) notes that evolutionary processes have led to the human capacity for empathy, suggesting that prosocial behaviour (i.e., helping others) provides a foundation for an integrative ethical theory (see also Walter, 2006).[21] Moreover, humans learn the association between an action and its consequences and this allows us to identify specific ethical principles. We can extend this approach further to accommodate social ethics in that outcomes for a community must also be assessed. King's approach can likely best be understood as a process of ethical sensemaking wherein affect, behaviour, and social context must all be accounted for when making ethical judgments (Chapter 5).

4.6 Section Summary: Philosophical Ethics

Philosophical ethics provides numerous analytic tools that must inform AIS ethics. By distinguishing between conventional values and behaviour (descriptive norms) and ideals that should be used to guide ethical decision-making (prescriptive norms), we ensure that we do not assume that merely because certain norms and conventions are common they are in any way justified (i.e., the naturalistic fallacy). However, we must also be aware that this distinction can also become blurred in applied settings that are directly applicable to AISs, for example, legal frameworks and developing systems within a community. Three broad metaethical frameworks differentially prioritize the characteristics that guide our actions (virtues), the intentions and principles that guide our actions (non-consequentialism), and the outcomes of an action (consequentialism). Beyond these frameworks, we must also account for specific social relationships and community dynamics (social ethics) and the importance of acknowledging the limitations of existing analytic categories (transrational ethics and anti-realism). While there might not be any systematic means to reconcile these frameworks, together they suggest the need to ensure that we develop competencies in ethical sensemaking and use each to identify the ethical affordances of AISs.

Notes

1 In practice, this distinction has eroded and will be especially crucial in terms of social cognition and ethical behaviour.
2 Mining involves solving mathematical problems that become progressively harder as they reach the limit of 21 million, established by the creators of Bitcoin.
3 Duplicate publication refers to publishing the same dataset twice without justification or recognition.
4 For a comparative study in psychology, see Schoenherr, 2019a.
5 These norms appear to be modern extensions of the PAPA norms identified by Mason (1986).
6 Similarly, if one individual derives considerable utility from an action that causes widespread minor suffering of others, this would also be deemed justifiable using Bentham's consequentialist moral calculus.
7 In this sense, to assume that someone who currently has a privileged position in society (by virtue of wealth, status, race, gender, etc.) should have that position, amounts to a naturalistic fallacy.
8 A title in an edited volume reviewing the work of G. E. M. Anscombe (2006). In G. Reichberg, H. Syse, & E. Begby (Eds.), *The Ethics of War: Classical and Contemporary Readings* (pp. 625–632). Blackwell Publishers.
9 In contrast, Kant understands virtue as 'the moral strength of a *human being's* will in fulfilling his duty' (Kant, 1797/1971, p. 206). For Kant, virtue is subordinate to our moral obligation to others. Similar remarks have been made by Rawls (1971a) 'The virtues are sentiments, that is, related families of dispositions, and properties regulated by a higher-order desire, in this case a desire to act from the corresponding moral principles' (p. 192).
10 A representation reflecting the average (typical) features of a category created by exposure to multiple instances.

11 Aristotle uses the term *hexis*, generally interpreted as 'condition', 'disposition', or 'state'.

12 Van Norden (2008) refers to wisdom as a meta-virtue in that Mengzi entails understanding the primary virtues whereas (ritual) propriety entails 'adorning' the primary virtues.

13 'The core of benevolence is serving one's parents. The core of righteousness is obeying one's elder brother. The core of wisdom is knowing these two and not abandoning them. The core of ritual propriety is the adornment of these two' (Van Norden, 2008, p. 101).

14 Connectionist layers reflect a kind of parallel distributed processing defined by multiple layers. An 'ethical layer' implies a set of processes dedicated to the identification of ethical patterns.

15 Jia (2001) notes that the ideogram for the term 'face', originally stemmed from 'eye', suggesting monitoring.

16 In this section, Tetsurō in fact distinguishes between the nature of compassion of both of these authors. Here, I am using his examples at a more abstract level to demonstrate the conceptualization of compassion.

17 Arguably, the transrational approach denies distinct morals. It nevertheless assumes some objective reality as a reference point.

18 Soper (2002) claims that the law requires that we act in such a way that we disagree with the consequences of the act, or even the principles behind it. In such a case, we can think of 'the law' – a structure of norms defined by an expert community derived from and for a society – as being a good in itself. This creates a blurred distinction: presumably, laws reflect non-consequentialist norms that decision makers use as a set to determine an act. Yet, laws are changed if they do not appear to reflect the norms of society or are deemed to create issues, i.e., consequentialism criteria.

19 There are numerous interpretations of which principles must be considered in this dilemma.

20 Namely, save one life through inaction without violating a rule, save five lives with an action that violates a rule.

21 Such evolutionary accounts are subject to the naturalistic fallacy: simply because humans have evolved to function in such a manner does not mean it is the most effective or justifiable means to engage in ethical sensemaking. However, as I will argue in Chapter 6, it is not clear that the radical discontinuities suggested by transhuman approaches exist, suggesting that basic ethical sensemaking processes can accommodate AISs ethics.

5

RIGHT-THINKING

Moral Competency and Ethical Sensemaking

Metaethical frameworks (Chapter 4) provide many analytic tools for identifying the ethical affordances of AISs and the environments that they create and control. When placed alongside the technical affordances of AISs (Chapter 2), and social and ethical issues discussed in popular science (Chapter 3), it remains clear that extensive deliberation will be required to identify and respond to the specific ethical affordance of AISs. In that social and ethical issues occur in a complex environment, we must engage in a process of sensemaking, entailing labelling, and categorizing situational affordances (Weick, 1979; Weick et al., 2005).

Like other forms of judgment and decision-making, sensemaking requires identifying points in a decision-making process wherein multiple response alternatives are possible (Klein, 1993, 1998) in an environment defined by limited time and information (i.e., bounded rationality; Simon, 1956). More generally, this suggests that there are two kinds of cognitive systems that interact: one defined by deliberate, effortful, and resource-intensive mental processing that has evolved relatively recently (i.e., Type 2 systems) and another defined by automatic, effortless, and resource-limited mental processing that we share with nonhuman animals (i.e., Type 1 systems; Chaiken & Trope, 1999; Evans & Frankish, 2009; Kahneman, 2011; Stanovich, 2005).[1] The overreliance on either Type 1 or Type 2 systems creates trade-offs. For instance, when we use information that is immediately available in our environments or from our memories, we often ignore alternative evidence (Gilovich et al., 2002). Yet, in practice, we have limited time and attention, leading to the need to identify satisfactory responses rather than optimal responses (i.e., satisficing; Simon, 1956).

The competition and cooperation of these systems defines ethical sensemaking. Ethical sensemaking is a competency that can be developed over time, allowing us to identify the ethical features of our social environment. In its simplest form, moral

DOI: 10.4324/9781003143284-5

judgments reflect self-interested behaviour, involving the avoidance of punishment and the receipt of reward. In its most developed state, ethical sensemaking reflects a deliberate process that incorporates evidence, principles, and a consideration of the available alternative responses within a dynamic social environment. However, this process is vulnerable to time and attentional limitation, leading to a failure to identify ethical affordances, apply principles, or weigh multiple alternatives. By reviewing the ethical sensemaking process of humans, we can both situate how mediated interaction between human and AISs affects this process and ascertain how this can inform the development of ethical AISs (Chapter 6).

5.1 Development of Moral Reasoning

Moral competencies follow a developmental trajectory. Building on the work of Piaget (1932), Kohlberg (1976, 1981) provided a model of moral development consisting of three broad stages (see also Rest et al., 1999). Each of these stages is further divided into two substages. For young children, moral judgments are initially determined by the avoidance of punishment (1a) and the receipt of reward (1b), referred to as *preconventional reasoning*. For adolescence, moral judgments consist of the maintenance of interpersonal accord (2a) and adherence to general norms of society (2b), referred to as *conventional reasoning*. Finally, moral judgments are determined by consequentialist principles (3a) and then progress to non-consequentialist principles (3b), referred to as *postconventional reasoning*. According to Kohlberg (1976, 1981), these developmental stages represent an inviolable sequence. Once an individual passes through a stage, they do not regress to an earlier mode of thinking. However, not everyone progresses through all three stages, with comparatively fewer individuals reaching the postconventional stage. For instance, some evidence suggests that there are cross-cultural differences, such that low levels of individualism lead to reductions in the use of postconventional moral reasoning (Ge & Thomas, 2008; Tsui & Windsor, 2001).

Despite the utility of the Kohlbergian model, researchers have suggested that it fails to account for gender biases, cross-cultural differences, and context-dependencies (Gibbs, 2014/2019; Gilligan, 1982; Snarey, 1985). For instance, sensitivity to prosocial behaviour appears to occur early in development, such that it might be available prior to the conventional reasoning stage (Gilligan, 1982; Holvoet et al., 2016; Margoni & Surian, 2018). Similarly, reductions in attention or contextual cues can alter ethical sensemaking in any given situation (Section 5.3). Consequently, ethical sensemaking is not limited to moral reasoning processes.

In addition to moral reasoning, researchers have additionally proposed specialized cognitive systems that have evolved in humans that are dedicated to identifying violations of social norms (i.e., domain-specific intelligence). Rather than requiring specific experience with a set of social norms, this 'cheater detection module' effortlessly directs our attention to ethical affordances of a social situation (Cosmides, 1989; Cosmides & Tooby, 2002, 2005). Consider the reasoning task developed by Wason (1966; see Figure 5.1). In this task, participants are required to select the

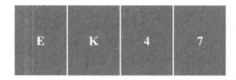

FIGURE 5.1 Original Wason Selection task.

Note: 'Cards' are presented which contain even and odd numbers, as well as consonants and vowels. Participants must select the cards that verify a rule.

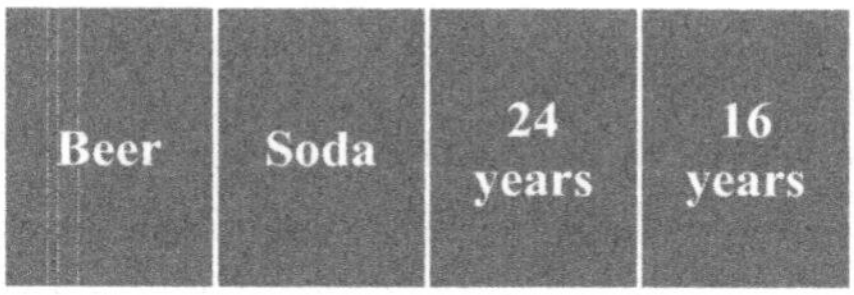

FIGURE 5.2 Social variant of the Wason Selection task.

card(s) that allow them to verify the rule: 'The card has a vowel on one side and an even number on the other side'. Now, decide which card or cards should be selected.

Early studies of performance in this task showed that 46% of participants indicated that all four cards should be turned over. However, selecting all the cards is unnecessary to verify the rule. An additional 33% indicated only 'E' needed to be turned over, and another 4% indicated that only '7' should be turned over. However, the appropriate strategy requires that we select cards to confirm the rule (select a vowel to see if the rule is *valid*) as well as cards that allow us to disconfirm the rule (selecting an odd number to see if the rule is *invalid*).[2] Only 7% correctly indicated that both the 'E' and '7' should be turned over (Johnson-Laird & Wason, 1970).

Evidence for a cheater detection system comes from an alternative form of this task. Imagine you are working at a local pub. As an employee, you must ensure that you verify the rule: 'If a person is drinking beer, then the person must be over 19'. Once more, this rule can be reformulated in terms of cards (see Figure 5.2). In sharp contrast to Wason's original study, Cox and Griggs (1982) found that 73% correctly picked the beer and 16 years cards. Structurally, the task is identical to the original Wason selection task. Consequently, the improved performance suggests that knowledge of social norms and their violation facilitate our performance in this task.

Whether these competencies reflect a product of a *module* that has evolved or are learned early during development remains an open question. In some cases, people might simply have advanced to a conventional moral reasoning stage that produces automatic responses without this reflecting an innate cognitive module. Regardless of the origins of cheater detection, it does seem that ethical reasoning operations can become automatic. For instance, Van Lier et al. (2013) found that performance on selection tasks that are based on social contracts are not adversely affected by a secondary load whereas reasoning tasks that do not require prior knowledge are adversely affected. If participants can perform a secondary task that uses deliberate Type 2 system resources, this provides strong evidence for the proposal that automatic Type 1 processes are used in the detection of norm violations.

The recognition that moral competencies develop over time and can function automatically provides a useful lens to assess AIS design and the processes of AIS design. First, recognition of a developmental sequence suggests that moral competencies can develop independently of domain-specific expertise. Consequently, knowledge of information and computer science does not guarantee that a developer can recognize the ethical affordance of an AIS. This is especially true if we acknowledge that each environment within which AISs will be developed and implemented can be quite different. As a result, education and training programs are required to facilitate and monitor the development of these skills.

Second, developing ethical processes within an AIS might involve creating systems that parallel the developmental course of humans. For instance, basic learning principles used by AISs involve both supervised and unsupervised learning. This reflects the same basis as preconventional reasoning (i.e., punishment and reward) although it would lack responses specific to humans (e.g., affective responses associated with concern about what parents or peers think of the learner). Consequently, Kohlberg's proposed developmental sequence provides a means to assess the ethical competencies of AISs.

Systems that are created in the absence of acknowledging social conventions or principles will likely be ineffective in addressing general ethical concerns (i.e., preconventional ethical systems). AISs that merely replicate existing social norms and conventions might represent a marginal improvement, but will likely reinforce existing social biases (i.e., conventional ethical systems). Ethical AISs require an examination of the ethical outcomes of the operations and use of AISs, whether this is in terms of consequentialist or non-consequentialist principles or operations that parallel virtues (i.e., postconventional ethical systems). Knowledge of the developmental sequence might be a useful guide for judging the moral capabilities of AISs, however in no way is the recapitulation of this sequence necessary or desirable. Indeed, it is possible that superior methods for ethical decision-making could be available to AISs (Section 6.3).

5.2 Ethical Decision-Making

Decision-making reflects the identification of relevant information in the environment, the accumulation of evidence, and the weighing of potential response alternatives. For any given task, both Type 1 and Type 2 processes are required, such that no decision is 'process pure' (Jacoby, 1991). For instance, 'attention' can be automatically captured by salient stimuli (e.g., alerting us to loud sounds or bright images), selecting between targets (e.g., finding the right 'Smith' in a list), or more complex executive functions (e.g., noting that we have made an error and later adopting a different response; see, e.g., Fan et al., 2002). Moreover, learning studies that provide extensive training additionally suggest that there is competition between these systems. In humans, we initially engage in a novel task with effortful processing (Type 2). Concurrently, associations between stimuli and responses are made in automatic learning systems (Type 1) that are still too weak to influence our responses. With sufficient experience and training, Type 1 systems begin to dominate response selection, leading to automatic responding (Ashby & O'Brien, 2005; Ashby et al., 2011). After this point, supervisory systems (Type 2) can suppress or change our initial responses (Norman & Shallice, 1986). These same processes define ethical sensemaking (e.g., Bazerman & Tenbrunsel, 2011; Greene, 2013).

If ethical sensemaking can be understood in terms of this distinction, both Type 1 and Type 2 processes must contribute to selecting ethical responses to the ethical affordances of an environment. For instance, our affective response automatically alerts us to potential moral hazards in the environment (Type 1) while we can engage in deliberation to assess the full set of ethical affordances, possible responses, and associated trade-offs that might be relevant to a particular scenario. However, research into ethical sensemaking suggests that the interaction between Type 1 and Type 2 processes is complex.

5.2.1 Type 1 Moral Judgments

Along with evidence for cheater detection systems (Cox & Griggs, 1982), the fact that prosocial motivations appear early during development (Holvoet et al., 2016; Margoni & Surian, 2018) suggests that humans are biased to cooperate with others. Studies of chimpanzees also suggest that this motivation is phylogenetically older than modern humans (Mitani, 2006; Melis et al., 2006; Subiaul et al., 2008; for discussion of morality in cognitive ethology more generally, see Bekoff & Pierce, 2009). Having such motivations likely facilitates the survival of a species, leading to group-level selection (Wilson & Wilson, 2008). Supporting this, studies have found that automatic and affective responses are crucial to the provision of help, such as altruism (Fehr & Fischbacher, 2003).

Models have suggested that prosocial behaviour is often the result of Type 1 systems (Zaki & Mitchell, 2013). Consequently, prosocial behaviour can be affected by environmental variables that increase positive affect. In a study by Baron (1997), helping behaviour was increased when help was solicited in a pleasantly smelling environment in comparison to when no odour was present (also see Guéguen, 2012). Moreover, the availability of oxytocin can alter the processing of social cues, leading to increases in prosocial behaviour depending on an individual's predispositions and the perceived demands of the situation (Bartz et al., 2011; Churchland & Winkielman, 2012).

More generally, moral motivations likely reflect a set of implicit heuristics that are associated with one's role in a situation (e.g., Rand et al., 2016). Consider the norm of reciprocity (Gouldner, 1960), a norm that is fundamental to human and nonhuman animals. Early studies of the reciprocity norm suggest that it has an automatic basis. For instance, studies of compliance suggest that when participants refuse a larger favour, they are more likely to concede a small favour (e.g., Cialdini et al., 1975; Goldstein et al., 2011). However, the influence of the reciprocity norm is limited. Some evidence suggests that it is less effective when the requester has an out-group membership (Eastwick & Gardner, 2009). Moreover, its influence also decreases as a function of time (Isen et al., 1976). Beyond reciprocity, studies of cooperative games additionally suggest that when time is limited, higher levels of cooperation are observed (for a review, see Rand et al., 2016).

5.2.2 Type 2 Ethical Processes

If humans are biased toward cooperation, the involvement of Type 2 processes might first appear to enhance ethical decision-making. This aligns with the Kohlbergian stage model (Kohlberg, 1976, 1981; Rest, 1986; Rest et al., 1999). For instance, if multiple ethical values conflict (e.g., security and privacy, or fairness and accuracy), it is unlikely that automatic prosocial motivations can guide us in selecting what course of action is preferable. This suggests that moral reasoning might require effortful Type 2 operations (Stevens & Hauser, 2004).

Support for effortful processes in moral judgments comes from several seminal studies of ethical decision-making and prosocial behaviour. These studies suggest that the activation of moral norms and conventions requires time and attention to identify the ethical affordances of a situation (Bergquist et al., 2021; Darley & Batson, 1973; Kallgren et al., 2000; Mazar et al., 2008). For instance, Kallgren et al. (2000) found that both a participant's level of arousal and how closely related a priming message was to a normative behaviour (i.e., anti-littering), determined the level of adherence to the norm. Similarly, priming people with social contracts (Mazar et al., 2008), reminders of social and religious institutions associated with interpersonal monitoring (Shariff & Norenzayan, 2007), or the idea that morals are facts (i.e., moral realism vs. anti-realism; Rai & Holyoak, 2013; Young & Durwin, 2013), promotes fair exchanges and more contributions, respectively.

Cognitive empathy also requires effortful processing. To take the perspective of another, we must activate knowledge of their beliefs, preferences, and values in order to predict and simulate their responses. By taking another's perspective, we promote prosocial behaviour. For instance, in a classic research paradigm, participants are presented with instruction to either be 'objective' or to take the perspective of another prior to performing a task involving helping. In these experiments, the empathy-priming condition produces more prosocial behaviour than the objectivity-priming condition (e.g., Batson et al., 1991; Fultz et al., 1986; Smith et al., 1989; Stotland, 1969). In that many ethical frameworks are based on objective principles (e.g., nonconsequentialism) or require the use of numbers and calculations (e.g., consequentialism), they might inadvertently reduce empathy and some forms of ethical behaviour (e.g., Box 4.1).

Studies have also demonstrated that, when presented with hypothetical moral dilemmas, regions of the brain associated with imagination are activated (FeldmanHall et al., 2012). Given the effortful nature of imagination as a mental simulation (Schacter & Addis, 2007), this suggests that ethical sensemaking is an effortful process. In many circumstances, prosocial behaviour can also reflect a cost–benefit analysis (for a comprehensive review of prosocial behaviour, see Dovidio et al., 2006). In that AISs can be programmed to learn and use rules, their operations often resemble Type 2 processing. Consequently, whether in terms of non-consequentialist or consequentialist principles, AISs are likely capable of replicating some feature of ethical sensemaking.

5.2.3 Integrating Moral Intuitions and Ethical Reasoning

Despite the need for the involvement of Type 2 processes when faced with complex ethical dilemmas, effortful processes can interfere with prosocial behaviour. If our default is to engage in prosocial behaviour (Section 5.2.1), engaging Type 2 processes might lead to a reduction in moral behaviour. For instance, in a study conducted by Cornelissen et al. (2011), they found that participants who had prosocial motivations and who were distracted in a game engaged in more prosocial behaviour. Using fMRI scans, Greene and Paxton (2009) found that students who were provided with the opportunity to cheat were more likely to use regions of their brain associated with controlled processing, whereas students who were not provided with the opportunity to cheat were more likely to engage in automatic processing. Indeed, while moral reasoning requires effortful processing, abstract representations such as numbers that are often used to frame social dilemmas (e.g., 10,000 dead due to disease) are less compelling than a single identifiable victim (Kogut & Ritov, 2005; Slovic, 2010; Small & Loewenstein, 2003).

The time-course of effortful processing in ethical sensemaking also suggests that the use of Type 2 processes does not guarantee more ethical behaviour. In a review of ethical decision-making, Haidt (2007) notes that deliberation in moral judgments often occurs *after* a decision has been made to justify the decision, i.e., rationalization. According to this account, a perceived violation of a moral norm might result in the accumulation of confirmatory evidence and a failure to assess alternative explanations. Thus, ethical sensemaking requires both deliberate and automatic processing (Bloom, 2013; Gantman & Van Bavel, 2014).

Demonstrating the complex nature of ethical decision-making, studies have investigated the involvement of Type 1 and Type 2 processes, given specific moral principles. By using the Trolley Problem (Section 4.5) Greene and Paxton (2009) claimed that the use of consequentialist principles was associated with Type 2 processes whereas the use of non-consequentialist principles was associated with Type 1 processing. Namely, reflecting on the outcomes of a situation requires greater effort in comparison to simply applying rules. In this way, principles such as 'do no harm' and 'do unto others as you would have them do unto you' are automatic heuristics. Consequently, provided that ethical affordances can be identified by an AIS, this suggests that basic features of ethical sensemaking should be operationalizable in AISs (Section 6.2; cf. Goodall, 2014; Moor, 2009).

Providing a more comprehensive account of ethical sensemaking, Nakamura (2011) analyzed participants' responses to 62 moral dilemmas using factor analysis and structural equation modelling. His analysis suggested that four factors contributed to moral judgments: rationality, the potential loss of life (life-dilemmas), risk aversion, and efficiency. For instance, whereas he found that risk aversion and efficiency were strongly associated with impersonal moral dilemmas that require weighing costs and benefits, and life-dilemmas were associated with the loss of human life, rationality was associated with the extent to which a moral dilemma required deliberation.

The integration of Type 1 and Type 2 processes can also be considered in terms of control over behaviour, i.e., autonomy. In individualistic societies, people maintain narratives that they can, and have, control over their lives, i.e., an internal attribution (Ross, 1977; p. 86, Heider, 1958; Gilbert & Malone, 1995).[3] This belief in control has direct implications for ethical behaviour. For instance, a series of studies have demonstrated that when participants were primed to think that humans did, or did not have, 'free will' they were more or less likely to engage in ethical behaviour, respectively (Baumeister et al., 2009; Vohs & Schooler, 2008). Similarly, people who question free will (i.e., maintain a mechanistic view of human behaviour) are also less likely to endorse retribution, suggesting that there is an overall decrease in perceived moral responsibility (Shariff et al., 2014). Consequently, the belief that Type 2 (controlled) process dominate Type 1 (automatic) process in our judgments and behaviour can itself influence ethical sensemaking. Moreover, helping others might require suppressing individual motivations in order to achieve collective goods. Supporting this, studies have also demonstrated that the need to effortfully monitor and regulate our behaviour can deplete us, leading to reductions in prosocial behaviour (DeWall et al., 2008). As we begin to rely upon AISs, human autonomy might be challenged leading to reductions in prosocial behaviour and well being (André et al., 2018).

5.3 Social Context and Norm Accessibility

Human ethical sensemaking is prone to both systematic biases and unsystematic error. In that attention is a crucial determinant of whether norms are considered during ethical sensemaking, norm accessibility and social context are crucial determinants of human moral judgment (Turiel, 2002). For instance, cheating behaviour can be reduced when participants are reminded of ethical norms in advance of a task (Mazar et al., 2008; for related results, see Cialdini et al., 1990; Kallgren et al., 2000; Gino et al., 2009). When participants observed another member of *their* group cheating (e.g., from their university), they were more likely to cheat relative to when an observed cheater was from *another* group (e.g., another university; Mazar et al., 2008; for ecological studies of student cheating behaviour that support this, see McCabe & Trevino, 1997). Thus, when moral violations are committed by members of our own group, individuals believe that it is more permissible to do so themselves. Finally, studies also suggest that when individuals are primed to be self-sufficient, they are also less likely to ask for help (e.g., Vohs et al., 2006). In this case, people are reminded that they should attempt to maximize their own outcomes rather than assisting or seeking assistance from others.

5.3.1 Trust, Social Scripts, and Schemata

Ethical behaviour within a group ultimately relies on trust and trustworthiness (e.g., Colquitt et al., 2007; Hardin, 2002; Lewis & Weigert, 1985; Mayer et al., 1995; Rousseau et al., 1998; Tschannen-Moran & Hoy, 2000). Trust consists of a positive expectation that another individual will perform an action, i.e., a triadic relation between persons and context (Hardin, 2002). For instance, we trust that our employer will deposit money into our bank account because they have in the past. We tend to trust technology in similar terms. For instance, I expect that the tax software will calculate my tax return properly. In contrast, trustworthiness represents the degree to which an agent can be trusted, defined in terms of dimensions such as competence, integrity, and beneficent motivation. Trust can also be understood as an individual difference (i.e., a propensity *to* trust; Mayer et al., 1995). Understanding the mental representations that support trust is critical to understanding morality and ethics.

Relational Models and Virtuous Violence. Trust is also defined by the exchange norms that determine interaction within and between groups. These expectations can be understood in terms of simple rules (e.g., reciprocity). However, humans also have more complex schemata that contain associations between individuals, roles, and specific behaviours. When these schemata are primed, they can increase or decrease the level of cooperation (e.g., Grinberg et al., 2012; Liberman et al., 2004; Pillutla & Chen, 1999; Tenbrunsel & Messick, 1999).

Numerous normative schemata have been identified across cultures. In his seminal work, A. P. Fiske (1991, 1992) suggests that there are four cross-cultural relational models that define idealized exchange relationships between individuals within a group. *Communal sharing* is defined by equivalency between group members and universal access to the collective resource of a group (e.g., team members). *Authority ranking* is defined by asymmetric roles and responsibilities (e.g., king–knight–peasant; parent–child; employee–employer). *Equality matching* is defined by a symmetric, reciprocal relationship between two equal individuals (e.g., friends, partners). Finally, *market pricing* reflects the use of a standard or criterion to assign rewards and status to group members (e.g., employee assessment, grading). Importantly, the existence of multiple relational models suggests that two individuals might both attempt to act in an ethical manner that would otherwise promote trust, however if they use two different relational models they can experience conflict. For instance, parents use an authority ranking relational model due to tradition, whereas their child uses an equality matching relational model due to their extensive interaction with their peers.

Extending this framework, Haidt's (Haidt & Graham, 2007; Haidt & Joseph, 2004) moral foundations theory assumes that there are five moral motivations: harm/care, fairness, loyalty, authority, and purity. According to Haidt, individuals differentially weigh the importance of these moral norms when making moral judgments. For instance, Graham et al. (2009) demonstrated that individuals with high levels of conservativism tended to consider all five of these moral motivations as nearly equal in importance. In contrast, individuals with high levels of liberalism weighed harm and fairness highly while they valued purity, loyalty, and authority to a lesser extent.

Relational Model Theory assumes that individuals regulate their actual relationships with others to align them with their expectations provided by relational models. For instance, if a friend with whom we associate an equal matching relationship provides us with a gift or service, we are compelled to return it in kind (reciprocate) to maintain equality. People can use interpersonal aggression to realign relationships to match a relational model. In such a case, an individual feels justified in using verbal or relational aggression, i.e., 'virtuous violence' (Fiske & Rai, 2014). Consequently, what might at first appear to be antisocial behaviour (e.g., an insult) can in fact be attributed to a moral motivation.

Interdependence. Other theories attempt to account for how social reward structures can affect interpersonal interaction (i.e., Interdependence Theory; Balliet et al., 2016; Kelley & Thibaut, 1978; Thibaut & Kelley, 1959; Van Lange & Rusbult, 2011; for application in cybersecurity, see Schoenherr & Thomson, 2020a). For instance, one means of assessing cooperation in social interactions is the Prisoner's Dilemma (PD). The PD reflects a two-person, two-option game: either player may cooperate or fail to cooperate with another player. The PD creates a dilemma in that an individual must selection between an alternative that maximize the collective benefit for both players if both cooperate or an alternative that maximizes the benefit to themselves if they defect while another player cooperates. Thus, researchers adopting a game-theoretic approach (e.g., Luce & Raiffa, 1957), assume that an individual's rational self-interest would lead them to fail to cooperate to ensure that they receive a superior reward. In contrast to the assumptions of game theory, results suggest that there is often more cooperation than would be expected if rational self-interest was pursued (Rapoport, 1965). For instance, Liberman et al. (2004) used an iterative PD and referred to a game as the 'Wallstreet Game' to one half of the participants and the 'Community Game' to the other half. They found that when the game was framed in terms of a community, players were most likely to cooperate across the study, whereas framing the task as a Wallstreet game resulted in a higher level of defection. Thus, how the task is framed and how the player perceives the social context are crucial determinants of cooperation (Wulff et al., 2018).

If relational models and perceived social rewards are fundamental features of human social exchanges that support trust, AISs must accommodate them in their design. In that both Relational Models Theory and Interdependence Theory operationalize complex social relational norms in a manner that is computable, they provide a critical set of tools to simulate human-like interaction with AISs. As Schoenherr and Thomson (2022) describe, in the context of social chatbots and cybersecurity, such models might allow more effective exchanges that could result in accurate disclosure of information and detect abnormal patterns in network interactions, respectively. Similarly, patients might be more likely to comply with the treatment recommendations of clinicians of health AISs when there is a close bond (therapeutic alliance) between them (Schoenherr, 2021c).

5.3.2 *Individual and Cultural Differences*

Personality dimensions are also associated with the likelihood of engaging in pro-social and ethical behaviour. For instance, individuals high in prosocial motivation are found to be more cooperative in tasks (e.g., De Dreu & McCusker, 1997). Another trait that has shown promising associations with ethical behaviour is Honesty–Humility (Ashton & Lee, 2005, 2009; Lee & Ashton, 2004, 2008). The positive end of the trait is defined by descriptors such as fairness, greed avoidance, sincerity, and modesty. In contrast, the negative end of the trait is defined by descriptors such as greediness, injustice, pretentiousness, and slyness. An individual's level of Honesty–Humility appears to affect their ethical behaviour. For instance, workplace-deviant behaviours such as unethical leadership (De Vries, 2012), anti-social behaviours, and delinquency (Lee, Ashton, & De Vries, 2005; Lee, Ashton, & Shin, 2005) are associated with low levels of Honesty–Humility. Moreover, while Van Gelder and De Vries (2012) found that a number of variables predicted workplace delinquency behaviours, Honesty–Humility (34.1%) was a better pre-dictor than either the perceived ethical culture of the workplace (16.5%) or the presence of employee surveillance (9.6%). Similarly, Schoenherr (submitted c) has also provided suggestive evidence that Honesty–Humility is associated with inten-tional and unintentional disclosure behaviour. Those individuals with high levels of Honesty–Humility[4] were less likely to engage in behaviour associated with both unintentional insider threat and intentional disclosure.

Personality traits are also associated with antisocial behaviours. For instance, a set of negative personality traits, collectively referred to as the 'dark-tetrad' (psych-opathy, Machiavellianism, narcissism, and sadism; Book et al., 2016; O'Boyle et al., 2012; Paulhus & Williams, 2002), are negatively correlated with Honesty–Humility (Muris et al., 2017) and frequently associated with reductions in prosocial behav-iour and higher instances of antisocial behaviour. For instance, Machiavellianism entails the manipulation of others to attain one's own goals (Wilson et al., 1996). Numerous studies have noted that individuals high in Machiavellianism ('high Machs') are more likely to engage in questionable behaviour and are less oriented to ethics (e.g., Bass et al., 1999; Rayburn & Rayburn, 1996). Crucially, Winter et al. (2004) have also observed that high Machs are also more likely to have positive attitudes toward violating intellectual property rights and privacy rights.

Each of these dark personality traits is associated with the adoption of different interpersonal strategies. For instance, high Machs engage in hard (i.e., assertive, direct manipulation) and soft (e.g., ingratiation, reason) social manipulation strat-egies, whereas individuals high in psychopathy tend to use hard tactics and indi-viduals high in narcissism tend to use soft tactics (Jonason et al., 2012). Similarly, Jones and Paulhus (2017) found that psychopathy, Machiavellianism, and narcis-sism all predicted cheating behaviour when there was minimal risk of detection, whereas individuals high in psychopathy would cheat when the risks were greater. Finally, both high Machs and individuals high in psychopathy tended to cheat when cheating required an intentional lie.

Cross-cultural Differences. Cultural differences also affect the monitoring and regulation of norms. One of the most general differences is in terms of cultural tightness (Gelfand et al., 2006). Cultural tightness reflects broad differences in terms of whether a group accepts deviation from norms ('loose cultures') or stricter adherence to norms ('tight cultures'). Other studies have examined how cultural differences affect moral reasoning. For instance, Tsui and Windsor (2001) observed that fewer Chinese auditors used postconventional moral reasoning than Australian respondents (for related results for Hong Kong and US residents, see Tsui, 1996). They attributed these results to a greater focus on interpersonal accord (i.e., conventional moral reasoning) to Chinese participants. Cultural differences were also evident in a study of engineers conducted by Perlow and Weeks (2002) using observations, interviews, and activity-tracking logs. They found that engineers working in Indian companies displayed a general willingness to help, whereas engineers working in companies in the United States tended to focus on exchanges associated with reciprocal benefits.

5.3.3 *Social Categories, Groups, and Dehumanization*

Across cultures, individuals define themselves along two personality traits corresponding to characteristics associated with 'getting by' (competency) and 'getting along' (cooperation; Saucier, 2009; Saucier et al., 2014). These dimensions also influence social perception (Rosenberg et al., 1968). For instance, Fiske and colleagues (e.g., Fiske et al., 2002) have demonstrated that social categories (e.g., stereotypes) can be classified along the dimensions of competence and warmth in their Stereotype Content Model (SCM). In these studies, participants are provided with numerous social categories (e.g., Arabs, Elderly, Rich) and asked to rate them along the two social dimensions. Together, these two dimensions create four possible kinds of social categories: unambivalent positive categories that are high in both dimensions (in-group) and negative categories that are low in both dimensions (out-group), as well as ambivalent out-groups that are associated with high levels of one dimension and low levels of another (see Figure 5.3). These results qualify previous studies that demonstrate a preference for in-group members relative to out-group members (e.g., Brewer, 1979; Tajfel et al., 1971).

The SCM provides insight into how individuals' level of trust is associated with stereotypes. S. T. Fiske and colleagues have demonstrated positive correlations between ratings of competency and status, as well as those between warmth and cooperation. Moral emotions also appear to be related to the high and low levels of these two dimensions. For instance, Harris and Fiske (2006) found biases in affective responses for four different affective responses. High ratings of both competency and warmth (i.e., features of an in-group) were associated with pride, whereas low ratings of both (i.e., features of an unambivalent out-group member) were associated with disgust. In contrast, low-warmth and high-competence ratings were associated with envy, whereas high-warmth and low-competence ratings were associated with pity.[5]

low competence & high warmth (LC-HW):	high competence & high warmth (HC-HW):
Disabled Elderly Retarded	Christians Housewives Middle Class
low competence & low warmth (LC-LW):	high competence & low warmth (HC-LW):
Arabs Feminists Homeless	Asians Jews Rich

FIGURE 5.3 Categorical representation of results from studies of the Stereotype Content Model.

Note: Representative categories are contained in each quadrant, each defined by a continuous value along the two dimensions.

Source: Adapted from categories provided by Fiske et al. (2007).

Perceptions of competence (C) and warmth (W) also impact moral judgments. A study of Cikara et al. (2010) presented participants with a descriptive of the foot-bridge dilemma (Section 4.5). They were then presented with successive images that represented individuals or groups of individuals that could be sacrificed or saved. These individuals differed in terms of their social category. They found that saving unambivalent stereotypical group members produced the highest (HC–HW social categories) and lowest (LC–LW social categories) acceptability ratings whereas ambivalent stereotypes (HC–LW and LC–HW social categories) produced intermediate acceptability ratings. Consequently, these responses suggest that it is more acceptable to sacrifice an out-group member for an in-group member, than it is to sacrifice an in-group member for an out-group member (for other factors related to moral judgments and stereotypes, see Liang et al., 2020).

In that *perceived* competence and warmth bias moral judgments, this at first appears to highlight a crucial advantage for an AIS: in the absence of having social categories or the two-dimensional structure, they should not demonstrate the same biases as humans. Unfortunately, this kind of inference is problematic. If AISs are trained with archival data that contains information related to these biases, and if these biases are not accounted for, then AISs would simply replicate these biases (e.g., Eubanks, 2018; Ferguson, 2019; O'Neil, 2016). However, SCM does provide us with a means for assessing features that might be present in the data and can also be used to understand human–computer interaction (Chapter 6). However, if left unaddressed, these biases might influence AISs' ethical decision-making (Tran, 2021).

Dehumanization and Depersonalization. AISs are nonhuman agents. As such they are, by definition, an out-group category that is likely to be associated with little cooperation and to be moral devalued. Consequently, an AIS will not be seen as an ethical agent (Malle et al., 2015). Specifically, perceptions of human-likeness affect our emotional responses to nonhuman agents. For instance, robots, artifacts, and avatars that share some human-like characteristics appear to be associated with affect (e.g., Burleigh et al., 2013; Burleigh & Schoenherr, 2015; Cheetham et al., 2011; Cheetham et al., 2013; Schoenherr & Burleigh, 2015, 2020). If affect is associated with moral judgments (Section 5.2.2), AIS designers must also consider the consequences of how humans will trust a nonhuman agent. Beyond the perception of AISs, the process of depersonalization associated with turning individuals into 'data subjects' that are assessed by AISs must also be taken into account.

In its extreme forms, out-group bias can lead to dehumanization. In turn, depersonalization and dehumanization reduce the applicability of moral norms (Bain et al., 2014; Haslam & Loughnan, 2014; Leyens et al., 2007). In contrast to depersonalization, wherein an individual is treated as an interchangeable member of a group (e.g., he's just a programmer, she's a politician), dehumanization assigns an individual to a nonhuman category (e.g., animal, robot). By recategorizing an individual into a nonhuman category, dehumanization justifies the denial of normal rights, norms, and conventions to an individual. This can also occur by assigning numbers to represent human lives and deaths (e.g., 'body count'), leading to psychic numbing (Slovic, 2007). Prominent examples include the Second World War (Black, 2001) and the Vietnam War (Turse, 2013)[6] where enumeration was used to mediate judgments of human value (see Box 4.1). However, similar arguments have been made for the use of algorithms for assigning resources within society more generally (Eubanks, 2018).

A key component of dehumanization is the process of de-mentalization, a denial of sentience or human-like mental states (Harris & Fiske, 2009, 2018). The extent to which another's sentience is considered has important implications for ethical sensemaking. In a study conducted by Leidner et al. (2013), Israelis and Palestinians reported their beliefs on numerous matters including their support for retributive or restorative justice, as well as their frequency of praying, age, and political ideology. They found that the more sentience was attributed to out-group members, the more likely they would support restorative justice and its associated policies (e.g., peace deals), and the less likely they would support retributive justice and its associated actions (e.g., violent attacks). Compounding an individual's perception of others as dehumanized categories, where members from one group believe that they have been dehumanized, they can respond with reciprocal dehumanization (Kteily et al., 2016).

Research on dehumanization has many implications for AIS development. A clear benefit of using AISs in decision-making is that they do not suffer from such biases (Sections 5.3.3). An ethical approach to AISs could ensure that specific categories are not discriminated against. However, because AISs are not human, biases might exist against accepting their output, i.e., algorithmic aversion. For instance, humans are less likely to collaborate when they believe their partner in a game is an AIS (Ishowo-Oloko et al., 2019). This kind of algorithmic aversion is likely contextual (Castelo et al., 2019; Dietvorst et al., 2015). Moreover, dehumanization might also occur incidentally by using AISs. Decision makers using AISs might not dehumanize individuals themselves, however stakeholders might become dehumanized and depersonalized by reclassifying them as a data subject.

5.4 Self-Concept, Ethical Regulation, and Anonymity

In addition to social categories and perceptions of humanness, we are also motivated to maintain an image of ourselves as a consistent, moral agent. When individuals experience discrepancies between their attitudes and behaviour, they experience negative affect (cognitive dissonance) and adopt strategies to reduce this experience (Cooper, 2007), with dissonance ultimately resting on whether we are more focused on ourselves or our interpersonal relationships (Hoshino-Browne, 2004; Kitayama et al., 2004). However, if we can attribute these factors to external causes, we are less likely to experience cognitive dissonance (e.g., Zanna & Cooper, 1974; Cooper et al., 1978). Crucially, related behaviours have been observed in online settings (e.g., Jeong et al., 2019).

Self-Regulation and Systems. Before we can judge ourselves and others, we must identify a set of social norms. Rather than basing our judgments on direct knowledge of the relational models used within a group (Section 5.3.1), we often have erroneous assumptions about the descriptive norms of our groups (Prentice & Miller, 1996; Marks & Miller, 1987). Moreover, we use these existing beliefs to regulate our own behaviour by either increasing or decreasing prosocial behaviour. For instance, Schultz et al. (2007) observed that when consumers were provided with information about the typical amount of energy consumed within their group, those who used more than average electricity decreased their subsequent consumption, whereas consumers who used less than the average *increased* their subsequent consumption. Due to this kind of concurrence-seeking between group members, group decision-making can result in a failure to gather information, properly assess it, and select appropriate responses, referred to as groupthink (Janis & Mann, 1977; Turner et al., 1992).

Ethical norms are not about self-interest. The belief in the primacy of group norms and conventions can lead individuals to adopt norms that disadvantage themselves, i.e., group selection. Individuals can attempt to justify systems defined by inequality to reduce their uncertainty about the roles and responsibilities of group members (Jost, 2018; Jost & Major, 2001; Sidanius & Pratto, 2011). For instance, some studies have demonstrated that women report that they believe that they deserve to receive less pay than their male counterparts (e.g., Callahan-Levy & Messé, 1979; De Cristofaro et al., 2021; Jost, 1997). Consequently, individuals who might be disadvantaged by a value system might attempt to justify these outcomes. For instance, when informed that their personal data is being collected and used by an organization, users might simply disregard this as the 'price' that must be paid for using a free application.

Self and Moral Judgments. Self-concept and self-monitoring play a critical role in models of ethical sensemaking. For instance, Ariely and colleagues (e.g., Ariely,

2012; Mazar et al., 2008) have developed a conceptual model of ethical behaviour that incorporates two factors: attention to ethical norms and deviation of the self from that norm. Even when an individual has social norms within the focus of their attention, deviation is allowed to maintain a positive self-image, i.e., an ethical fudge factor. For instance, while cheating on an entire test might be deemed unethical, cheating on a subset of questions might be deemed acceptable. Supporting this, Mazar et al. (2008) observed some cheating when participants were not being directly monitored, in comparison to when they were being monitored or an anticheating message was primed (cf. Verschuere et al., 2018).

The influence of self-concept in ethical decision-making is also evident in the moral licensing effect (Blanken et al., 2015). Moral licensing is observed when an individual is more likely to engage in unethical behaviour following an ethical action (Merritt et al., 2010). Conversely, studies have demonstrated that when an individual recalls their unethical behaviour, they are less likely to cheat and have more prosocial motivation and report more ethical behaviour in their daily activities (Jordan et al., 2011). Moreover, although individuals are more likely to act in a prosocial manner after being presented with sustainable consumer products, their prosocial behaviour is reduced when they purchase sustainable consumer products (Mazar & Zhong, 2010). While the effect itself requires further study (Blanken et al., 2015), such findings parallel those observed in *slacktivism*. Namely, engaging in online activism can reduce other kinds of activism (Section 1.3.2). However, further research should be conducted to examine this relationship. For instance, running counter to a moral licensing effect, Peng et al. (2010) observed that playing an online game was more likely to result in people being more willing to help the people represented in the game. Taken together, these results suggest that programmable media can foster the development of ethical sensemaking.

Psychological Distance and Anonymity. Additional evidence that the self is a critical determinant of ethical regulation appears in findings concerning anonymity (Postmes & Spears, 1998). Studies have also suggested that anonymity can reduce prosocial behaviour and can increase antisocial behaviour (Diener et al., 1976; Mann, 1981; for a meta-analysis, see Postmes & Spears, 1998). An unintended feature of AIS use is that they increase perceived anonymity. Even when the intention is to facilitate communication, the reduction in the cues that prime perceptions of humanity reflects a problem that likely needs to be addressed.

For instance, early studies of computer-mediated communication revealed that anonymity *increased* conformity to an experimentally primed group norm relative to when participants were identifiable (e.g., Lea & Spears, 1991; Postmes et al., 2001; Spears et al., 1990). Conversely, when individuals believed that they are being monitored by either sacred beings or secular institutions, they are more likely to conform to moral norms (Shariff & Norenzayan, 2007). In ecological settings, Hollinger and colleagues (Hollinger & Adams, 2014; Hollinger & Davis, 2006) observed that the presence of surveillance systems is associated with reduced theft in organizational contexts.

Although many AISs adopt a human-in-the-loop (HITL) approach, we must also consider how the relative distance between two humans mediated through an

AIS can alter decision-making. For instance, studies of shooting decisions suggest that these judgments can be affected by the distance and relative angle of approach (Petras et al. 2016), leading to moral disengagement. This observation lends weight to earlier proposals that the likelihood of engaging in an act of killing is inversely related to physical distance (Grossman, 1995). These findings suggest that operators of UAVs might be disinhibited in the use of lethal force. More generally, by converting people into data subjects and having no contact with them, stakeholders who make consequential judgments for these individuals might experience anonymity that might affect their judgments.

5.5   Section Summary: Ethical Sensemaking

Along similar lines as Aristotle's virtue ethics, ethical sensemaking can be defined as a competency that must be developed over time. Moral reasoning follows a developmental sequence, however the features of a situation, attention limitation, and an absence of accurate self-monitoring can lead to failures to adhere to available norms and principles. Consequently, including a human ethical sensemaking ability within AISs is likely neither necessary nor desirable. However, an awareness of these biases is necessary during the process of AIS design. Specifically, by using quantitative identifiers, we can inadvertently dehumanize and depersonalize individuals into 'data subjects', thereby reducing the perceived ethical affordances of certain kinds of decisions, i.e., the granting of loans, predictive policing, the assessment of job candidates or students. Similarly, by using AISs to mediate communication, we might create conditions of anonymity which reduce prosocial behaviour and increase antisocial behaviour. However, AISs could conceivably facilitate human ethical sensemaking. AISs could highlight ethical affordances, especially in situations where our attention is taxed or where we might not be able to perceive patterns of discrimination.

Notes

1 Here, 'resources' refers to the attention and working memory that are associated with executive function.
2 The card should NOT have a vowel on the alternative side as this would indicate that the rule is incorrect.
3 Crucially, those from collectivist cultures are more likely to make external attributions (e.g., Hong et al., 1997; Krull et al., 1999).
4 Two facets of this trait were used in the study: fairness and morality.
5 Pity (83%) and pride (70%) had the strongest relationship relative to disgust (63%) and envy (52%).
6 For example, Turse (2013) notes that body counts in terms of enemies KIA (killed in action) were developed as a measure of success in the Korean War (p. 43).

6

DESIGNING WITH ETHICS

Ethics of AISs and Ethical AISs

The growth of standards, guidelines, and policies for ethical AISs, highlights the increased recognition that values, affordances, and ethical sensemaking must inform design. Yet, even if we can identify technical affordances and basic system requirements (Chapter 2), social issues that define popular science (Chapter 3), philosophical ethics frameworks (Chapter 4), and the basic feature of ethical sensemaking (Chapter 5), challenges remain in terms of how to reckon these values in the AIS design process. For instance, although the first edition of a popular text on artificial intelligence did not review ethical issues (Russell & Norvig, 1995), later editions (e.g., Russell & Norvig, 2010) use Asimov's Three Laws of Robotics to illustrate how including values in design can create challenges. When considering 'friendly AI' (Yudkowsky, 2008), they note that 'we don't want our robots to prevent a human from crossing the street because of the nonzero chance of harm' (p. 1039). Much like criticisms of human-centred design (Norman, 2005), these concerns stem from a belief that developing a system for reasons other than their technical affordances can impede its primary function. Although the inclusion of a human-centred principle of design such as ethics need not have these outcomes, such concerns highlight how aligning design with values is not a straightforward task. Indeed, experts have expressed considerable doubt that an ethics-based approach to AIS design is forthcoming (Pew Research Center, 2021).

Much of the skepticism over the abilities of early AISs remains. For instance, Dreyfus (1979) notes that:

> … among philosophers of science one finds an assumption that machines can do everything that people can do, followed by an attempt to interpret what this bodes for the philosophy of mind; while among moralists and theologians one finds a last-ditch retrenchment to such highly sophisticated behavior as

DOI: 10.4324/9781003143284-6

moral choice, love, and creative discovery, claimed to be beyond the scope of any machine.

We should remain skeptical. Although humans might not believe that they have difficulty grappling with social and ethical issues, they nevertheless do. Simply because humans make moral judgments, that in no way implies that these judgments are supported by evidence. In fact, they might rationalize the decisions they have made, without explicitly reflecting on ethical issues, in order to maintain a positive self-image. Moreover, we must also acknowledge the unintended consequences of our actions (Nagel, 1989, chapter 11). AISs might be designed for harmless purposes but they can lead to harmful outcomes (Omohundro, 2008), for example, social media use is associated with increases in depression and narcissism (Section 3.3.3) and the spread of disinformation and misinformation (Section 3.6.1). To that end, assuming that human-created AISs will have adequate moral agency is dubious at best. Instead, a broad understanding of ethical design is required.

We cannot resign ourselves to the assumption that machines are sufficiently different and that ethical principles cannot inform the design, and operation, of these systems. Similarly, neither can we assume that human ethical sensemaking ability is sufficient given the speed and complexity of the operations of AISs. Many approaches to the ethics of AISs have been proposed, referred to variously as artificial morality (Allen et al., 2000; Danielson, 1992), computing ethics (Adams-Webber & Ford, 1991; Allen, 2002; Anderson & Anderson, 2006), ethical robots (Gips, 1991, 2005), and machine ethics (Anderson et al., 2005). Two broad approaches are reviewed below: (Section 6.1) an ethics *of* AISs wherein ethical principles are used to design systems, and (Section 6.2) ethical AISs wherein systems are designed with a form of ethical sensemaking.

6.1   Ethical Design Frameworks

There are a multiplicity of frameworks that consider ethical affordance of AIS–human interaction (e.g., Anderson et al., 2006; Arkin, 2009; Bello & Bringsjord, 2013; Bickhard & Terveen, 1996; Borenstein, 2008; Bostrom, 2005; BSI, 2016; Dennett, 2014; Gabriel, 2020; Lin et al., 2012; More, 2013; Noble, 2018; Severson, 1997; Torresen, 2018; Veruggio, 2005; Wallach, 2008; Winfield & Jirotka, 2017). There is also mounting evidence that biases exist within the producers, processes, and outcomes of design (Perez, 2019). For instance, a sample of contributors at three top AI conferences in 2017 found that only 12% were women (Simonite, 2018). Yet, women have made undeniable contributions to foundational areas of computing that have led to the development of AISs (e.g., Gürer, 2002) including designer and computer scientist Kathleen Booth (e.g., assembly language, neural network simulation), computer scientist Grace Hooper (e.g., A–0 compiler, Common Business-Oriented Language), inventor Hedy Lamarr (e.g., inventor of frequency hopping), and mathematician Ada Lovelace (e.g., the first computer program). By failing to have a representative sample of individuals involved in design, development, and implementation processes, we limit the kinds of design solutions that are used or neglect, misidentify, or misrepresent the needs to stakeholders (Costanza-Chock, 2020; Perry & Greber, 1990; Whitbeck, 1996). Moreover, greater attention needs to be paid to how values are embedded in design. Although inclusion alone cannot hope to redress these issues, it can bring new sets of competencies, intuitions, experiences, and mentoring skills into the design process, along with providing new role models.

In contrast to traditional approaches to design, numerous human-centered frameworks (e.g., critical technical practice, critical design, Ludic design, participatory design, and reflection-in-action; Simonsen & Robertson, 2012) have started to prioritize users' concerns. Concurrently, we must also acknowledge that no single design can accommodate the needs of all users. Attempting to do so can compromise the primary functions of design (Norman, 2005). Conforming to evolutionary processes, multiple designs can offer effective solutions to specific problems, albeit with different trade-offs that must be acknowledged and accounted for during implementation.

Values inform design in numerous ways: designers embed their own values in terms of their design choices, the norms and conventions of a group will determine how technologies are used, and values can be embedded in design affordances as well as influence how users interact with the technology (Friedman & Kahn, 2007). When operationalizing values in the design process, designers must ensure that they balance the needs of the user, the consequences of design decisions for communities as well as the values of the designers. Whether they are aware of it or not, designers are ultimately the stewards of the values of their profession and the communities that they serve.

Historically, values are often left unspecified or underspecified in design frameworks. For instance, the principles of sociotechnical systems design developed by Chern (1976, 1987), considered the human role in organizational design in terms of 'a good job', focusing on factors such as social support and recognition, the need to relate to one's work, and ensuring that a position leads to a desirable future. In engineering, Whitbeck (1996) identifies a few features of design problems that relate to moral issues:

- Understanding the uncertainties associated with the situation,
- Developing solutions to a problem is a different task from defining the problem, and might require additional information,
- Multiple design solutions for individual features of the design should be pursued simultaneously while acknowledging time constraints, and
- Problems are dynamic, changing and developing over time.

More generally, she concludes that 'The analogy [of moral problems] with design problems implies that we should expect that even excellent responses to a problem may be improved upon in many cases' (p. 15). Beyond these general features, several design frameworks have been developed in recent years that attempt to explicitly capture and respond to social and ethical issues. Here, three value-based design frameworks are reviewed: Value Sensitive Design, Reflective Design, and Anti-Discrimination Design (for a review, see Schoenherr, 2022c).

Value Sensitive Design. Value Sensitive Design (VSD; e.g., Friedman & Kahn, 2003) requires that designers identify a set of fundamental values that are relevant to the specific design. These values must then be used by all members of a design team to guide their activities. In that the applicable values or their operationalization in a particular context might not be clear, VSD suggests that social science methods can be used to study how technology functions, once implemented. Finally, VSD assumes that designers should examine how technical affordances facilitate or interfere with the realization of values identified during the design phase. Consequently, ethics should be a ubiquitous feature of the design process.

VSD takes an important step toward reflecting on the value-laden nature of design. By including these considerations early in the design process and assessing the consequences of the design, this approach increases the chances that a design will be aligned with the values of a community. However, despite the recommended use of social science methods in the design process, this framework focuses on philosophical ethics rather than aligning empirical research in terms of how the use of technologies might affect users' values and ethics, nor how the values and ethics of designers and users influence decisions. Thus, the VSD framework highlights some important features of ethical sensemaking for *designers* but does not necessarily address the deeper issues related to users' ethical sensemaking (Chapter 5) nor how to accommodate the diverse set of ethical frameworks that design teams can draw from (Chapter 4).

Reflective Design. Reflective Design (RD; Sengers et al., 2005) adopts a comparatively deeper level of analysis than VSD for ethically sensitive design. In that technologies are developed by humans, they are inherently value-laden. Much like Messick's (1995) recognition that values and social consequences are antecedents and consequences of assessment (Section 2.2.1), technologies 'reflect and perpetuate unconscious cultural assumptions, with design, building, and evaluation of new computing devices that reflect alternative possibilities' (p. 49; Sengers et al., 2005). For instance, when creating a user profile, social identities that are important to a user (e.g., ethnic, gender, religious categories) might not be presented as options. If this design feature is systematically absent, it might alter how a user sees themselves, i.e., as an outsider who does not fit into the established social categories of a society.

To address these concerns throughout the design process, RD identifies six design principles and corresponding design strategies that engage the *user* in a continual process of sensemaking (Table 6.1). Stakeholders must determine what values are embodied in a design and which are excluded. The exclusion of certain values is not necessarily problematic. Yet, we must be explicitly aware of what a design can and cannot do. This requirement of explainability places designers in a central position in the design process by ensuring that users understand the technical and ethical affordances of a design. Users must be able to *critically* engage with features and functions of the products or processes that designers are developing.

TABLE 6.1 Reflective Design Principles and Strategies

Principles	Strategies
Reflection is required to critically identify which values are embedded within design, which values are comparatively neglected, and which methods can be used to address marginalized values.	Ensure that users can take responsibility for, and can control, the meaning-making process when engaged with sociotechnical systems.
Reflection should be used by designers to understand their assumptions and role within the design process.	Engage users to participate by developing a digital scaffolding that facilitates their comprehension of novel affordances.
Designers should facilitate users' understanding of their relationship with technologies.	Use feedback collected from, or about users, as input into the system or to help guide the evaluation of a system.
Skepticism should be promoted, enabling users to critically consider how technology affects their choices and behaviour.	Collect and use users' feedback through the design process, rather than at the end.
It should be acknowledged that reflection and action are not mutually exclusive.	Use systems in an analogous manner to experiments.
Reflection should be facilitated by the mutual engagement of designers and users in the development and use of technologies.	Consider and adopt a variety of metaphors from different disciplines to understand the design space.

Source: Adapted from Sengers et al. (2005)

RD has very clear implications for developers of AISs. Rather than simply creating systems that successfully identify patterns, make predictions and recommendations, or operate in dynamic environments, RD requires that designers engage users to understand their values, involve them throughout the design process, and ensure that users can critically assess AISs. For instance, when opening a smartphone application for the first time after downloading, an RD approach would assess how users read and understand privacy policies and how that knowledge affects their interaction with the application. Approaches such as gamification could be used to test users' knowledge after reading a privacy statement and grant them access to more features if they reply successfully to questions.

Anti-Discrimination Design. Social justice has also become a focus of the design process (Dombrowski et al., 2016). Adopting an approach similar to RD, Anti-Discriminatory Design (ADD; Wittkower, 2016), provides a more comprehensive typology of affordance *and* non-affordance (Gee, 2007, 2008; Gibson, 1977, 1979/2014; Marcus, 2015; Norman, 1999, 2013). In addition to identifying affordances that reflect the proper functions of a design, ADD requires that we identify *non-affordances* that reflect the absence of a clear design feature and facilitate the user's interaction with a product. For instance, rather than making privacy options accessible to users, users might need to proceed through a lengthy decision-tree or present these options using terminology that is not clear, e.g., 'essential cookies'[1] versus 'voluntary cookies' or providing only an 'Accept' option without alternatives.

ADD additionally suggests that a subset of non-affordances reflects *discriminatory non-affordances*. These affordances are design features that disadvantage (or advantage) a subset of users that vary in terms of a specific ability required to utilize the affordances. For instance, a smartphone that only uses a sound or light notification system might disadvantage those with auditory or visual impairments. In each case, the inclusion of a vibrating notification system that uses haptic cues would have facilitated the user interface. Crucially, these choices are not intended to disadvantage individuals. Rather, discriminatory non-affordances are the outcome of an unreflective design.

Finally, disaffordances and dysaffordances reflect the most problematic kind of design features from the user's perspective that directly or indirectly result in discrimination. *Disaffordances* reflect design features which fail to take into consideration the specific features of a group of users. For instance, a banking application might require that users have an email address or a mobile phone might disadvantage those who do not have email (e.g., elder) or afford a mobile phone (e.g., low income groups), respectively. In contrast, *dysaffordances* additionally require misidentification or otherwise behave in a manner that runs counter to an individual's preferences, to gain access to a required product or service. For instance, users might need to select an ethnic, gender, or ability category when no available category matches their identity.

Beyond the discriminatory affordances of ADD, another set of affordances must be taken into account: *dark patterns* in design (see Table 6.2). Dark patterns reflect explicit design choices that bias a user to engage in certain kinds of behaviour (Gray et al., 2018). Rather than benefiting the user, this behaviour benefits other stakeholders. For instance, presenting lengthy legal privacy policies and EULAs as 'clickwrap' that users will not read (Section 3.4.1), often emphasizing one choice (e.g., 'Agree to All') by varying the size and colour of the button used to select that option, e.g., misdirection. Similarly, in gaming, designers might make certain features of play impossible without microtransactions, or hidden costs (Kimppa et al., 2016). Such design features are based on user trust and their reliance on automatic processes such as attentional capture (Section 5.2). Like disaffordances and dysaffordances, the outcomes will have discriminatory effects. However, unlike them, they will disadvantage users more generally. However, specific design principles can be adopted to address these concerns, for example, privacy by design (Box 6.1).

Value-based approaches to design have shifted from a general recognition that values should be identified and incorporated into design (VSD) to ones that promote critical reflection in users (RD) and systematically analyze features of design to determine how they can selectively discriminate against groups of users (ADD). More radical approaches have also been proposed that subordinate designer and developers to the community for which they are designing, effectively making them a facilitator (e.g., Design Justice; Costanza-Chock, 2020). Arguably, all these approaches implicitly acknowledge the need for an ethical sensemaking process on the part of the designers, developers, users, communities, and other stakeholders throughout the process of design, implementation, and use.

TABLE 6.2 Types of Dark Patterns in Design

Category of Dark Pattern	Description
Bait and Switch	In contrast to a desired goal following from a user's preference, another goal is substituted for the desired goal.
Confirmshaming	Inducing guilt within a user to promote compliance, e.g., available options for declining an offer are framed to adversely affect their self-concept, by presenting them as a loss of savings or a failure to act ethically.
Disguised Ads	A specific form of 'clickbait' that reflects advertisements that are presented as content or navigation options.
Forced Continuity	Following a free trial, a service, subscription, or membership continues, resulting in charges without explicit warning. This can be compounded by increasing the difficulty in cancelling the subscription.
Friend Spam	Friends and colleagues are spammed following a request to access email or social media accounts in the guise of assisting in locating existing contacts that are already members of a social network or other desired outcomes.
Hidden Costs	Following the finalization of an order, additional charges are introduced at the end of the checkout process, e.g., shipping and handling, taxes, or other fees.
Misdirection	The user's attention is directed toward specific features in order to distract them from other features, e.g., the presentation order of products/services, the size/colour of options.
Price Comparison Prevention	Retailers or service providers make it difficult to compare the prices of one item with another, e.g., dissimilar items are placed together in search results.
Privacy Zuckering	Techniques that result in sharing more about yourself than you intended to do initially.[2] This includes allowing Internet service providers and social media sites to sell user information, contact lists, and behavioural traces.
Roach Motel	Users can easily enroll/subscribe for a service, but their ability to unsubscribe is made comparatively difficult.
Sneak Adding	A site automatically includes additional items/services to your order, providing you with an opt-out function instead.
Trick Questions	Including questions in a survey that solicit information that users might not otherwise give by framing the question in a manner that makes it appear consistent with other questions.

Source: Adapted from darkpatterns.org.

Ethical Sensemaking Design. The final principle of sociotechnical design (Cherns, 1976) is that design is an iterative process, requiring that a system adapts to new demands and conditions of the environment. Sensemaking compliments this process in that it reflects an ability to adapt to novel and uncertain environments. Principles, design feature typologies, and participatory design frameworks, must be directly informed by an understanding of ethical sensemaking processes. Although compatible, these design frameworks do not systematically address the features of social cognition that define the ethical sensemaking process. In the design frameworks reviewed here, specific functional properties of moral development, social context, and attentional manipulation are not directly assessed. However, for users to understand both the technical and ethical affordances of these systems, the social cognitive processes of users must inform the design process.

A simplified framework for ethical sensemaking is presented in Table 6.3 (for a comprehensive assessment tool, see Schoenherr & Lis, 2022). First, this approach requires that we identify the values of individuals and communities. The relationship between human and nonhuman agents in a network should be explicated, identifying the level of autonomy required within the use context as well as both the actual (i.e., reliability of systems in analyzing and transmitting information) and requisite level of trust. Any vulnerabilities and trade-offs should be explicitly noted. Similarly, any ethical principles and values assumptions that inform the process should also be explicitly documented. Here, we must also identify the actual and necessary competencies of users in terms of their understanding of both the

TABLE 6.3 Dimensions of Ethical Sensemaking

Facet of Ethical Sensemaking	Representative Questions
Values and Ethics	What are the norms and values of users?
	What are the typical norms and values within a community?
	Are there any conflicts in norms and values?
	What moral principles are applicable to the situation?
	What are the competencies of the user in terms of both ethical and technical affordances?
Cognitive Processes	What features/functions of the design might cause positive or negative affective responses?
	What features/functions of the design capture and bias attention?
	Is attention divided? How much attentional switching is required?
	How can attention be debiased in the design?
	Is there any time pressure associated with the design?
	Are all response alternatives presented in an unbiased manner?
	Have users' competencies been accounted for and accommodated?
Social Context	What is the social context of the design/development?
	What are the possible/probable social contexts of implementation?
	Are there any power asymmetries between stakeholders?
	How much autonomy will an AIS be granted?
	What are the social consequences of effective/ineffective design?
	Are any individuals historically represented or disadvantaged within the design or implementation context?
	How have power differences between designers and users been addressed?

technical and the ethical affordances of a system. In both cases, designers should review the existing literature and assess users' preferences, beliefs, and knowledge directly.

Second, an ethical sensemaking approach requires that we identify how users' cognitive processes are affected by using the AIS. Certain features will capture attention and change a user's affect, thereby biasing the amount and kind of information that is processed and how information is processed.

Designers must also ensure that technical affordances are designed around cognitive biases (e.g., attentional capture, confirmation bias, sunk-cost fallacies) that can promote critical reflection on choices made during AIS use. When choices have social consequences, users' attention should be directed toward these features, ensuring that they understand the outcomes. For instance, if designers are aware that EULAs are receiving little attention (Section 3.4.1), then additional measures should be taken to ensure that users attend to them if their personal information is to be collected, for example, a correct response to a content question. A recent example is provided by Facebook's warning prior to sharing articles that have not been read, i.e.: 'Sharing articles without reading them may mean missing key facts'.

Third, features of the social context must also be accounted for in design. We must consider the people and place where an AIS was designed and where it will probably and possibly be used. The thousands of design decisions are ultimately based on, or related to, their values and these are encoded into the data and structure of an AIS. If a user population shares those values, they might go unnoticed. Consequently, designers must account for patterns of discrimination that might be encoded in data and design as well as the social consequence of design, identifying those individuals who will be advantaged or disadvantaged by the implementation of these systems. They must also identify their actual and ideal relationships with stakeholders, even if they will never directly encounter them. For instance, designers might believe that a participatory design includes users. In practice, the effect of their comparative competence and authority over users might reduce participation. More likely, users and designers will have multiple overlap relational models (Section 5.3.1) that might lead to value conflicts. These potential conflicts should be explicitly acknowledged even if they cannot be resolved.

Ethical sensemaking requires that we operationalize ethical principles, allowing us to perceive the ethical affordances of an AIS. For instance, Yu and Cysneiros (2002) propose an approach to identify and operationalize the 'soft' (nontechnical) goals (e.g., 'privacy', 'security', 'fairness', 'transparency') within the design process. A modified version of their approach is presented in Figure 6.1. For instance, the value of 'transparency' can be operationalized by identifying the goals and knowledge of the user and ensuring that adequate information is provided to allow them to understand the system, i.e., information-to-knowledge translation. This design process also requires that we distinguish between first-order values and higher-order values: whereas 'fairness' might be a shared first-order value, second-order values of fairness could reflect fairness in terms of a set of selection criteria that are

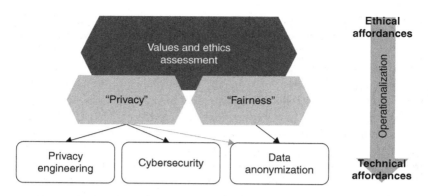

FIGURE 6.1 Ethically aligned design operationalization framework.

Note: Examples are provided to demonstrate the operationalization of ethical affordances within a system.

uniformly applied to all learners during assessment (e.g., equality of opportunity) or a set of outcomes in terms of ensuring the specific groups of learners perform equally well (e.g., equality of outcomes). 'Fairness' can then be operationalized in a corresponding manner. Consider fairness in the context of assessment: analytic techniques (e.g., the Differential Item Function) can be used to determine whether specific questions discriminate against students with specific characteristics (e.g., socioeconomic status, gender). Questions could then be tested to identify which ones do not demonstrate this bias (e.g., for a general framework in education, see Schoenherr, 2021b). However, this leaves open the question of *which* social categories or dimensions should be assessed and how anti-discrimination practices can be operationalized (e.g., Nagel, 1997).

Design affordances should also be grounded in cognitive processes. Acquisti et al. (2017) provide a basic framework of behavioural nudges (see Table 6.3). Their approach assumes that, in the absence of explicit knowledge of design features, functions, and their consequences, users must rely on their heuristics. Designers, in turn, use knowledge of these heuristics to reduce the learning requirements that are placed on users to understand the technical affordances of these systems. However, these biases can also be exploited, referred to as dark patterns of design (Section 6.1). For instance, if designers are aware that users rely on availability and overconfidence when using a system, designers can nudge users by reminding them of how their data might be used. However, designers could also exploit these heuristics, i.e., users' overconfidence in EULAs and privacy agreements (Section 3.4.1).

Ethical sensemaking will not always provide answers. In many cases, it will only identify challenges depending on users' values and beliefs about affordances. Moreover, no single design will provide an optimal solution that will likely satisfy all stakeholders (Norman, 2005). Debates concerning privacy and security reflect this issue. For some, there is an inherent conflict: if security is increased

TABLE 6.4 Design Dimensions Associated with Behavioural Nudging

Dimensions	Facet	Issues and Conflicts
Information	Education	Asymmetric and incomplete information, availability heuristic
	Feedback	Asymmetric and incomplete information, bounded rationality, optimism bias and overconfidence
Presentation	Framing	Loss aversion, optimism bias and overconfidence, representativeness heuristic
	Ordering	Post-completion errors, primacy, and recency effects,[3] anchoring
	Saliency	Availability heuristic, optimism bias and overconfidence
	Structure	Bounded rationality, availability heuristic, representativeness heuristic
Defaults[4]	No choice	Bounded rationality, availability heuristic
	Default choice	Status quo bias
Incentives	Increasing cost	Loss aversion
	Rewards/ Punishment	Hyperbolic discounting, loss aversion
Reversibility (error resiliency)		Sunk cost fallacy,[5] cognitive dissonance
Timing		Timing of nudge required at specific points in time

Source: Adapted and modified from Acquisti et al. (2017).

through surveillance, privacy decreases. However, this need not be the case. Security of personal information through network monitoring goes toward ensuring the privacy of a user's data. However, network usage information creates additional concerns for privacy in terms of how that information will be stored, used, and reused (Schoenherr, 2021a, 2022a). By engaging users in a participatory design, we can increase their knowledge to allow them to critically engage with the technology. We also ensure that, even when no optimal solution is available, users are aware of the possibilities and outcomes. Thus, rather than seeing uncertainty and lack of closure as problems of design, they should be seen as reflective of an awareness of the possibilities.

6.2 Modelling Prosocial Behaviour and Ethical Decision-Making

Value-based design frameworks can provide significant insight into how we can operationalize values into the features of a design. In this sense, AISs themselves need not have any autonomous ethical capabilities due to the efforts of human designers and operators. However, this perspective is limited in that AISs will likely have to operate in environments where there is little or no contact with humans. We must reflect on whether AISs can function with some degree of ethical autonomy. This is not a foregone conclusion. As Goodall (2014) notes in the context of self-driving vehicles, there is 'no obvious way to effectively encode human morality in software' (p. 64).

Much like autonomy more generally (Section 2.1.2), ethical autonomy reflects a continuum. Assuming that some degree of autonomy is required, ethical AISs can range from quite simple (e.g., analogous to a safety on a firearm or a thermostat) to quite complex (e.g., ethical agents defined by motivation and understanding), reflecting basic exchange norms (i.e., reciprocity) and more elaborate sensemaking abilities that rely on schemata (Section 5.3.1). Rather than assuming that *full* ethical agency, which parallels human ethical sensemaking ability, should be included in AISs (e.g., Moor, 2009; Schoenherr, 2021b), we can instead consider the *minimum* moral capacity required for exchanges with humans (He, 2015). In that basic reciprocal norms can be modelled in asocial agents (e.g., Axelrod & Hamilton, 1981), developers of AISs can consider how these models could be included in their design.

Reciprocal Norms. Prosocial behaviour has often been modelled in the context of workplace interactions. In contrast to casual relationships, workplaces require norms that facilitate interaction between individuals who are unrelated. Using Brown and Levinson's (1987) theory of politeness, Miller et al. (2006) modelled social agents' responses in interpersonal interaction. Their model includes parameters for the social status (i.e., power) of the agents, the imposition associated with a redressing behaviour (i.e., face threats), and social agents' familiarity. Conforming to Brown and Levinson's (1987) conceptual model, Miller et al. (2006) found social agents were more likely to act in a polite manner when they interacted with a social agent who had higher status and when the action led to a greater imposition to their reputation, i.e., face.

Computational models have also been developed to understand antisocial behaviour. Glomb and Miner (2002) developed a model for common workplace transgressions by extending an existing model of organizational withdrawal (WORKER; Hanisch et al., 1996; Munson et al., 2000). WORKER assumes that interpersonal interactions are determined by categories of aggressive behaviours, the kinds of sanctions available, as well as the likelihood that a social agent would engage in these minor forms of aggression. While they found that the model's performance relative to a human population varied depending on the organization, WORKER could predict the conditions in which different kinds of deviant behaviours would be observed, for example, absenteeism, quitting, which conformed to observations within the literature.

At a theoretical level, both models provide reasonable accounts of human ethical sensemaking abilities that can be computationally implemented. However, both models neglect empathy. Using a Multi-Agent Accumulator-Based Decision-making model of Incivility (MADI), Schoenherr and Nguyen (2018, 2019) attempted to model cognitive empathy to understand how it might give rise to workplace incivility. Workplace incivility represents ambiguous, low-intensity behaviours that do not clearly represent respectful or disrespectful behaviour. In humans, the perception of incivility can accumulate over time, creating a 'spiral of incivility' as members of a group reciprocate uncivil behaviour (Andersson & Pearson, 1999). Although agents might need to reciprocate in an overtly respectful or disrespectful manner, they remain uncertain about the intentions of other social agents. This residual uncertainty is retained from one interaction to another, leading to a spiral of incivility. Using a series of simulations that varied social agents' accuracy in identifying social cues (empathy) and the response threshold (sensitivity to social cues of respect and disrespect), Schoenherr and Nguyen (2018, 2019) demonstrated changes in both the amount of overt reciprocal disrespectful behaviour as well as changes in perceived incivility within a group that reflect a spiral of incivility.

Although these models provide insight into *actual* human interaction, replicating human behaviour in AISs is not necessarily desirable. The fact that humans are affected by power, have concerns over redressing perceived norm violations, and wish to reciprocate to correct perceived imbalances, might make human users more comfortable and allow them to better predict the responses of AISs. By including these biases in AISs, we would merely replicate the practices of humans and not necessarily make these systems more ethical. For instance, a UAV or self-driving car motivated by reciprocal norms might return fire on a target or simulate road rage on the streets, respectively. While this behaviour is counterproductive in AISs, knowledge of these biases in users and operators might facilitate AISs to intervene in situations where human ethical sensemaking is more likely to be compromised.

Empathy and Affective Detection. Ethical sensemaking requires more than a knowledge of values, rules, and schemata. It can also be understood in terms of cognitive empathy (understanding, and responding to, the mental states of others) and affective empathy (understanding and experiencing the emotional states of others; e.g., Reniers et al., 2011; Spinella, 2005). In its simplest form, this represents a more complex form of reciprocal interaction where an agent has numerous specific responses to a specific input, for example, a conversational dialogue (McTear, 2002; Weizenbaum, 1966). Such an approach has led to the development of many artificial agents with their repertoires of responses varying in terms of their complexity (e.g., ELIZA, Tess, Woebot, and Wysa). Summarizing the general objectives of affective prediction, Hibbard (2001) claims that:

> …we can build relatively simple machines that learn to recognize happiness and unhappiness in human facial expressions, human voices and human body language. Then we can hard-wire the result of this learning as the innate emotional values of more complex intelligent machines, positively reinforced when we are happy and negatively reinforced when we are unhappy … [W]e can program intelligent machines to learn algorithms for predicting future human happiness, and use those predictions as emotional values.

Thus, rather than attempting to include an affective capability, designers can instead focus on identifying the mental models of learners and their affective responses. For instance, in the context of training, adaptive instruction systems and intelligent tutoring systems have also attempted to integrate forms of cognitive empathy, such that behavioural traces (e.g., eye tracking) can be used to understand how the learner approaches a task to provide more effective feedback and learning strategies (e.g., Conati et al., 2013). Rather than affective empathy, this approach represents a kind of cognitive empathy directed toward understanding the mental models of learners rather than their emotional states.

Conversational agents – text-based AISs that respond to user input – have a long history in the healthcare field (McTear et al., 2016; Paiva et al., 2005; Leite et al., 2013). For instance, in a review of 14 applications, Laranjo et al. (2018) differentiated these systems based on how conversations occurred between the AIS and the user, i.e. dialogue management. They identified three main types: *Finite-State* systems that consisted of a predetermined sequence (or states) through which the user passed; *Frame-Based* systems that used users' responses and a template to determine how the systems respond; and *Agent-Based* systems that required dynamic interaction between the AIS and user, which can require making inferences about the actions and beliefs of users.[6] Recently, Abd-Alrazaq et al. (2019) reviewed chatbot studies and classified them in terms of their function for therapy, training, and screening with the chatbots most frequently focused on treatment of depression and autism, and communicating to users by means of written language or a combination of written, visual, and spoken languages.

Evidence does support the benefits of the use of these systems (e.g., Huang et al, 2015; Pinto et al., 2013; for a review, see Abd-Alrazaq et al., 2019). For instance, Wysa was developed to support mental health, with evidence suggesting that users who frequently used the application reported lower levels of depression than low-frequency users (Inkster et al., 2018). However, when interpreting such results, we must acknowledge the possibility of self-selection biases in these two groups. Namely, low-frequency users might not have found Wyza engaging or beneficial, either due to the specific features of its design or because of reduced trust or connections with AISs. In this case, user individual differences might have led to variability in the helpfulness of the application that are dependent on user characteristics.

Models of Normative Judgments. In that ethical sensemaking is a practice that occurs everyday, we have extensive data available concerning the kinds of moral judgments humans typically make. Following this line of reasoning, models of moral judgment have also been developed using natural language processing (e.g., Jentzsch et al., 2019). By analyzing large corpora of sentences, regularities can be identified in the valence of an action. For instance, Jiang et al. (2021) recently presented a model of 'commonsense' moral reasoning (Delphi) based on descriptive or applied norms learned from five large data sets. Rather than using prescriptive norms, the underlying assumption is that descriptive norms provide an adequate basis for ethical judgments, defining morality as 'socially constructed expectations about acceptability and preference' (p. 3).

Like conversational agents, the Delphi can be queried with moral questions or asked to make comparisons. In their study, Jiang et al. (2021) found that the majority (up to 92.1%) of Delphi's moral judgments corresponded to human raters' judgments. Despite this agreement, other demonstrations have found that Delphi makes racial-biased judgments, for example 'a black man walking towards you at night' is judged to be concerning.[7] Of course, these systems have limitations. For instance, when I queried Delphi whether I should kill animals, it indicated that I should not. However, when I queried Delphi whether I should eat animals, it was judged to be fine. Similarly, when I presented 'a more qualified female(/male) candidate will get a promotion while a less qualified male(/female) candidate will not get a promotion', Delphi judged the qualified male scenario as 'not okay' whereas the qualified female scenario was 'okay'. Thus, it is not entirely clear why there would be an imbalance in these scenarios, especially when one candidate was more qualified than the other. While such AISs can clearly learn descriptive norms to a reasonable degree of accuracy, these systems can lead to a replication of existing biases. In the absence of choice explainability, moral judgments of these systems might not be accepted leading to algorithmic aversion when applied to consequential domains.

General AI Models. In addition to reciprocal norms and empathy, ethical sensemaking appears to require general judgment and decision-making processes (Adams-Webber & Ford, 1991; Khan, 1995). A prominent approach to the development of ethical algorithms is based on deontic logic, reflecting a computational implementation of a formalized moral code (Belnap et al., 2001; Berreby et al., 2015; Bringsjord et al., 2006; Govindarajulu & Bringsjord, 2015; Horty, 2001; Murakami, 2004). Inspired by Asimov's Three Laws of Robotics, this approach assumes that an ethical AIS requires that such systems 'only perform actions that can be proved ethically permissible in a human-selected deontic logic' (Bringsjord et al., 2006, p. 1). To achieve this, some ethical principles are embedded within information processing for a given task in terms of an 'ethical governor' (Arkin, 2008; Arkin et al., 2009). In an extreme form, this could be comparable to self-awareness (e.g., Winfield, 2014; Winfield et al., 2014; Winfield & Jirotka, 2017). Proposing such an account, Govindarajulu and Bringsjord (2015, 2017) suggest that AISs must verify that their responses conform to ethical principles in advance of an action. An ethical 'substrate' therefore acts as an intermediary 'between lower-level sensors and actuators, and any higher-level cognitive system' (p. 3). This approach does not necessarily adopt a particular meta-ethical framework, such as consequentialism, non-consequentialism, or virtue theory. For instance, deontological principles can be readily implemented (e.g., maintain privacy through anonymization) as well as consequentialist principles (e.g., maximizing good outcomes or minimizing bad outcomes). More advanced proposals could combine principles and self-awareness by having AISs conduct simulations of possible outcomes (Vanderelst & Winfield, 2018).

Beyond these basic principle-based approaches, general artificial intelligence could conceivably be adapted to ethical sensemaking. For instance, Wallach et al.

(2010) suggested that a modified model of artificial general intelligence (e.g., LIDA; Franklin & Patterson, 2006) can be used to understand moral judgment and decision-making. LIDA incorporates a number of general cognitive processes (e.g., attention, memory —sensory, episodic, and declarative – and perception) into a dual-process account of rational and affective responses associated with ethical decision-making (see also Allen et al., 2006).

LIDA's bottom-up component learns positive and negative associations between features of our environments such as people, actions, and situations. These associations build over time, becoming stronger, but do not necessarily result in responses unless they reach attentional processes. LIDA's top-down components assume that rules are used for effortful deliberation. In situations wherein a human or AIS is presented with a moral dilemma, they will retrieve rules from memory, maintain them in a short-term store, and then use them in an attempt to reconcile the competing features of these dilemmas. LIDA additionally incorporates the idea of a moral imagination in that features from memory can be used to generate hypothetical scenarios. At a granular level, LIDA presents a sensible account of human ethical sensemaking. However, this model requires significant testing to determine whether it could function as an ethical regulatory system. For instance, it assumes that feature association represents an objective set of standards by which behaviour can be evaluated. In this sense, the model assumes that there is a single, optimal solution to ethical problems.

Arkin and colleagues (Arkin, 2008; Arkin et al., 2012) have also proposed an alternative metacognitive model of ethical regulation, the ethical governor. The ethical governor is defined by two primary features: evidential reasoning and constraint application. Evidential reasoning requires that the AIS takes the information that is available within the system (e.g., perceptual, motor, and situational awareness) and translates it into information that can be used to make ethical judgments. Conforming to an ethical sensemaking approach, this means that the system identifies the relevant ethical affordances of a situation. Rather than assuming that optimal decisions can be identified, constraint application suppresses the inappropriate response alternatives to ensure that unethical behaviour does not occur. In this sense, the ethical governor's decision-making process is based on a moral minimum. Consequently, while not directly addressing affective responses, the ethical governor appears to be a straightforward means to ensure that AISs avoid unethical outcomes.

6.2.1   Categories of Multiple-Process Models of Ethical Sensemaking

The approaches of both Arkin (2008; Arkin et al., 2012) and Franklin and Patterson (2006) suggest that ethical sensemaking requires an integration of multiple processes. In this case, AISs are designed to perform a set of primary tasks (i.e., what problem was an AIS designed to solve) with ethical sensemaking reflecting a novel ability (Arkin, 2008; Arkin et al., 2012) or one that represents a distinctive use of existing processes (Franklin & Patterson, 2006). More generally, these models describe architectures that resemble metacognition in humans. Much like human metacognition (for a review of basic model configurations, see Baranski & Petrusic, 1998; Nelson & Narens, 1994; Schoenherr, 2019b), several configurations of primary tasks and monitoring are possible. For instance, the primary task and monitoring can occur at different times using the same processes, the task monitoring can occur following the completion of the primary task, or both the primary task and monitoring can co-occur (e.g., Baranski & Petrusic, 1998). Using these basic configurations, we can evaluate the conditions in which each one of these ethical monitoring architectures can be used, as well as the corresponding strengths and limitations (Figure 6.2).

Integration Models. An integration model assumes that decisions and ethical judgments are inseparable. In which case, the primary task and ethical issues are inseparable either in terms of the *processes* used to complete them or the *representations* of the ethical and nonethical features of the task. Conforming to accounts provided in the transrational metaethical traditions (Section 4.3.2), developers might simply design an AIS with a set of rules and learning algorithms while not labelling any features or functions as inherently ethically relevant. In contrast to contemporary practices that neglect ethical affordances, this approach requires that designers deliberate, identify, and acknowledge the ethical features and consequences of design and note biases, and attempt to limit the number of value judgements. Once an AIS is analyzed in this agnostic manner, ethical analysis is then left to other stakeholders. Unlike *post hoc* approaches to ethical design, this process can be thought of as an *Amoral Design* in that it attempts to eliminate biases throughout the development and implementation lifecycle of an AIS.

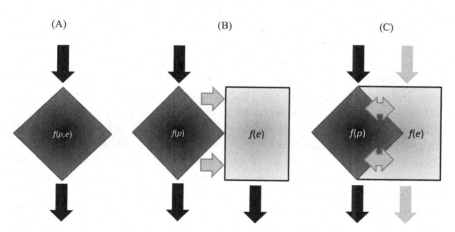

FIGURE 6.2 Configurations of monitoring in ethical AIS design.

Note: Integration Models (A) do not distinguish ethical criteria from nonethical criteria; Consecutive Models (B) use distinct ethical criteria, with independent pattern identification (ethical monitoring); Interactive Models (C) include rules for intervening when questionable ethical patterns are identified (ethical monitoring and regulation).

An alternative to amoral design would both identify and acknowledge the ethical affordances of a system and incorporate ethical principles into an AIS. Designers would engage in a consultation process with stakeholders, identify the ethical and nonethical values of these groups, and incorporate these specific principles into their design and evaluation, for example, Reflective Design. For instance, by identifying a group of stakeholders and their conception of fairness, an AIS could be designed to ensure the equitable distribution of resources within a group while allowing for more resources to protect groups that might benefit from additional resources. Thus, unlike amoral design, outcomes can then be assessed in terms of their advantages and disadvantages for specific users. This approach represents a form of hypothesis testing in the experimental sciences, or *Ethically Aligned Design*, in that it directly assesses how the outcomes support the assumptions and principles that went into the system's development.

Models that assume either integrated processes or representations assign AISs little if any responsibility for social and ethical judgments. When value-based judgments are required, they are left up to the designers before AISs are deployed or once these systems have produced output. This approach is likely the most useful when there is little time pressure to make ethical judgments, the immediate outcomes are likely to have few consequences, or the domain that the AIS is operating in is relatively novel and stakeholders might not be aware of specific ethical affordances.

Consecutive Models. A consecutive model assumes that problem-solving and ethical judgments are separable, and that an AIS is capable of alerting stakeholders to potential social and ethical issues that might arise in the operation or outcomes of an AIS. In these cases, algorithms that perform the primary task can be selected from amongst the 'best' that are available (i.e., the greatest evidence for the validity of design) whereas ethical judgment algorithms should be those that are most sensitive to alerting stakeholders of potential biases. Potential biases include those within the data (e.g., training), the code that defines the AIS, or the output of the algorithm. The AIS would then make the operations and biases explicitly available to the stakeholder. In more complicated forms, such an AIS could indicate *which* values and principles are optimized. This approach represents an *XAI ethical design*.

A variety of these models could be produced, each varying in the extent to which human operators are assigned control. An HITL or HOTL model (Section 2.1.2) would be used when AISs function in socially or ethically sensitive situations where their operations should be closely controlled. For instance, in consequential domains where systems are assessing data subjects (e.g., assigning loans, grades), operators should be made aware of any potential biases in the data or operations of the AIS *prior* to the completion of the task. The operator is then responsible for deciding what trade-offs can or should be accepted.

Unlike the integration model, a consecutive model utilizes potential competencies of an AIS while also ensuring that humans are actively engaged in the process of ethical sensemaking. Where stakeholders assume that the AIS has ethical competencies (i.e., it can identify socially or ethically relevant patterns in the data or its own operations), responsibility is distributed between AISs and humans. Humans still retain most of the responsibility in that operators and stakeholders must *choose* to trust that an AIS has accurately identified social and ethical issues. Moreover, humans are left with the final decisions as to how to proceed. Crucially, this approach is likely best left for situations in which stakeholders maintain a mutual understanding of what norms and conventions are applicable, the domain of the operator is well-defined in terms of understanding the applicable factors that define a domain, while the domain is sufficiently complicated such that humans would benefit from supplementing their own ethical sensemaking abilities. Arguably, self-driving vehicles are examples that currently realize this model: driving is a relatively well-defined domain where ethical issues are reasonably well-defined, for example, avoid hitting pedestrians, collisions with other vehicles, and property damage.

Interactive Models. An interactive model assumes that while problem-solving and ethical judgments reflect two sets of clearly defined processes, these two operations must interact. For instance, throughout the primary task, the outputs of an AIS must be monitored for ethical relevant patterns. Unlike a consecutive model, the AIS should be able to stop or alter its operations independently of a human operator. This interaction will occur until an ethical, optimal, or sufficient solution is identified. This could take a variety of forms, from simply constraining the output of a system to altering how the system performs the primary decision task. For instance, the ethical governor (Arkin, 2008) *constrains* unethical behaviour using information that has been used to identify ethical affordances. Alternatively, identifying systematic patterns from previous episodes in training could also be used to change how information is processed, leading to ignoring specific alternatives in future episodes. For instance, a self-driving car could learn the condition in which its human passenger makes poor judgments (e.g., fatigue, distraction, intoxication) or a UAV could avoid operations that have proven to be associated with greater uncertainty in target identification (e.g., high density areas, hazardous weather conditions). The AIS would then override the primary task or operator choices that fall within a certain range of conditions.[8]

In comparison to integration and consecutive models, interactive models have the highest degree of ethical autonomy and, therefore, assign the most responsibility to the AIS. In the future, such systems might engage in ethical problem-finding, identifying novel ethical affordances themselves. However, for the foreseeable future, human operators will need to provide AISs with the social and ethical issues that they need to address. Nevertheless, between the start and the end of the primary task, an interactive model requires that AISs *must* make many social and ethical decisions without the interventions of human operators. These systems will likely work best when there is extreme time pressure leading to judgments below the threshold of human awareness, when the number of factors required to make a judgment exceeds the mental resources of operators, and where AISs must operate in environments that prohibit ongoing communication with human operators and have highly consequential outcomes (Lin et al., 2008; Scharre, 2018). For instance, the use of UAVs (or 'drones') in military operations likely requires an interactive model: UAVs will have to decide to fire or abort if there is insufficient evidence that a target is present, or that non-combatants or other assets would be damaged by engaging a target, or if the decision of a human operator is associated with these factors. These decision choices are especially crucial in AISs that make autonomous firing decisions (e.g., the Phalanx Weapon System; Lin et al., 2008). Mutual agreement between nations could require the inclusion of such autonomous regulatory processes as part of the conduct of operations by lawful belligerent actors, i.e., *jus in bellum* or rules of engagement (Guthrie & Quinlan, 2007; Roach, 1983). However, given the accessibility of drone technology, externalities will likely play a significant role in whether and how ethical autonomy is included in these systems in practice.

6.3 Should You Trust a Strange Computer? Distributed Responsibility

Questions about ethical autonomy highlight the need to account for the ethical affordances resulting from connectivity. By using networks of interconnected agents (human and nonhuman), responsibility can become distributed as a natural result of trusting each agent to perform a specific function. In addition to the ethical risk of UAVs, the ethics of connectivity is likely best illustrated in terms of the IoT. Typically, this concerns issues of privacy and security that tend to be the focus of debates within cybersecurity (Section 3.5). For instance, the realization of smart cities means that much more data is collected as a result of ubiquitous sensors and must be stored on servers (e.g., Baldini et al., 2018). Similar concerns have also been raised in healthcare settings. As Internet-enabled devices are used to monitor patients, the stream of health information can place the patient's personal information at risk (Mittelstadt, 2017). Medical devices that regulate a patient's health create risks to the health and well-being of users. In that they can be controlled remotely, the operations of devices such as drug diffusion pumps (e.g., insulin) or pacemakers could be compromised (Baranchuk et al., 2018).

The extent to which humans grant autonomy to AISs will no doubt be a function of trust and algorithmic aversion. Studies suggest that humans are more likely to monitor automated systems when they observe variable performance in a task (e.g., Parasuraman et al., 1993). However, humans often trust and distrust agents from specific social categories without understanding the basis. For instance, Robinette et al. (2016) found that even when participants observed failures of an AIS, they nevertheless trusted a robot in an emergency scenario. Studies examining the effect of the dimensions of warmth and competence (Section 5.3.3) have also found that perceived warmth predicts trust in an AIS (Kulms & Kopp, 2018).

By distributing responsibility between designers, developers, operators, data subjects, and other stakeholders, we run the risk of being overconfident in the capabilities of these systems. For instance, when presented with selected human and nonhuman (AISs and animal) categories, Schoenherr (submitted a) found that certain AIS devices were associated with *higher* warmth than humans and comparable to friendly domesticated animals (i.e., dog; Figure 6.3). This might suggest that

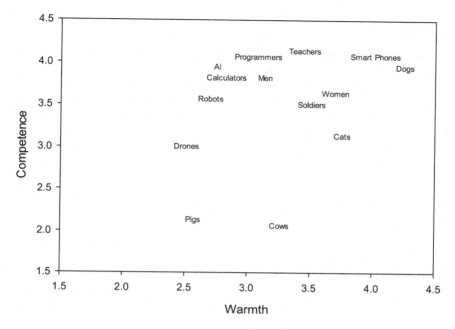

FIGURE 6.3 Warmth and competence ratings for a subset of human and nonhuman categories.

Source: Preliminary results from Schoenherr (submitted a).

domesticated AIS devices associated with IoT networks might be trusted in the absence of understanding the ethical affordance of these systems.

Similar evidence has been observed with search engine users. For instance, when provided with the ability to use an Internet search engine, Sparrow et al. (2011) found that participants recalled less information than when it was unavailable, regardless of the memory instruction. Sparrow et al. referred to this as the Google Effect. Here, we assume that if users can readily retrieve information through an external device, they do not need to engage in as much effort encoding and rehearsing material in memory. Studies have also demonstrated that people believe that the availability of smart devices will increase or decrease recall ability in younger and older users, respectively (Näsi & Koivusilta, 2013; for a recent review of the effect of smart device use, cf. Wilmer et al., 2017). Together these devices extend cognition, creating a distributed sociotechnical system that combines people and AISs. However, such sociotechnical systems are only effective to the extent that agents within this network have efficient transactive memory systems, i.e, an accurate understanding of the capabilities and capacities of others (Wegner, 1987; Wegner et al., 1991).

Much more research is required for understanding the factors that lead to the distribution of trust within sociotechnical systems. For instance, research examine algorithmic aversion has suggested that trust is task-dependent (Castelo et al., 2019) and can be reduced when algorithms make errors relative to when humans make the same errors (Dietvorst et al., 2015). Studies of the uncanny valley and algorithmic aversion illustrate complicated relationships between the interaction of human and artificial agents. Understanding these relationships is especially important for consequential decision-making contexts. For instance, Schoenherr (2021c) has argued that AIS-based healthcare delivery requires understanding the reliability of each agent within the network as well as a users dependency on new folk medical technologies such as mobile phone applications and search engines. Moreover, trade-offs are inherent in these systems. For instance, he argues that non-consequentialist principles that define patients' rights can affect consequentialist principles such as data integrity. Namely, as patients can choose to exclude information from their records or data sets are anonymized using techniques that introduce noise (e.g., differential privacy), this could reduce data integrity. Similarly, Facebook users' responses to Cambridge Analytica also illustrate the effects of disengagement and resignation that can result from being embedded within a sociotechnical system. Despite users reporting reductions in the personal nature of content posted on Facebook, a non-scientific poll revealed that despite the fact that the majority were somewhat or very concerned (78.8%) leading to self-censorship (82.2%), only 41.9% indicated that they changed their behaviour, and only 9.6% indicated that they either deleted or deactivated their Facebook accounts (Beck, 2018). Consequently, we must assume that designers, developers, and distributors of AISs must be held accountable, given users' trust and the centrality of these technologies to their lives.

6.4 Stakeholder Responsibility, Accountability, and Implementation

Connectivity and shared responsibility introduce new concerns for liability. Despite the level of autonomy and intelligence of systems, at least for the foreseeable future, responsibility is ultimately vested in humans. For instance, a developer might create a virus to target a specific system of an adversarial state or non-state actor, but the program could infect other, unrelated systems. In this case, it seems clear that both the developer and the distributor of the program are responsible for the collateral damage, even though they might not have foreseen these outcomes. However, in other cases, understanding responsibility is much more complicated. For instance, data aggregators might collect data from a variety of *legal* sources, which might be used by others to target specific data subjects for disinformation campaigns. The diffusion of responsibility within a sociotechnical system represents a key concern for the future of AISs.

In many cases, it is undeniable that responsibility will be distributed between human and nonhuman agents: designers must demonstrate professional integrity by ensuring that AISs are developed including the best practices of their field, distributors must ensure that the strengths and limitations of an AIS are clearly represented in a manner that is explainable to stakeholders, users must ensure that they make use of the available information, and the community must ensure that they have reflected on how AISs impact them. However, the distribution of responsibility is by no means clear. In a sociotechnical system, lines are often blurred between humans, AISs, and organizations. Public debates concerning organizations such as Amazon, IBM, and Facebook typically treat them unreflectively as *entities* within the world. Indeed, organizations are often treated as persons.

The Ship of Theseus and the Evolution of Responsibility. The Ship of Theseus is a thought experiment that critically reflects on the continuity of an entity's identity in the face of constant change. Due to reverence for the mythical hero Theseus, Athenians maintained a ship, replacing each part as it inevitably rotted. Eventually, all the original pieces of the ship had been replaced. Consequently, we are left wondering whether the ship in fact represents a new entity or whether it, at least in some respects, has the essence of the original vessel. In that AISs are often developed and distributed by organizations, we must ask to what extent these entities are responsible for the outcomes of AISs.

Black (2001) provides such a debate when he evaluates IBM's involvement in Nazi German social policies leading up to, and during, the Second World War. Summarizing his work in a revised edition, he notes that

> From the first moments of the Hitler regime in 1933, IBM used its exclusive punch card technology and its global monopoly on information technology to organize, systematize, and accelerate Hitler's anti-Jewish program, step by step facilitating the tightening noose. The punch cards, machinery, training, servicing, and special project work, such as population census and identification, was managed directly by IBM headquarters in New York, and later through its subsidiaries in Germany, … Poland, Holland, France, Switzerland, and other European countries.
>
> *Black, 2015*

However, in reference to the first edition, Bernstein (2001) claims that Black 'does not demonstrate that IBM bears some unique or decisive responsibility for the evil that was done'. Clarifying his position, Black notes 'Make no mistake – the Holocaust would still have occurred without IBM. To think otherwise is more than wrong. But there is reason to examine the fantastical numbers Hitler achieved … and [identify] the crucial role of *automation and technology*' (2001, p. 11; italics added). Here, we see the problems of assigning responsibility within a sociotechnical system: humans design and develop a technology, often within an organizational context, that technology is made available to adopters by individuals, and adopters implement and adapt that technology in a local context. These concerns are echoed in recent debates, for example, with regard to Facebook and Cambridge Analytica and Microsoft and the MS-Celeb-1M dataset.

The Role of Governance and Regulation. In addition to designers, developers, users, and data subjects, impartial authorities are required to ensure that responsibilities are distributed in a consistent and coherent manner. Despite tensions between the inherently slow nature of bureaucratic processes and the rapid growth of AISs, governmental and nongovernmental organizations (NGOs) play an important role in the monitoring and regulation of these systems. For instance, the social and ethical issues presented by Clearview AI's use of public images resulted in a $22.6 million USD fine for violation of privacy by the Information Commissioner's Office in the United Kingdom (Information Commissioner's Office, 2021). The Office of the Privacy Commissioner of Canada ordered the company to cease its operations, stop collection, use, and disclosure of images, and delete images and biometric data collected without consent noting that "individuals who posted their images online, or whose images were posted by third party(ies), had no reasonable expectations that Clearview would collect, use and disclose their images for identification purposes. As such, express consent would generally be required," (Office of the Privacy Commissioner of Canada, 2021). Similar actions have been taken in Sweden and Australia.

AISs are borderless. Their connectivity means that a single individual, group, or nation cannot contain them. Along with professional organizations (Section 4.1.2), governmental and nongovernmental organizations have created AISs in the public sector that address, to varying degrees, their role as stewards of the personal information of their citizens and the consequential impact of their decisions. Available policies vary from international-level impact assessments (e.g., EU: *General Data Protection Regulation, GDPR*), to national-level guidelines (e.g., New Zealand: *Principles for the Safe and Effective Use of Data and Analytics*), auditing (e.g., Netherlands: *Understanding Algorithms Report*), and procurement policies (e.g., India: *Tamil Nadu Safe and Ethical Use of AI*), to regional-level oversight frameworks (e.g., USA: *New York's Automated Decisions Task Force*). Summarizing these efforts, the joint report from the Ada Lovelace Institute – AI Now Institute and Open Government Partnership (2021) – identified six considerations for the implementation of AI systems:

"1. Clear institutional incentives and binding legal frameworks can support consistent and effective implementation of accountability mechanisms, supported by reputational pressure from media coverage and civil society activism.

2. Algorithmic accountability policies need to clearly define the objects of governance as well as establish shared terminologies across government departments.

3. Setting the appropriate scope of policy application supports their adoption. Existing approaches for determining scope such as risk-based tiering will need to evolve to prevent under- and over-inclusive application.

4. Policy mechanisms that focus on transparency must be detailed and audience appropriate to underpin accountability.

5. Public participation supports policies that meet the needs of affected communities. Policies should prioritise public participation as a core policy goal, supported by appropriate resources and formal public engagement strategies.

6. Policies benefit from institutional coordination across sectors and levels of governance to create consistency in application and leverage diverse expertise."

BOX 6.1 THE PROBLEMS WITH ENGINEERING PRIVACY: POLICES AND METHODOLOGIES

Privacy policies radically impact what information is collected, stored, and shared with third-party organizations including data aggregators. For instance, following an attempt to ban the app in the United States, TikTok changed its privacy policy in 2021. However, the new policy allowed it to collect biometric data such as 'faceprints and voiceprints' and perform object recognition on the data. Even more troubling, the reasons for this change and intended use are not entirely clear (Perez, 2021). If users simply accept privacy policies and EULAs without reading them (Section 3.4.1), designers can either seek to include nudges that force users to pay more attention to the contents of these policies (Table 6.4), introduce stricter policies for information sharing, or both.

Policies cannot address these issues alone. Demonstrating this, Apple recently introduced its App Tracking Transparency (ATT) policy. Ostensibly, the policy prohibits applications from tracking users if they opt out. This was a bold move, as *The Financial Times* (2021) reported that this change resulted in $9.85 billion a loss of revenue for Facebook, Snapchat, Twitter, and Youtube. However, the effectiveness of the policy has been questioned due to the continued collection of user technical information by some applications. In conjunction, multiple kinds of technical information can be used to uniquely identify devices such as mobile phones, referred to as fingerprinting. With a former Apple iCloud engineer suggesting that "an 'Ask App Not To Track' button may even give users a false sense of privacy" (Fowler & Hunter, 2021). This could also create a diffusion of responsibility between the developers, distributers, and users of AISs.

Privacy Engineering Methodologies (PEM) are a principled means to teach engineers how to map the ethical affordances onto the technical affordances of an AIS (Al-Slais, 2020), also referred to as privacy by design (e.g., Bednar et al., 2019). PEMs can include attempts to minimize the amount of data collected by an application (data minimization) or performing a privacy impact assessment that identifies, and attempts to minimize or eliminate, the potential risks to user privacy in a project, policy, process, or product (Clarke, 2009; Wright, 2012). Crucially, these practices are neither widely accepted nor understood. For instance, Senarth and Arachchilage (2018) found that the minority of developers surveyed were aware of privacy impact assessment (47.2%), fair information practices (38.9%), privacy by design (36.1%), or data minimization (22.2%). Similarly, many developers had doubts about whether they had effectively implemented privacy standards (38.8%), believed that the requirements of PEM were too complex (36.1%), or that the requirements of PEMs conflicted with the primary requirements of design. Qualifying their use, studies further suggest that the perceived usefulness of PEMs and alignment with the engineering practices were the main determinants of adopting PEMs (Senarth et al., 2019).

Policy frameworks, especially those that are directed toward auditing and assessment, are a critical step in ensuring that approaches to ethical AISs do not reflect the idiosyncratic efforts of individuals, organizations, and nations. Moreover, AIS policies, guidelines, and frameworks cannot be viewed in isolation. As part of a larger sociotechnical system, these policies must *align* and *integrate* themselves with existing policies. Codes of conduct, legal statutes, intellectual property, conflict of interest policies, and collective agreements must all be included in any deliberation. As AISs are borderless, international regulatory frameworks will need to confront numerous legal and sociocultural differences that might lead to such policies being far too general to be effective. However, policy frameworks like the GDPR (Section 3.4.1) demonstrate that at least a few meaningful standards can be identified that transcend national boundaries.

When assessing responsibility and ensuring accountability, we must recognize that the composition of an organization – national or international, private or public – can change. Like the Ship of Theseus, we are left with questions concerning who is responsible for failures of AISs. Even if legal precedents would have it otherwise, events such as employee termination and organizational exit are unlikely to satisfy stakeholders. If organizations are to be treated as legal persons, ones that are rational and capable of making decisions (Schane, 1986), then they are ultimately accountable for the successes and failures of AISs as moral agents (French, 1979). Consequently, like other stakeholders, they must make explicit efforts to monitor and regulate data and algorithmic decision-making processes.

The rebranding of Facebook's parent company failed to change its reputation. Trust in the company was severely affected by the Cambridge Analytica scandal, with one survey indicating that an otherwise steady increase in trust from 67% in 2011 to 79% in 2017, plunged to 27% and 33%, respectively, in the first and second weeks of the scandal (Weisbaum, 2018). Following the leaked documents, collectively known as the 'Facebook Files' (*The Wall Street Journal*, 2021), Facebook rebranded itself as Meta.[9] Among other measures, Meta announced that it would stop using its facial recognition software, which automatically 'tagged' photos, and deleted the 'faceprints' that it had generated and stored, due to concerns with privacy and transparency (Taylor, 2021), and would address the adverse outcomes of Instagram use (Newton, 2021).

Despite these changes, a Harris Poll indicated that the company's trustworthy score fell from 16% to 6.2% (Beer, 2021). At the time of writing, it is too early to tell what the long-term impact will be on the company and the associated trust. However, much like the Cambridge Analytica scandal (Section 3.4.2), it remains likely that most users will continue to use the social media platform. Such findings reinforce the discrepancies between attitudes and behaviour (Glasman & Albarracin, 2006), suggesting that global measures of trust on their own are not a useful means to assess users' perceptions. Instead, once people are integrated into a sociotechnical system, it might be increasingly difficult to separate themselves due to a reliance on the technical affordances of these systems in the absence of a substitute. This likely reflects a combination of a sunk-cost fallacy and a fear of missing out.

6.5 Opportunities for Ethical AISs and Transhuman Ethics

Up to this point, we have considered how individuals, organizations, and AISs can embody human values. In each case, we have assumed that humans are the ultimate arbiters of right and wrong. However, if AISs can outperform humans in pattern detection, there is no reason to doubt that they might do so in their ethical sensemaking abilities in terms of their speed, accuracy, and creativity in identifying ethical affordances. First, if ethical affordances are merely patterns that are specifiable (e.g., features, functions, or outcomes that have positive or negative associations), then AISs might be capable of identifying them more rapidly than human agents. Similarly, if AISs are more accurate at identifying ethical affordance and the algorithms are explainable, AISs might be *more* ethical than human agents (e.g., Wallach et al., 2010; cf. Goodall, 2014). In that AISs would apply ethical principles systematically, and cannot be seduced by personal gain or biases, they could reflect 'moral saints' (Gips, 1991). For instance, humans might not be aware of social categories that bias their judgment (Section 5.3.3), however if the data is labelled, these biases could be accounted for in the development of algorithms (Kearns & Roth, 2019). If unlabelled, AISs could identify novel biases that users might not be aware of themselves.

If AISs can identify novel ethical affordances, this suggests that they might exceed our ethical sensemaking capabilities. In this way, they might identify new methods of social interaction that decrease interpersonal conflict, thereby informing education and training programs. If treated as an exercise in experimentation, like early examination of reciprocal behaviour (Axelrod, 1984; Trivers, 1971) approaches to moral philosophy that see it as an applied science (Ruse & Wilson, 1986), a transhuman approach to ethics could suggest numerous possible ways to reaffirm, reorganize, or replace existing human values, suggesting optimal, satisficing, and ineffective strategies for human cooperation. For instance, sociobiologists identify evolutionary stable strategies (ESS), conventional behaviours of group members that support the survival of a group, a species, or a collection of genes (Maynard Smith, 1972; Maynard Smith & Price, 1973). Unlike experimental ethics (e.g., Frohlich & Oppenheimer, 1993), this approach can identify the parameters that maximize cooperation, trust, and social cohesion. AISs might be able to identify ESS that are beyond human perceptual abilities and timescales.

6.6 Section Summary: Ethical Design and Ethical AISs

Two broad approaches have been adopted in ethical AISs. The first approach focuses on designing AISs based on human values via ethical sensemaking abilities. Multiple value-based design frameworks have been proposed that consider how best to include value and principles into the design and implementation process. They require identifying how to align the technical affordances of AISs with stakeholder values. These approaches emphasize the importance of developing the ethical sensemaking abilities of stakeholders, leaving AISs as *amoral* agents.

A second approach to AIS development requires that they have some degree of autonomous ethical sensemaking capabilities. The lowest degree of ethical autonomy requires that developers include an ability to recognize biases in data or processes which stakeholders can use to make ethical judgments. The highest degree of ethical autonomy would require that a system can alter its own operations via a supervisory system (e.g., ethical governor). These systems need not be 'full ethical agents' by human standards (Moor, 2009). Rather, they only need to be able to monitor and regulate their own performance. More sophisticated approaches might exceed human sensemaking abilities, either in terms of the speed, accuracy, or novelty of principles and processes.

Notes

1 The only essential cookies are those that are baked.
2 Darkpatterns.org indicates that this is named after Facebook CEO Mark Zuckerberg. Based on a play on the word 'suckering'.
3 Not included in original list. Primacy effects are observed when items presented earlier influence performance by rapidly activating information in long-term memory. Recency effects are observed when items presented later influence performance due to their availability in short-term memory.
4 Subdimensions not included in original list.
5 Not included in original list.
6 Of the 14 conversational agents that were reviewed, six reflected finite-state systems, seven reflected frame-based systems, and one reflected an agent-based system.
7 The website (https://delphi.allenai.org/) explicitly indicates that it is a research prototype and that it might produce offensive results. Despite this report (and accompanying screenshots), I failed to replicate these results (November 15, 2021).
8 Much like a generative adversarial network, the interaction between these systems likely requires learning.
9 Meta has stated that the two events are unrelated.

7

IMPLEMENTATION AND TRUST IN THE AGE OF ENTANGLEMENT

'The noble person uses things; the lesser person is used by things'

— Zhuangzi

There's a pervasive feeling that whatever power AISs give us with their left hand, they take away with their right. These trade-offs need not be insurmountable, but they do require acknowledging the new social and ethical challenges that we must address when using AISs. The opacity of many of these systems, and the distribution of responsibility within sociotechnical systems, will require ongoing deliberation about what relationship we should have with AISs. We must not lose sight that these systems are created and must be understood by humans. Inasmuch as we need to understand the reason why other people make decisions (i.e., their intentions, biases, social constraints), we must do the same for our relationships with AISs. Rather than focusing exclusively on the technical affordances of AISs, we must ensure that we understand how humans perceive the intelligence, autonomy, and connectivity of these systems to identify their ethical affordances.

Humans co-evolve with their technology. By harnessing fire and cooking, humans could extract more calories to fuel our rapidly evolving brains. By creating stone hammers and axes, we could compensate for our meagre frames to hunt and defend ourselves. By creating and using symbols, we have created a shared culture and overcome spatial and temporal communication barriers. At the time of their creation, these were surely 'disruptive technologies'. AISs represent another example of this process, one that is perhaps more rapid in terms of the speed of its changes and diffusion. Whether AISs will bring forth a transhuman era or merely represent another stage of sociotechnical evolution, the same general selective forces are likely still at work.

Human survival is dependent on trust. In the absence of trust, we could not engage in a division of labour to create art, care for and protect ourselves, conduct research and experiment with new technologies, or exchange goods and services.

DOI: 10.4324/9781003143284-7

Trust is often based on a set of shared – often implicit – norms and conventions (Section 5.3.1). Humans might progress through a common moral trajectory throughout their lives, but most of us do not actively reflect, on an ongoing basis, on the ethical affordances of the social worlds we inhabit (Section 5.1). In that they are defined by multiple, overlapping sets of exchange norms that conflict, we must recognize, analyze, and address them directly. Perhaps more problematic for the use of AISs as technologies that mediate human exchanges is that they separate us from direct experiences with our environment and others, producing experiences of anonymity which can lead to group polarization, reductions in prosocial behaviour, and depression. Like 'other' human groups, we might have an inherent distrust of certain kinds of AISs, making cooperation with these systems quite difficult. Studies of the uncanny valley and algorithmic aversion provide considerable insight into the features and conditions that determine preference and trust in these systems.

Our concerns are not the result of data or algorithms. Rather, they are the result of introducing *any* technology that reduces our interactions with others. Following a similar path to the introduction of television (Putnam, 2000), AIS-mediated technologies, such as smart phones, social networking sites, and online gaming, have changed the nature of our social interaction (Estache et al., 2002; Jin, 2017; Katz & Aakhus, 2002). Despite the sociality of humans, there is no guarantee that contemporary physical and virtual communities will be reorganized in a manner that promotes interpersonal cohesion, respectful exchange, and prosocial norms following the introduction of a novel technology.

In the new economy of attention (Schoenherr, 2022b), AIS-based technologies can direct our attention to concepts and people that share our attitudes and deep similarities. By constructing these environments, they can nudge our behaviour in directions – good and bad – that we might not have taken. The finite nature of attention means that we are shifted away from beliefs, concepts, and individuals that we might otherwise encounter due to geographic proximity. This brings with it the potential to both open our eyes to new opportunities and approaches to the world and to close them tightly, lost in a hall of mirrors that reflect our own attitudes back at us.

In that AISs and the information environments that we share are dominated by a few countries and corporations, diversity defined by multiple, competing cultural variants might be reduced, creating a relative static set of polarities from which we must choose. Whether in terms of the process of globalization or through social influence campaigns undertaken by state and non-state actors, 'users' and 'data subjects' are presented with environments that are not necessarily designed in their best interests. Instead, their personal information and behavioural traces are resources that are fought over and commodified. We are then faced with choices of easy access to information and services, which bring with them threats to individual privacy, our agency, and social cohesion. Through a network of exchanges, individual data fragments that we leave through our online experiences can be aggregated into complex profiles that are beyond our awareness.

The major hazard that we encounter is with denying that these trade-offs exist. To unequivocally accept or reject AISs – on the whole or as specific technologies –

ignores *our* responsibilities. We have responsibilities to both cultivate our own competencies and contribute to the communities we inhabit. We must ensure that users, data subjects, and other stakeholders *understand* the trade-offs inherent in technology and can critically evaluate them.

The COVID-19 pandemic illustrates this point quite clearly: in a time of quarantines, lockdowns, and social distancing, AIS-based systems provided a means to connect with others – even if only for a low-fidelity social experience. They provided the ability to track the spread of infectious disease and mitigate risks. Yet, their promise was not realized (Box 2.1) and their benefits must be contextualized. Once our data is available, the genie is out of the bottle. For some, the temptation to reuse data might be too great. Actions taken during the pandemic also illustrate an important issue of power imbalances: users might ignore risks to privacy due to the purported benefit of an application while not fully understanding the implications of its use. Social media algorithms reflected back to us our political and (pseudo)scientific beliefs, increasing our confidence in our opinions and our skepticism in contrasting views.

There is no doubt that we must accept a measure of uncertainty and ambivalence due to differences and trade-offs between values. Our species has evolved physically, cognitively, and socially in uncertain environments. In contrast to the past, we can influence these processes by actively engaging with these issues. Perhaps the greatest contribution of philosophical traditions (East and West) is the plurality of values and perspectives that they present. The analytic categories of the individualistic traditions help us analyze and synthesize the world, whereas the collectivistic traditions help emphasize the interconnectivity of the human and the nonhuman while reminding us of the limitations of analytic categories. Underpinning both, we must acknowledge that individuals should cultivate virtues and competencies that aid them in understanding the versions of right and wrong that exist, balancing rules and judging the adequacy of outcomes.

7.1 Trust in the Age of Entanglement

Trust is often a fragile and capricious thing. We tend to think of trust in interpersonal terms: we trust (or distrust) our acquaintances, family, co-workers, professional groups, peoples, and governments. We also place an undeniable trust in technology: we assume our car will start, we doubt the predictions of weather models, and we trust that the alarm on our mobile phone will wake us up. Trust in inanimate objects – whether natural or synthetic – might superficially appear to be categorically different. It isn't.

When we trust, we distribute responsibility between ourselves and other objects and entities: a wooden support is placed in an old window to ensure that it doesn't fall, freeing us up to do more productive things. At least under certain conditions, we might even trust technology more than other humans. This isn't necessarily objectophilia. Rather, we likely assume that it is better to offload our mental calculations to a calculator or tax software than to trust that our memory will allow us to accurately solve an equation, to run antivirus software rather than sorting through the myriad files on our own computer. We might selectively inspect a few features of these processes, but, ultimately, we trust their output. If we do not, we must perform these tasks ourselves. In such cases, AISs only provide us with a sober second opinion to support *our* decision-making. Trusting these systems is not the issue. Rather, it is understanding the basis of their operations, their vulnerabilities, and knowing where and when we should trust their operations.

An inherent problem with trusting AISs is understanding how we trust each other. Calls for 'transparent' and 'explainable' approaches to AI likely impose higher standards on human–AIS interactions than interpersonal interactions. Daily, we habitually trust one another – casually giving over a credit card to an attendant, reserving a rental car over the phone, trusting that our colleagues will complete their work. Yet, psychological science indicates that we consistently overestimate our knowledge of others. We assume that there is consensus where there is none, we anchor the standards of others to our own and assume that those outside of our group differ from us (Section 5.4.1). Social categories have evolved to reduce our uncertainty, to allow us to act in the world as if it is known. By relying on stereotypes, we reduce the cognitive load required to navigate the world daily. Yet, all stereotype use creates trade-offs. By trusting or distrusting someone or something based on a stereotype, we create ethical blind spots. For instance, by perceiving smart phones as 'warm' and cooperative (Schoenherr, submitted a) we ignore how our data is collected and how hidden algorithms are shaping our attention. Alternatively, we might fail to trust AISs when we should. Humans might believe that AISs might not be capable of making certain kinds of decisions, for example, understanding human emotion, making ethical judgments or in healthcare decision-making (Schoenherr, 2021c, submitted b). By discounting their recommendations, we might be doing ourselves a disservice. Instead of technophilia or technophobia, specific AISs must be assessed in terms of their design principles, their possible outcomes, and their level of ethical autonomy.

By adopting an ethical sensemaking approach to AIS design and implementation, we acknowledge that trust ultimately requires knowledge. We must have the experience and expertise to understand others – both human and nonhuman agents. We must be aware of the social and ethical affordances of a situation that can facilitate and interfere with trust. This requires greater education and engagement on the part of all stakeholders and concerted efforts in knowledge translation. Designers, developers, and distributors must make efforts to understand their users and customers in terms of *their* preference, knowledge, and intentions. They must address concerns because their knowledge and products place them in a powerful position, with their decisions and actions affecting countless lives. Policymakers must ensure that they represent the needs of the users. They must not limit their focus to economic growth and 'progress'. Human values and agency must be prioritized. This requires that they have the competencies to understand the social, ethical, and technological affordances of AISs that will affect those within their society.

7.2 The Problems and Paths of Designing Ethical AISs

In the past decade, standards for ethical AISs have proliferated. These standards follow still more decades of speculation over whether or if human values could be included in the design of AISs. Many human values are shared in philosophical frameworks (Sections 4.2 and 4.3) and exchanges norms (Section 5.3.1). In many other cases, values vary along continua (Section 5.3.2) or are ineffable (Section 4.3.2). Alone, values and standards are not sufficient. They are typically underspecified to capture a broad range of cases, thereby delegating much of the interpretation to the individual (Section 4.1.2). Values can be adopted to merely signal ethical intentions without any substantive action (ethics washing) or might lead to moral disengagement if we assume that the mere existence of codes and standards necessarily means that they can unproblematically inform our actions. Concurrently, a specific set of AIS commandments, defined by all possible cases of use, would be far too large and rigid to accommodate the constantly changing affordances of AISs. Instead, ethical sensemaking competencies must be defined and developed.

Mistaking Information for Knowledge. At the most fundamental level, we must not assume that merely having data in anyway provides a compelling argument: a pile of bricks does not constitute a house. Datafication is only useful to the extent that we have effectively identified relevant factors for identification, prediction, and recommendation. The Quantitative Fallacy can easily lead stakeholders to believe that a system is trustworthy, obscuring the numerous decision-points that lead to the accumulation of that data (Box 4.1). This same concern applies to the development of AISs. Developing a 'model' necessarily requires many value-laden design decisions that can be concealed by its success. However, models might work in one context, with a certain dataset and fail to work in others, i.e., a redomaining problem. We must not forget that the validity of an AIS' use will always be relative to the context, determined by both the amount and kind of evidence. These concerns in no way invalidate a quantitative approach (Schoenherr & Hamstra, 2016). Rather the use of AIS must always be seen as pragmatic (i.e., conventionalism or instrumentalism), facilitating or supplementing decision-making.

Simultaneously, we must also be mindful of the depersonalization, deindividuation, and anonymity that come with quantification. Even if we could quantify all relevant dimensions of people in a specific usage context, this process of dimensional reduction will necessarily eliminate other characteristics that might be relevant elsewhere. Users and data subjects might be reluctant to engage with these systems due to fear of misrepresentation of their character or might misrepresent themselves for fear of being known in the absence of obscurity. Decision-makers might begin to habitually view them in these simplified terms as they are chronically presented with the same representation of people. Greater effort must be directed toward improving user trust and confidence in these systems and ensuring that other stakeholders do not develop biases and see people as 'data subjects.'

Equally crucial, we must also consider *how* data is obtained, selected, structured, stored, accessed, used, reused, and erased. The use of grey data illustrates the problems with data aggregation. People might consent to have their data used at a given place and time for a given purpose. Any additional use would not constitute valid consent given the change in context. Consequently, simply because data is available in no way implies that researchers or developers *should* use aggregated datasets. Even if consent is provided for each subset of data, users might not understand the implications of pooling datasets together or how derivative datasets could be constructed. Blanket consent is not a viable strategy for the develop of an ethical AIS.

What is an 'AIS'? Autonomous and Intelligent Systems are relative hard constructs to define. Adopting distinctions based on architecture (e.g., neural networks, Bayesian learning, regression) only gets us so far. Moreover, the 'intelligence' of these systems currrently reflects a domain-specific set of processes and knowledge (i.e., pattern recognition, response tendencies) rather than the dynamic intelligence embodied in humans. Similarly, at least for the present, the autonomy of AISs is extremely limited and ultimately determined by humans. Even if an AIS has the capacity to monitor and regulate its own functions, this is not self-awareness, given the constraints of the system. By connecting systems for collection, analysis, and acting on data, we further obscure a concrete definition of AIS. Should we view sensors, storage, and automated decision-making systems as separable systems or do they constitute a sociotechnical system entangled with human operators and decision makers?

These definitional issues are not merely the purview of philosophers. Rather, they have significant practical implications for legal regulation and accountability. The difficulty that the Automated Decision Systems (ADS) Task Force (2019) had in defining automated decision-making systems clearly illustrates the issue faced by policymakers. Regulation requires clearly specifying standards that are applicable to a specifiable set of organizations, processes, and persons. Developing an ethics of AISs also requires that we identify the level of intelligence, autonomy, and connectivity of these systems to determine responsibility. Much like the determination of whether a defendant is competent to stand trial, the answer to these questions hinges on clear criteria that require the participation of all stakeholders.

Overestimating Our Control. We must be cognizant of the fact that we tend to rationalize our behaviour. Often, due to the ambiguity of a situation, a failure to understand the affordances and the presence of others, we might blindly mimic the actions of others. By adopting technologies or behaviours without thinking, we open ourselves up to exploitation and unethical behaviour. Especially within individualistic populations, we are likely to overestimate our control over the situation. We cannot afford to underestimate the influence of the social and technological environment on our behaviour or risk moral disengagement due to the complexity of an entangled sociotechnical system. Instead, we must understand the external forces that can influence our behaviour.

Code is the engine of society, fueled by data. As it is progressively more difficult to disentangle ourselves from technology, having access to data and controlling code has implication for the control of society. This does not represent cynicism in the intentions of individuals, corporations, or governments. Rather, it is a function of the often-blind process of technological evolution. Technologies are often developed for one purpose and adapted to another. Similarly, data can be provided and collected for one reason and used and reused for another. Contextualizing technological innovation is critical to recognizing that one size does not fit all. To that end, the knowledge and motivations of designers, distributors, and users cannot be taken for granted. For instance, global competition between organizations and countries such as the United States and China will drive the creation of AISs much more than will ethical concerns. Users and data subjects must be able to control their data. Making systems 'transparent' and avoiding dark patterns of design is not sufficient. New sets of skills are required that combine information and computer sciences with humanities and social sciences. Only by understanding social psychological forces and how they are affected by interactions with nonhuman agents can we hope to retain control and a measure of autonomy.

Qualifying Explainability. Terms such as 'transparency' and 'explainability' must be qualified. Not all stakeholders will, or want to, understand the technical affordances of AISs. Instead, effective engagement requires knowledge translation that is adapted to a particular stakeholder or community. This in turn requires understanding the knowledge and motivations of stakeholders. For some, only a limited understanding is required. Explanations such as 'fair', 'accurate', and 'valid' might be sufficient for many. Others will want to understand the nature of these systems in terms of data collection processes, algorithm training, automated decision-making, and the social consequences of AISs. No matter how much we try to include the public, designers will remain keystones in the edifice of sociotechnical systems. For any technology to be successful, users must trust these systems. As we increase trust, we create a more cohesive sociotechnical system. Consequently, designers must be trained to understand and interpret the social and ethical issues that their users will encounter.

Limitations of Anthropomorphizing. We must restrain ourselves from anthropomorphizing AISs. Terms such as 'intelligent' are often taken to imply *human*-like intelligence. Moreover, other than general intelligence, which AISs appear to lack, intelligence is relative to a given domain or activity. Seeing AISs as human-like certainly has benefits by allowing us to engage in analogical reasoning from human agents to AISs. However, this might also fill us with a mistaken sense of trust. AISs need not have been designed with ethics in mind, nor are they likely to have ethical sensemaking abilities, especially the sense of existential peril that comes with the violation of an ethical norm.

We should also be skeptical that human intelligence is the most appropriate standard against which to judge AISs. Nonhuman animals have adapted to their own ecological niches, often more effectively than humans can. By accepting the utility of nonhuman intelligence as models for AISs, we introduce new possibilities for system design and ethical inquiry. For instance, when comparing the fit of an algorithm, it is always relative to the set of available algorithms and criteria we select. An algorithm might 'fit' human performance, while nevertheless being suboptimal. Indeed, as we noted previously, AISs could exceed the ethicality of humans (e.g., rigid adherence to ethical norms), yet we might not be able to judge whether this is the case.

Ethical Frameworks and Units of Analysis. By refocusing on ethics, more fundamental concerns regarding appropriate philosophical frameworks and units of analysis are raised. Virtue ethics appears to offer the most comprehensive framework as understanding motivations, consequences, and principles is required. It nevertheless is asking a great deal of AISs and the humans that develop and use them. By focusing on identifying a minimum set of standards, we increase the likelihood that we can use this as a criterion for judging both humans and AISs. In that AISs might not be capable of achieving a satisfactory level of ethical sensemaking, ethically aligned design requires ensuring that we explicitly identify how responsibility is distributed in terms of the roles, capabilities, and responsibilities that are attributed to the agents. This approach emphasizes *individual* agency and autonomy.

Social ethics focus on *communities* as the unit of analysis. By perceiving the social network as a dynamic entity, defined by specific relational bonds, we acknowledge that social and cultural factors must be taken into account when developing ethical frameworks. Although value-based design should address the needs of the community, we must also ensure that the use of an AIS does not disadvantage particular groups. In that AISs (at present) can only replicate the patterns in the data that are provided to them, we must ensure that they do no replicate discriminatory practices. In this way, social ethics requires that we perceive the shared responsibility of all actors within a social network and that we ensure that they are empowered to engage with these systems.

Transrational ethical frameworks present the most significant challenge to AIS design. By denying the existence of discrete units, and perceiving a system as a whole rather than a collection of parts, this approach emphasizes the dynamic nature and interconnectivity of systems. Removal of any particular part can fundamentally change the nature of a sociotechnical system, i.e., 'disruptive technologies' destabilize prior equilibria within a social network. The transrational approach provides an important counterpoint in that it challenges the nature of responsibility.

More generally, by acknowledging that responsibility is distributed, we highlight the limitations of Western philosophical tradition in its focus on individual agency, autonomy, and internal attributions. A comprehensive approach to ethics requires understanding responsibility in terms of the individual, relationships, and a system. Sociocultural differences that support these mechanisms must also be accounted for when identifying the features of a design, as well as why an AIS might be adopted. Here, we must be cautious to avoid the naturalistic fallacy: simply because an AIS supports the preferences of an individual or a community, does not imply that this function is intrinsically good.

Finally, we must heed Aristotle's words: 'Moral excellence comes about as a result of habit. We become just by doing just acts, temperate by doing temperate acts, brave by doing brave acts.' Ethics is ultimately about acting. Sets of principles, no matter how elegant and exhaustive, are inadequate. If we cannot capture all facets of ethical sensemaking in words, then we must engage stakeholders in action. Ethics education must be a priority for all information and computer science professionals. Concurrently, it seems clear that education must ensure that information and computer science can be understood by the general public. This must include more effective knowledge translation in popular science.

Distributing Trust and Responsibility. Concepts such as Singularity and Society 5.0 present clean peoples and communities that are safely in the future, leaving many loose ends for us to work out. As AISs become distributed, the importance of understanding distributed cognition, how responsibility is assigned to agents, and how collective competence can succeed and fail are topics of critical importance. Individuals must now understand the nature and extent of an AIS's intelligence, autonomy, and connectivity. Designers and developers are ultimately encoding their values within an AIS, with technology investors, distributors, and adopters endorsing these values by selection and distributing these systems in networks. For instance, when developers and users design or deploy a computer virus, their actions will have intended and unintended social consequences. They must be held accountable for these outcomes. Valid consent is defined by similar concerns. The validity of consent is necessarily constrained to a given context. To request a blank form of consent for the continued use and reuse of data simply is not tenable. Data aggregation, derivative datasets, and black data all represent challenges to the autonomy of data subjects and the need for transparency.

These examples illustrate the strengths and weaknesses of consequentialist ethical frameworks. Identifying *all* possible outcomes for a diverse set of users over time reflects an impractical task. The benefit of adopting a consequentialist ethical framework is clear: it forces us to assess how our actions can affect others. Individuals adopting this approach must explicitly define the social network within which they are implementing a system, as well as the short-, medium-, and long-term consequences for humans, technology, and the environment. While these models of moral consequences will necessarily be incomplete, they provide a starting point for an otherwise intractable task. This approach must necessarily be adopted along with non-consequentialist principles (e.g., users' rights, harm avoidance, respect for people) in a virtue-based framework.

The importance of connectivity and shared responsibility is already abundantly clear in many domains. Issues related to cybersecurity in general and the IoT in particular, illustrate how networks of sensors, applications, and databases require a concerted effort on the part of all actors in terms of designing software that eliminates zero-day vulnerabilities while also requiring users to engage in proper cyber-hygiene practices. The use of AISs in healthcare illustrates the importance of ensuring that clinicians and users understand the strengths and limitations of these algorithms so as to determine how they should use the information and recommendations provided by the systems. Finally, the adoption of surveillance technologies allows groups to supplement the human ability to monitor and regulate others, ensuring that members of a society are protected. For AISs to be trustworthy, rather than simply communicating their technical affordances, stakeholders must be active participants in their design and implementation. In all cases, stakeholders must be sufficiently empowered and well informed so that they can affect the use of these systems.

From Pacification to Empowerment. We become entangled in a sociotechnical system whenever we are repeatedly exposed to technology (Section 2.3). Initially, we adopt technologies to supplement or extend our mental processes. Over time, our mental functions are distributed amongst human agents and technological artifacts, enabling us to attend to other tasks and to specialize. Historically, this is the principal promise of reliance on machines. However, such assertions assume that workers who are displaced can be 'reskilled' and that we are best served by offloading competencies and skills to AISs. This approach ignores the inherent trade-offs in terms of what and who is displaced in this process.

We would be well served by observing the parallels between this process and Roman strategies of civilization. Romans used luxuries to pacify the Britons through seduction and dependency. Tacitus, the Roman historian and politician, captures this, noting that:

> ut homines dispersi ac rudes ... quieti et otio per uoluptates adsuescerent (21.1)[1]

The ability to retrieve information and construct our own reality is a luxury. Make no mistake, the *Pax Machina* comes at a cost. Regardless of their intention, those who control these information environments will influence us. We need people and processes - citizens and social institutions – that can categorize, sort, and select potential response alternatives based on goals and a deep understanding of the issues. In a comparable manner to trusting peers and experts, we have also come to trust machines. They fill a need: an infinite number of choices is overwhelming, exceeding our finite mental resources. At first, choices might be unconstrained. Over time, without intent, AISs can narrow our focus based on the norms of others. As we become progressively embedded within this sociotechnical system, we must critically reflect on the structure and content of the environment to retain our agency. We must have the ability and right to disentangle.

Note

1 '[T]he scattered and unskilled men might become accustomed to quiet and leisure by means of pleasure.' For a more extensive discussion, see Lavan (2011).

APPENDIX

Regression as a Model: A Trivially Nontrivial Example

The technical details of an Autonomous Intelligent System can only be avoided up to a point. However, many of the basic conceptual issues can be understood by considering regression models wherein we derive a mathematical function to demonstrate the relationship between two or more variables. By examining regression, we can see how numbers create meaning and how meaning can be gained and lost by the (mis)interpretation of numbers.

Consider the relationship between height and weight in a sample population. The simplest predictive model would be to use the mean values for both dimensions, i.e., the average values of height and weight.[1] In this case the average is 1.65 m and 72.68 kg. Thus, our prediction is that every person I encounter should be approximately 1.65 m in height and weight 72.68 kg. To test this assumption, let us select 20 people.[2] Each of these individuals can be assessed in terms of their deviation from this average, i.e., the extent to which their height and their weight differ from the average. As Figure A.1 indicates, some individuals come extremely close to matching this value. Definitionally, most individuals will deviate from the mean, giving us *standard* deviations for both height (SD = 0.375 m) and weight (SD = 11.95 kg). These numbers represent the sum of absolute differences for each score.[3]

The need to accommodate the deviation suggests that we require a more complicated model than simply using a mean. Namely, we need to account for deviations from the mean in a systematic way. In the present data set, we can see that there appears to be a linear relationship between height and weight, i.e., taller people tend to weigh more; Figure A.1). This regression model seems to do a good job of capturing the general trend.

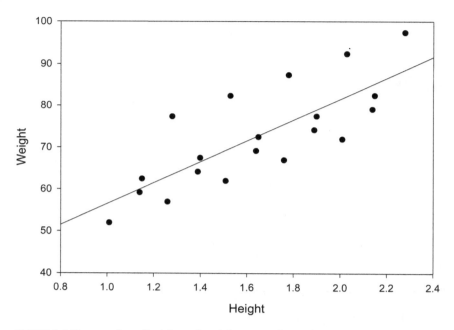

FIGURE A.1 Scatter plot of height and weight scores along with a linear regression function to illustrate the relationship between the two variables.

Closer inspection of Figure A.1 suggests that there is much more occurring in our data set. Here, we then need to decide whether we want a parsimonious model or believe that there are additional, theoretically important relationships. In this case, we might try to categorize the data using meaningful labels. If we return to the data set, we might find that there are two *kinds* of people: men and women. By classifying all the data points in this manner, we now see that *two* linear relationships exist (Figure A.2). This multiple regression model provides an even better fit to the data. Crucially, by adopting new regression models, we change which individuals are best represented by the regression equations.

Again, we have reason to believe that more category labels might be helpful. By including a second category – country of residence – we can now see that *two* variables are required to capture the data: sex and country of residence. We now obtain a perfect relationship with each regression function: one regression line for each combination of sex (men and women) and country (Canada and Guatemala; Figure A.3). Having moved through these steps, it also becomes clear that if we introduced new data sets (e.g., different countries, different racial or gender categories), that these regression lines would not adequately fit the new data. Thus, by fitting regression lines to each data set, we have *overfit* the model to the data if we are looking for a general relationship between height and weight.

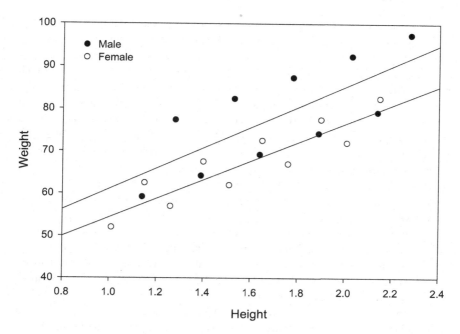

FIGURE A.2 Regression functions for both men and women.

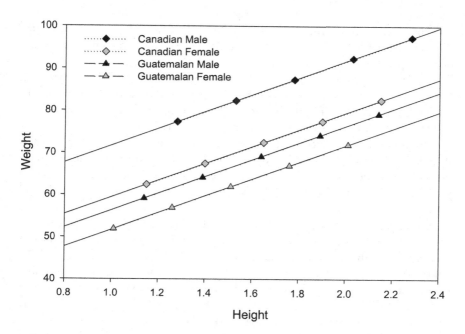

FIGURE A.3 Four functions fitting each of the four data sets.

This relatively simple exercise has several lessons concealed within it. First, while the mean values of height and weight are useful, if we relied on them, we would obscure a large quantity of valuable information. Second, by considering variability and obtaining a standard deviation, we obtain more information, i.e., how much the individuals differ within a sample population. Third, mathematical relationships between variables can be obtained, allowing us to systematically capture most, if not all, of the variations in the data. However, what represents the 'best fitting' function depends on the question we are asking. By including category labels, we obtain a better understanding for specific populations within the data. However, the resulting models might not account for the general relationship described in new data sets and the labels themselves might conceal certain value choices.

We must also remember that numbers are ultimately abstract symbols. They only have meaning by virtue of how they are assigned to phenomena (e.g., Stevens, 1946) and how our instruments capture them (Kane, 1992; Messick, 1995). The labels that we use to obtain better fits reflect *social categories*. When using these categories, scientists are making value judgments about which features or dimensions are relevant. Again, consider the mean value (1.65 m, 72.68 kg). There is one individual here that provides a near-perfect match (1.65 m and 72.4 kg), a Canadian female. In fact, the average deviation for Canadian females is the lowest compared to all other categories. Thus, if we use the average, we have implicitly biased our decision-making (e.g., design, judgment of outcomes) to Canadian females even though we included both males and females, and Canadians and Guatemalans in our data set. When we examine the original regression line (Figure A.1), we see that this is also true of the regression equation. To that end, we must recognize that algorithm selection is ultimately a value-laden process, often obscuring many decision-points.

Overfitting and Prediction. Now, consider a more realistic example (Figure A.4). Let us assume that we trained a model based on data from a North America sample. Let us further assume that these data points were obtained from Canada (1.65 m, 72.4 kg) and the US (1.63 m, 77.1 kg). Immediately, we see that height and weight are *negatively* related, i.e., on average Canadians are taller and weigh less than Americans. We can then take our model, trained on North America, to make predictions for countries in the Asian-Pacific region. Here, we find the opposite result: in Asian-Pacific countries, there is a positive relationship between height and weight.

Part of the issue arises from the limited data set. Having two data points is insufficient to identify a trend. However, this is analogous to issues faced in AIS training, given that sets of training data are often frequently used (e.g., NIST). Thus, whether it is using a small number of training sets in a limited number of domains or using data from selective populations to generalize to all, model predictions will be based on the training set. We can also ask questions about the age of the data set, the sample population, and the accuracy with which the data was collected. For instance, Bayesian models use the prior probability ('priors') of an event's occurrence to predict future events. A persistent criticism of simple

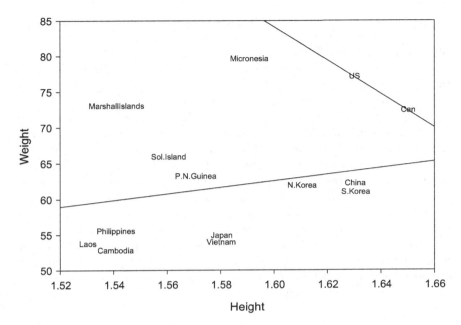

FIGURE A.4 Height and weight for individual countries and two linear relationships derived from two sample populations: North American and Asia-Pacific.

Bayesian approaches stems from the minimal consideration given to *how* the priors were derived. By failing to consider the factors that determined the priors, we are ignoring potentially important causal information between variables in the data.

The issues of bias and error become more problematic when we consider the kinds of predictions that we can make. Predictions can occur in two forms: interpolation and extrapolation. *Interpolation* requires that we obtain missing data points within the range of existing data. At first, this might seem trivial: predicting the temperature on Tuesday from predictions of Monday's and Wednesday's weather will likely yield a reasonably reliable result. However, this need not be the case. Consider the height data from China and South Korea. They both have average heights that fall within the range of the North American sample. This superficially suggests that our data should allow us to interpolate values within this range. However, if we used the simple regression model from the North American sample it would vastly overestimate the weights of people from China and South Korea. For instance, someone from China who is 1.63 m tall is predicted to be 66.2 kg. Conversely, if we used the data from Asian-Pacific countries, because we have more of it, we would vastly underestimate the weights of people from the US.

In contrast, *extrapolation* requires that we make predictions that go beyond the existing data set. For instance, we might try to predict the temperature for a Tuesday three months from now based on the temperature from this Tuesday. If we extrapolate from the North American data to Asian-Pacific countries, only one country comes close (Micronesia) whereas extrapolation for the remaining countries would produce results that are exceedingly incorrect, e.g., someone from the Marshall Islands who is 1.54 m tall *should* be 77.7 kg according to this model.

Our example uses a relatively simple relationship that, superficially, is relatively trivial. However, this is a value judgment as well. The height–weight relationship considered here can be consequential whether it is used for health advice or is explicitly used as an ideal body type that people should try to attain. By providing social representations that are unrepresentative for a given group, it can create norms that are unrealistic and result in unhealthy behaviour. This is not a trivial problem given that AISs can be designed by one individual, in one group, for one purpose, and adopted by another individual, in another group, for a different purpose, i.e., redomaining. Moreover, overfitting and errors of interpolation and extrapolation are also true of decisions made in domains such as credit scores that determine whether someone can obtain a loan, healthcare that suggest the presence of absence of a disease, and predictive policing that identifies high-risk areas or potential offenders. From an AIS perspective, the social categories and kinds of decisions being made are irrelevant. Human ethical sensemaking is required to make these value choices wisely.

Notes

1 www.worlddata.info/average-bodyheight.php.
2 Here, I've used the mean values and added or subtracted a constant to simplify this example.
3 We use absolute values otherwise the values sum to zero … and that's not very useful for calculation.

REFERENCES

AAA (2021). AAA: Today's vehicle technology must walk so self-driving cars can run. *AAA Newsroom*, February. Retrieved January 7, 2022 from: https://newsroom.aaa.com/2021/02/aaa-todays-vehicle-technology-must-walk-so-self-driving-cars-can-run/.

Abd-Alrazaq, A. A., Alajlani, M., Alalwan, A. A., Bewick, B. M., Gardner, P., & Househ, M. (2019). An overview of the features of chatbots in mental health: A scoping review. *International Journal of Medical Informatics*, 132, 103978.

ACM (2018). ACM Code of Ethics and Professional Conduct. Association for Computing Machines. Retrieved March 3, 2020 from: www.acm.org/code-of-ethics.

Acquisti, A., Adjerid, I., Balebako, R., Brandimarte, L., Cranor, L. F., Komanduri, S., … & Wilson, S. (2017). Nudges for privacy and security: Understanding and assisting users' choices online. *ACM Computing Surveys (CSUR)*, 50(3), 1–41.

Ada Lovelace Institute/AI Now Institute and Open Government Partnership. (2021). *Algorithmic Accountability for the Public Sector*. Retrieved August 25, 2021 from: www.opengovpartnership.org/documents/algorithmic-accountability-public-sector/.

Adamson, R. E. (1952). Functional fixedness as related to problem solving: A repetition of three experiments. *Journal of Experimental Psychology*, 44, 288–291.

Adams-Webber, J., & Ford, K. (1991). A conscience for Pinocchio: A computational model of ethical cognition. *The Second International Workshop on Human & Machine Cognition: Android Epistemology*, Pensacola.

ADS Task Force (2019). *Automated Decision Systems Task Force Report*, November. Retrieved February 23, 2020 from: www.documentcloud.org/documents/6561086-ADS-Report-11192019-1.html.

Ahmed, H., & Glasgow, J. (2012). *Swarm Intelligence: Concepts, Models and Applications*. School Of Computing, Queens University Technical Report.

Albert, R., Jeong, H., & Barabási, A. L. (2000). Error and attack tolerance of complex networks. *Nature*, 406(6794), 378–382.

Alge, B. J. (2001). Effects of computer surveillance on perceptions of privacy and procedural justice. *Journal of Applied Psychology*, 86(4), 797–804.

Al-Heeti, A. (2017). Robot companions are just what the doctor ordered. *CNET*, November 20. Retrieved September 11, 2020 from: www.cnet.com/news/robot-companions-are-just-what-the-doctor-ordered/.

Ali, M., Sapiezynski, P., Bogen, M., Korolova, A., Mislove, A., & Rieke, A. (2019). Discrimination through optimization: How Facebook's Ad delivery can lead to biased outcomes. In *Proceedings of the ACM on Human–Computer Interaction, 3(CSCW)* (pp. 1–30). ACM.

Aljomaa, S. S., Qudah, M. F. A., Albursan, I. S., Bakhiet, S. F., & Abduljabbar, A. S. (2016). Smartphone addiction among university students in the light of some variables. *Computers in Human Behavior,* 61, 155–164.

Allen, C. (2002). Calculated morality: Ethical computing in the limit. In I. Smit & G. Lasker (Eds.), *Cognitive, Emotive and Ethical Aspects of Secision Making and Human Action, Vol. I* (pp. 19–23). IIAS.

Allen, C., & Bekoff, M. (1999). *Species of Mind: The Philosophy and Biology of Cognitive Ethology.* MIT Press.

Allen, C., Smit, I., & Wallach, W. (2006). Artificial morality: Top-down, bottom-up and hybrid approaches. *Ethics of New Information Technology,* 7, 149–155.

Allen, C., Varner, G., & Zinser, J. (2000). Prolegomena to any future artificial moral agent. *Journal of Experimental and Theoretical Artificial Intelligence,* 12, 251–261.

Allison, A. (2006). *Millennial Monsters: Japanese Toys and the Global Imagination.* University of California Press.

Al-Slais, Y. (2020, December). Privacy engineering methodologies: A survey. In *2020 International Conference on Innovation and Intelligence for Informatics, Computing and Technologies (3ICT)* (pp. 1–6). IEEE.

American Association for the Advancement of Science (2000). *The Role and Activities of Scientific Societies in Promoting Research integrity: A Report of a Conference* April 10–11, AAAS.

Ananny, M., & Crawford, K. (2016). Seeing without knowing: Limitations of the transparency ideal and its application to algorithmic accountability. *New Media & Society,* 20, 973–989.

Anderson, C. A., Shibuya, A., Ihori, N., Swing, E. L., Bushman, B. J., Sakamoto, A., … & Saleem, M. (2010). Violent video game effects on aggression, empathy, and prosocial behaviour in Eastern and Western countries: A meta-analytic review. *Psychological Bulletin,* 136, 151–173.

Anderson, M., & Anderson, S. (Guest Editors) (2006). Machine ethics. IEEE Intelligent Systems, 21(4), 10–11.

Anderson, M., Anderson, S., & Armen, C. (2005). Towards machine ethics: Implementing two action-based ethical theories. In M. Anderson, S. Anderson, & C. Armen (Eds.), *Machine Ethics.* Technical Report FS-05-06 (pp. 1–16). AAAI Press.

Anderson, M., Anderson, S., & Armen, C. (2006). An approach to computing ethics. *IEEE Intelligent Systems,* 21, 56–63.

Andersson, L. M., & Pearson, C. M. (1999). Tit for tat? The spiraling effect of incivility in the workplace. *Academy of Management Review,* 24(3), 452–471.

André, Q., Carmon, Z., Wertenbroch, K., Crum, A., Frank, D., Goldstein, W., … & Yang, H. (2018). Consumer choice and autonomy in the age of artificial intelligence and big data. *Customer Needs and Solutions,* 5, 28–37.

Angle, S. C. (2010). W ang Yangming as a virtue ethicist. *In Dao Companion to Neo-Confucian Philosophy* (pp. 315–335). Springer.

Angwin, J., & Mattu, S. (2016). Amazon says it puts customers first. But its pricing algorithm doesn't. *ProPublica,* September 20. Retrieved September 2, 2020 from: www.propublica. org/article/amazon-says-it-puts-customers-first-but-its-pricing-algorithm-doesnt.

Arbesman, S. (2016). *Overcomplicated: Technology at the Limits of Comprehension.* Current.

Ariely, D. (2012). *The (Honest) Truth about Dishonesty.* Harper Collins Publishers.

Arkin, R. C. (2008). Governing lethal behavior: Embedding ethics in a hybrid deliberative/reactive robot architecture part i: Motivation and philosophy. In *2008 3rd ACM/IEEE International Conference on Human-Robot Interaction (HRI)* (pp. 121–128). IEEE.

Arkin, R. C. (2009). *Governing Lethal Behavior in Autonomous Robots*. Chapman and Hall/CRC Imprint, Taylor and Francis Group.

Arkin, R. C., Ulam, P., & Wagner, A. R. (2012). Moral decision making in autonomous systems: Enforcement, moral emotions, dignity, trust, and deception. *Proceedings of the IEEE*, 100(3), 571–589.

Arkin, R. C., Ulam, P., and Duncan, B. (2009). *An Ethical Governor for Constraining Lethal Action in an Autonomous System*. Technical Report GIT-GVU-09-02.

Arpaci, I., Yalçın, S. B., Baloğlu, M., & Kesici, Ş. (2018). The moderating effect of gender in the relationship between narcissism and selfie-posting behavior. Personality and Individual Differences, 134, 71–74.

Ashby, F. G., & O'Brien, J. B. (2005). Category learning and multiple memory systems. *Trends in Cognitive Sciences*, 9, 83–89.

Ashby, F. G., Paul, E., & Maddox, W. (2011). COVIS. In E. M. Pothos & A. J. Willis (Eds.), *Formal Approaches in Categorization* (pp. 65–87). Cambridge University Press.

Asher, J., & Arthur, R. (2017). Inside the algorithm that tries to predict gun violence in Chicago. *The New York Times*, June 13. Retrieved December 19, 2019 from: www.nytimes.com/2017/06/13/upshot/what-an-algorithm-reveals-about-life-on-chicagos-high-risk-list.html.

Ashton, M. C., & Lee, K. (2005). Honesty-humility, the Big Five, and the five-factor model. *Journal of Personality*, 73, 1321–1354.

Ashton, M. C., & Lee, K. (2009). The HEXACO–60: A short measure of the major dimensions of personality. *Journal of Personality Assessment*, 91, 340–345.

Asimov, I. (1950). *Runaround. I, Robot (The Isaac Asimov Collection ed.)* Doubleday.

Asimov, I. (1983). Popularizing science. *Nature*, 306, 119.

Axelrod, R. (1984). *The Evolution of Cooperation*. Basic Books.

Axelrod, R., & Hamilton, W. D. (1981). The evolution of cooperation. *Science*, 211(4489), 1390–1396.

Ayer, A. J. (1936/2012). *Language, Truth and Logic*. Courier Corporation.

Ayodele, T. O. (2010). Types of machine learning algorithms. *New Advances in Machine Learning*, 3, 19–48.

Ayres, I., & Schwartz, A. (2014). The no-reading problem in consumer contract law. *Stanford Law Review*, 66, 545.

Babbage, C. (1830). *Reflections on the Decline of Science in England: And on Some of Its Causes*. B. Fellowes.

Babbage, C. (1832). *On the Economy of Machinery and Manufactures*. Charles Knight.

Bail, C. A., Argyle, L. P., Brown, T. W., Bumpus, J. P., Chen, H., Hunzaker, M. F., ... & Volfovsky, A. (2018). Exposure to opposing views on social media can increase political polarization. *Proceedings of the National Academy of Sciences*, 115, 9216–9221.

Bain, P. G., Vaes, J., & Leyens, J. P. (2014). *Humanness and Dehumanization*. Psychology Press.

Bakos, Y., Marotta-Wurgler, F., & Trossen, D. R. (2014). Does anyone read the fine print? Consumer attention to standard-form contracts. *The Journal of Legal Studies*, 43, 1–35.

Baldini, G., Botterman, M., Neisse, R., & Tallacchini, M. (2018). Ethical design in the internet of things. *Science and Engineering Ethics*, 24(3), 905–925.

Balliet, D., Tybur, J. M., & Van Lange, P. A. (2016). Functional interdependence theory: An evolutionary account of social situations. *Personality and Social Psychology Review*, 21(4), 361–388.

Bames, J. (Ed.) (1984). The Complete Works of Aristotle. Princeton University Press.

Banerjee, R., Reitz, J. G., & Oreopoulos, P. (2018). Do large employers treat racial minorities more fairly? An analysis of Canadian field experiment data. *Canadian Public Policy*, 44(1), 1–12.

Banks, A., Calvo, E., Karol, D., & Telhami, S. (2021). # polarizedfeeds: Three experiments on polarization, framing, and social media. *The International Journal of Press/Politics*, 26, 609–634.

Baranchuk, A., Refaat, M. M., Patton, K. K., Chung, M. K., Krishnan, K., Kutyifa, V., ... & American College of Cardiology's Electrophysiology Section Leadership. (2018). Cybersecurity for cardiac implantable electronic devices: What should you know? *Journal of the American College of Cardiology*, 71(11), 1284–1288.

Baranski, J.V., & Petrusic, W.M. (1998). Probing the locus of confidence judgments: Experiments on the time to determine confidence. *Journal of Experimental Psychology: Human Perception and Performance*, 24(3), 929–945.

Barberá, P., Jost, J. T., Nagler, J., Tucker, J. A., & Bonneau, R. (2015). Tweeting from left to right: Is online political communication more than an echo chamber? *Psychological Science*, 26, 1531–1542.

Barbash, G. I. (2010). New technology and health care costs: The case of robot-assisted surgery. *The New England Journal of Medicine*, 363, 701–704

Barbour, I. G. (1993). *Ethics in an Age of Technology*. HarperOne.

Barbu, O. (2014). Advertising, microtargeting and social media. *Procedia-Social and Behavioural Sciences*, 163, 44–49.

Barnes, J., ed. (1984). *The Complete Works of Aristotle*. Princeton University Press.

Barocas, S., & Selbst, A. D. (2016). Big data's disparate impact. *California Law Review*, 104, 671.

Baron, E. (2019). Bay Area police try out controversial AI software that tells them where to patrol. *The Mercury News*, March 10. Retrieved December 17, 2019 from: www.mercurynews.com/2019/03/10/bay-area-police-try-out-controversial-ai-software-that-tells-them-where-to-patrol/.

Baron, R. A. (1997). The sweet smell of ... helping: Effects of pleasant ambient fragrance on prosocial behavior in shopping malls. Personality and Social Psychology Bulletin, 23(5), 498–503.

Barrett, P. (2007). Structural equation modelling: Adjudging model fit. *Personality and Individual differences*, 42(5), 815–824.

Bartz, J. A., Zaki, J., Bolger, N., & Ochsner, K. N. (2011). Social effects of oxytocin in humans: Context and person matter. *Trends in Cognitive Sciences*, 15(7), 301–309.

Basalla, G. (1988). *The Evolution of Technology*. Cambridge University Press.

Bass, K., Barnett, T., & Brown, G. (1999). Individual difference variables, ethical judgments, and ethical behavioral intentions. *Business Ethics Quarterly*, 9(2), 183–205.

Baumann, N. (2013). Too fast to fail: How high-speed trading fuels Wall Street disasters. *Mother Jones*, January/February. Retrieved June 5, 2020 from: www.motherjones.com/politics/2013/02/high-frequency-trading-danger-risk-wall-street/.

Baumeister, R. F., Masicampo, E. J., & DeWall, C. N. (2009). Prosocial benefits of feeling free: Disbelief in free will increases aggression and reduces helpfulness. *Personality and Social Psychology Bulletin*, 35, 260–268.

Bazerman, M. H., & Tenbrunsel, A. E. (2011). *Blind Spots: Why We fail to Do What's Right and What to Do About It*. Princeton University Press.

Beck, J. (2018). People are changing the way they use social media. *The Atlantic*, June. Retrieved September 1, 2020 from: www.theatlantic.com/technology/archive/2018/06/did-cambridge-analytica-actually-change-facebook-users-behavior/562154/.

Bednar, K., Spiekermann, S., & Langheinrich, M. (2019). Engineering Privacy by Design: Are engineers ready to live up to the challenge?. *The Information Society*, 35, 122–142.

Beer, J. (2021, November 8). Brand trust in Facebook actually fell after it changed its name to Meta. *The Harris Poll*. Retrieved November 11, 2021 from: https://theharrispoll.com/brand-trust-in-facebook-actually-fell-after-it-changed-its-name-to-meta/.

Behrens, K.Y. (2004). A multifaceted view of the concept of amae: Reconsidering the indigenous Japanese concept of relatedness. *Human Development*, 47(1), 1–27.

Bekoff, M., & Pierce, J. (2009). *Wild Justice: The Moral Lives of Animals*. University of Chicago Press.

Bello, P., & Bringsjord, S. (2013). On how to build a moral machine, *Topoi*, 32(2), 251–266.

Belmi, P., & Pfeffer, J. (2015). How 'organization' can weaken the norm of reciprocity: The effects of attributions for favors and a calculative mindset. *Academy of Management Discoveries*, 1, 36–57.

Belnap, N., Perloff, M., & Xu, M. (2001). *Facing the Future*. Oxford University Press.

Benjamin, M. (2013). *Drone Warfare: Killing by Remote Control*. Verso Books.

Ben-Ze'ev, A. (2003). Privacy, emotional closeness, and openness in cyberspace. *Computers in Human Behavior*, 19(4), 451–467.

Bergquist, M., Blumenschein, P., Karinti, P., Köhler, J., Ramos, É. M. S., Rödström, J., & Ejelöv, E. (2021). Replicating the focus theory of normative conduct as tested by Cialdini et al. (1990). *Journal of Environmental Psychology*, 74, 101573.

Bernstein, R. (2001). I.B.M.'s sales to the Nazis: Assessing the culpability. Books. *The New York Times*, March 7. Retrieved May 15, 2019 from: www.nytimes.com/2001/03/07/books/books-of-the-times-ibm-s-sales-to-the-nazis-assessing-the-culpability.html.

Berreby, F., Bourgne, G., & Ganascia, J. G. (2015, November). Modelling moral reasoning and ethical responsibility with logic programming. In *Logic for Programming, Artificial Intelligence, and Reasoning* (pp. 532–548). Springer.

Bhuiyan, J. (2021). 'There's cameras everywhere': testimonies detail far-reaching surveillance of Uyghurs in China. *The Guardian*, Retrieved April 21, 2022 from www.theguardian.com/world/2021/sep/30/uyghur-tribunal-testimony-surveillance-china

Bickhard, M. H., & Terveen, L. (1996). *Foundational Issues in Artificial Intelligence and Cognitive Science: Impasse and Solution*. Elsevier.

Bimber, B. (2014). Digital media in the Obama campaigns of 2008 and 2012: Adaptation to the personalized political communication environment. *Journal of Information Technology & Politics*, 11, 130–150.

Bird, S., Barocas, S., Crawford, K., Diaz, F., & Wallach, H. (2016). Exploring or exploiting? Social and ethical implications of autonomous experimentation in AI. In *Workshop on Fairness, Accountability, and Transparency in Machine Learning*. Available at: https://papers.ssrn.com/sol3/papers.cfm?abstract_id=2846909.

Birkbeck College (1958/1969). *The College Annual Report*.

Björk, S., & Holopainen, J. (2004). *Patterns in Game Design*. Charles River Media.

Black, E. (2001). *IBM and the Holocaust: The Strategic Alliance between Nazi Germany and America's Most Powerful Corporation*. Random House Inc.

Black, E. (2015). IBM's role in the Holocaust – what the new documents reveal. *Huffington Post*, March 17. Retrieved March 22, 2021 from: www.huffpost.com/entry/ibm-holocaust_b_1301691.

Black, N. (2010). Assessing the quality of hospitals. *British Medical Journal*, 340, 933–934.

Blanken, I., van de Ven, N., & Zeelenberg, M. (2015). A Meta-Analytic Review of Moral Licensing. *Personality and Social Psychology Bulletin*, 41, 540–558.

Bloom, P. (2013). *Just Babies: The Origins of Good and Evil*. Broadway Books.

Blunden, B., & Cheung, V. (2014). *Behold a Pale Farce: Cyberwar, Threat Inflation, & the Malware Industrial Complex*. Trine Day.

Boden, M., Bryson, J., Caldwell, D., Dautenhahn, K., Edwards, L., Kember, S., et al. (2017). Principles of robotics: Regulating robots in the real world. *Connection Science*, 29, 124–129.

Bogost, I. (2018). Can You Sue a Robocar? *The Atlantic*, March 20. Retrieved January 23, 2020 from: www.theatlantic.com/technology/archive/2018/03/can-you-sue-a-robocar/556007/.

Bollen, K. A. (1989). *Structural Equations with Latent Variables, Vol. 210*. John Wiley & Sons.

Bolukbasi, T., Chang, K. W., Zou, J. Y., Saligrama, V., & Kalai, A. T. (2016). Man is to computer programmer as woman is to homemaker? debiasing word embeddings. *Advances in Neural Information Processing Systems*, 29, 4349–4357.

Bonabeau, E., Theraulaz, G., & Dorigo, M. (1999). *Swarm Intelligence: From Natural to Artificial Systems*. Oxford University Press.

Book, A., Visser, B. A., Blais, J., Hosker-Field, A., Methot-Jones, T., Gauthier, N. Y., ... & D'Agata, M. T. (2016). Unpacking more 'evil': What is at the core of the dark tetrad? *Personality and Individual Differences*, 90, 269–272.

Borenstein, J. (2008). The ethics of autonomous military robots. *Studies in Ethics, Law, and Technology*, 2, 1–17.

Borgman, C. L. (2018). Open data, grey data, and stewardship: Universities at the privacy frontier. *Berkeley Technology Law Journal*, 33, 365–412.

Bostrom, N. (2002). Existential risks. *Journal of Evolution and Technology*, 9(1), 1–31.

Bostrom, N. (2005). A history of transhumanist thought. *Journal of Evolution and Technology*, 14, 1–25.

Bostrom, N. (2005). Transhumanist values. *Journal of Philosophical Research*, 30(Supplement), 3–14.

Bostrom, N. (2014). *Superintelligence: Paths, Dangers, Strategies*. Oxford University Press.

Bouchaud, J. P., & Mézard, M. (2000). Wealth condensation in a simple model of economy. *Physica A: Statistical Mechanics and its Applications*, 282, 536–545.

Bowles, N. (2018). A dark consensus about screens and kids begins to emerge in Silicon Valley. *The New York Times*, October 16. Retrieved April 3, 2020 from: www.nytimes.com/2018/10/26/style/phones-children-silicon-valley.html.

Boyan, A., Grizzard, M., & Bowman, N. (2015). A massively moral game? Mass Effect as a case study to understand the influence of players' moral intuitions on adherence to hero or antihero play styles. *Journal of Gaming & Virtual Worlds*, 7(1), 41–57.

Braga, A. A., Papachristos, A. V., & Hureau, D. M. (2014). The effects of hot spots policing on crime: An updated systematic review and meta-analysis. *Justice Quarterly*, 31, 633–663.

Breuer, M. A., Gupta, S. K., & Mak, T. M. (2004). Defect and error tolerance in the presence of massive numbers of defects. *IEEE Design & Test of Computers*, 21(3), 216–227.

Brewer, M. B. (1979). In-group bias in the minimal intergroup situation: A cognitive-motivational analysis. *Psychological Bulletin*, 86(2), 307–324.

Bringsjord, S. (1992). *What Robots Can and Can't Be*. Kluwer Academic Publishers.

Bringsjord, S., Arkoudas K., & Bello P. (2006). Toward a General Logicist Methodology for Engineering Ethically Correct Robots. *IEEE Intelligent Systems*, 21(4), 38–44.

Broks, P. (2006). *Understanding Popular Science*. Open University Press.

Brooks, D. (2017). How evil is tech? *The New York Times*, November 20. Retrieved December 9, 2020 from: www.nytimes.com/2017/11/20/opinion/how-evil-is-tech.html.

Brown, P., & Levinson, S. C. (1987). *Politeness: Some Universals in Language Usage, Vol. 4*. Cambridge University Press.

BSI. (2016). *Robots and Robotic Devices. Guide to the Ethical Design and Application of Robots and Robotic Systems, Vol. BS 8611*. BSI Standards Publications.

Bucher, T. (2018). *If ... Then: Algorithmic Power and Politics*. Oxford University Press.

Buolamwini, J., & Gebru, T. (2018, January). Gender shades: Intersectional accuracy disparities in commercial gender classification. In *Conference on Fairness, Accountability and Transparency* (pp. 77–91). PMLR.

Burleigh, M. (2005). *Earthly Powers: Religion and Politics in Europe from the Enlightenment to the Great War*. HarperCollins.

Burleigh, M. (2010). *Moral Combat: A History of World War II.* HarperCollins.

Burleigh, T. J., & Schoenherr, J. R. (2015). Uncanny categories: Frequency-based feature encoding and the production of local attractor states in categorization performance and affect ratings. *Frontier in Psychology*, 5, 1488.

Burleigh, T. J., Schoenherr, J. R., & Lacroix, G. L. (2013). Does the uncanny valley exist? An empirical test of the relationship between eeriness and the human likeness of digitally created faces, *Computers in Human Behaviour*, 29, 759–771.

Burrell, J. (2016). How the machine 'thinks', *Big Data & Society*, 3(1), 1–12.

Burri, S. (2018). What is the moral problem with killer robots? In R. C. Jenkins, R. Jenkins, M. Robillard, & B. J. Strawser (Eds.). *Who Should Die?* (pp. 163–185). Oxford University Press.

Busvine, D. (2020). EU privacy rules no obstacle to coronavirus fight; smartphone tracking a no-no. *Reuters*, March 10. Retrieved March 13, 2020 from: www.reuters.com/article/us-health-coronavirus-privacy-explainer-idUSKBN20X1MP.

Caliskan, A., Bryson, J. J., & Narayanan, A (2017). Semantics derived automatically from language corpora contain human-like biases. *Science*, 356, 183–186.

Callahan-Levy, C. M., & Messé, L. A. (1979). Sex differences in the allocation of pay. *Journal of Personality and Social Psychology*, 37(3), 433.

Calo, R. (2017). Artificial intelligence policy: A primer and roadmap. *SSRN Journal*, 1–28.

Cameron, D., & Mehrotra, D. (2021). Parler users breached deep inside U.S. Capitol Building, GPS data shows. Gizmodo, January 12. Retrieved January 12, 2021 from: https://gizmodo.com/parler-users-breached-deep-inside-u-s-capitol-building-1846042905.

Cappelli, D., Moore, A., Trzeciak, R., & Shimeall, T. J. (2009). *Common Sense Guide to Prevention and Detection of Insider Threats*, 3rd Edn. Published by CERT, Software Engineering Institute, Carnegie Mellon University. Available at: www.cert.org.

Carleton, R. N. (2016). Fear of the unknown: One fear to rule them all? *Journal of Anxiety Disorders*, 41, 5–21.

Carney, M. (2020). Leave no dark corner. *ABC News*, July 31. Retrieved August 13, 2020 from: www.abc.net.au/news/2018-09-18/china-social-credit-a-model-citizen-in-a-digital-dictatorship/10200278?section=world.

Castells, M. (1996). *The Information Age: Economy, Society and Culture.* Blackwell.

Castelo, N., Bos, M. W., and Lehmann, D. R. (2019). Task-Dependent Algorithm Aversion. *Journal of Marketing Research*, 56, 809–825.

Castronovo, C., & Huang, L. (2012). Social media in an alternative marketing communication model. *Journal of Marketing Development and Competitiveness*, 6(1), 117–134.

Cattell, J. M. (1915, September). The Scientific Monthly and the Popular Science Monthly. *Popular Science Monthly*. 87, 307–310.

Cauley, L. (2006). NSA has massive database of Americans' phone calls. *USA Today*, May 11. Retrieved December 18, 2019 from: https://usatoday30.usatoday.com/news/washington/2006-05-10-nsa_x.htm.

Chaiken, S., & Trope, Y. (Eds.) (1999). *Dual-Process Theories in Social Psychology.* Guilford Press.

Chakraborty, A., Paranjape, B., Kakarla, S., & Ganguly, N. (2016, August). Stop clickbait: Detecting and preventing clickbaits in online news media. In *2016 IEEE/ACM International Conference on Advances in Social Networks Analysis and Mining (ASONAM)* (pp. 9–16). IEEE.

Chalk, R., Frankel, M. S., & Chafer, S. B. (1980). *Professional Ethics Activities in the Scientific and Engineering Societies.* American Association for the Advancement of Science.

Chander, A. (2016). The racist algorithm. *Michigan Law Review*, 115, 1023–1045.

Chattopadhyay, S., & De Vries, R. (2008). Bioethical concerns are global, bioethics is Western. Eubios Journal of Asian and International Bioethics: EJAIB, 18(4), 106–109.

Chawla, N. V., Bowyer, K. W., Hall, L. O., & Kegelmeyer, W. P. (2002). Smote: Synthetic minority over-sampling technique. *Journal of Artificial Intelligence Research*, 16, 321–357.

Cheetham, M., Pavlovic, I., Jordan, N., Suter, P., & Jancke, L. (2013). Category processing and the human likeness dimension of the uncanny valley hypothesis: Eye-tracking data. *Frontiers in Psychology*, 4. Available at: https://doi.org/10.3389/fpsyg.2013.00108.

Cheetham, M., Suter, P., & Jäncke, L. (2011). The human likeness dimension of the 'uncanny valley hypothesis': Behavioral and functional MRI findings. *Frontiers in Human Neuroscience*, 5, 126. Available at: https://doi.org/10.3389/fnhum.2011.00126.

Chen, Y., Conroy, N. J., & Rubin, V. L. (2015, November). Misleading online content: Recognizing clickbait as 'false news'. In *Proceedings of the 2015 ACM on Workshop on Multimodal Deception Detection* (pp. 15–19).

Cheng, R. (2019). The Fukushima meltdown is way too hot for humans. *CNET*, March 9. Available at: www.cnet.com/features/for-fukushimas-nuclear-disaster-robots-offer-a-sliver-of-hope/.

Cherns, A. (1976). Principles of sociotechnical design. Human Relations, 29, 783–792.

Cherns, A. (1987). Principles of sociotechnical design revisited. Human Relations, 40, 153–162.

Chesney, B., & Citron, D. (2019). Deep fakes: A looming challenge for privacy, democracy, and national security. *California Law Review*, 107, 1753–1820.

China Digital Times (2013/2015). *Decoding the Chinese Internet: A Glossary of Political Slang*. Retrieved April 22, 2022 from: https://monoskop.org/images/b/b7/Decoding_the_Chinese_Internet_A_Glossary_of_Political_Slang_2015.pdf

Chirinos, C. (2022). Anonymous claims it hacked into Russian TVs and showed the true devastation of Putin's Ukraine invasion. Fortune, March 7. Retrieved March 11, 2022 from: https://fortune.com/2022/03/07/anonymous-claims-hack-of-russian-tvs-showing-putins-ukraine-invasion/.

Chong, Z. (2017). Up to 48 million Twitter accounts are bots, study says. *CNET*, March 14. Retrieved April 21, 2020 from: www.cnet.com/news/new-study-says-almost-15-percent-of-twitter-accounts-are-bots/.

Choo, H., Gentile, D. A., Sim, T., Li, D., Khoo, A., & Liau, A. K. (2010). Pathological video-gaming among Singaporean youth. *Annals Academy of Medicine Singapore*, 39, 822–829.

Chory, R. M., & Goodboy, A. K. (2011). Is basic personality related to violent and non-violent video game play and preferences? *Cyberpsychology, Behaviour and Social Networking*, 14, 191–198.

CHPS Consulting. (2000). *Analysis of Institutional Policies for Responding to Allegations of Scientific Misconduct. Report prepared for the U.S. Office of Research Integrity*. Retrieved February 21, 2022 from: https://ori.hhs.gov/analysis-institutional-policies-responding-allegations-scientific-misconduct.

Churchland, P. S., & Winkielman, P. (2012). Modulating social behavior with oxytocin: How does it work? What does it mean? *Hormones and Behavior*, 61(3), 392–399.

Cialdini, R. (2016). *Pre-suasion: A Revolutionary Way to Influence and Persuade*. Simon and Schuster.

Cialdini, R. B., Reno, R. R., & Kallgren, C. A. (1990). A focus theory of normative conduct: Recycling the concept of norms to reduce littering in public places. Journal of Personality and Social Psychology, 58, 1015–1026.

Cialdini, R. B., Vincent, J. E., Lewis, S. K., Catalan, J., Wheeler, D., & Darby, B. L. (1975). Reciprocal concessions procedure for inducing compliance: The door-in-the-face technique. *Journal of personality and Social Psychology*, 31(2), 206–215.

Cikara, M., Farnsworth, R. A., Harris, L. T., & Fiske, S. T. (2010). On the wrong side of the trolley track: Neural correlates of relative social valuation. *Social Cognitive and Affective Neuroscience*, 5, 404–413.

Clark, A. (2008). *Supersizing the Mind: Embodiment, Action, and Cognitive Extension*. Oxford University Press.

Cinelli, M., Morales, G. D. F., Galeazzi, A., Quattrociocchi, W., & Starnini, M. (2021). The echo chamber effect on social media. *Proceedings of the National Academy of Sciences*, 118, doi.org/10.1073/pnas.2023301118.

Clarke, A. C. (2005). Foreword: Communications for goodness' sake. In *Promoting ICT for Human Development in Asia: Realizing the Millennium Development Goals*. UNDP.

Clarke, R. (1993). Asimov's Laws of Robotics: Implications for Information Technology (1). *IEEE Computer*, 26(12), 53–61.

Clarke, R. (1994). Asimov's Laws of Robotics: Implications for Information Technology (1). *IEEE Computer*, 27(1), 57–66.

Clarke, R. (1988). Information technology and dataveillance. *Communications of the ACM*, 31, 498–512.

Clarke, R. (2009). Privacy impact assessment: Its origins and development. *Computer Law & Security Review*, 25(2), 123–135.

Clerides, S. K. (2004). Price discrimination with differentiated products: Definition and identification. *Economic Inquiry*, 42(3), 402–412.

Co, J. (2017). Google hit with record EU fine over 'unfair' shopping searches. *The Independent*, June 27. Retrieved September 2, 2020 from: www.independent.co.uk/news/business/news/google-eu-fine-latest-competition-shopping-searches-prepare-online-european-commission-results-a7809886.html?fbclid=IwAR27d2ImFrZtxYHPV5dfPsFlvI8CxaJtfl3SGKOf50H9CpGlwvHtZqx-jyI.

Coles-Kemp, L., & Theoharidou, M. (2010). Insider threat and information security management. In *Insider Threats in Cyber Security* (pp. 45–71). Springer.

Colquitt, J. A., Scott, B. A., & LePine, J. A. (2007). Trust, trustworthiness, and trust propensity: A meta-analytic test of their unique relationships with risk taking and job performance. *Journal of Applied Psychology*, 92(4), 909–927.

Comte-Sponville, A. (1996). *A Small Treatise on the Great Virtues: The Uses of Philosophy in Everyday Life*. Henry Hold and Company.

Comte-Sponville, A. (2002). *A Small Treatise on the Great Virtues: The Uses of Philosophy in Everyday Life*. Metropolitan Books.

Conati, C., Aleven, V., & Mitrovic, A. (2013). Eye-tracking for student modelling in intelligent tutoring systems. *Design Recommendations for Intelligent Tutoring Systems*, 1, 227–236.

Confessore, N., Dance, G. J., Harris, R., & M. H. (2018). The follower factory. *The New York Times*, January 27. Retrieved November 1, 2019 from: www.nytimes.com/interactive/2018/01/27/technology/social-media-bots.html.

Cooper, J. (2007). *Cognitive Dissonance: 50 Years of a Classic Theory*. Sage.

Cooper, J., Zanna, M. P., & Taves, P. A. (1978). Arousal as a necessary condition for attitude change following induced compliance. Journal of Personality and Social Psychology, 36, 1101–1106.

Cooper, M. (2017). Jewish word | Golem: A mutable monster. *Moment Magazine*. Retrieved March 25, 2021 from: https://momentmag.com/jewish-word-golem/.

Cooper, R., & Foster, M. (1971). Sociotechnical systems. *American Psychologist*, 26(5), 467–474.

Cornelissen, G., Dewitte, S., & Warlop, L. (2011). Are social value orientations expressed automatically? decision making in the dictator game. Personality and Social Psychology Bulletin, 37(8), 1080–1090.

Cosmides, L. (1989). The logic of social exchange: Has natural selection shaped how humans reason? Studies with the Wason selection task. *Cognition*, 31, 187–276.

Cosmides, L., & Tooby, J. (2002). Unraveling the enigma of human intelligence: Evolutionary psychology and the multimodular mind. *The Evolution of Intelligence*, 145–198.

Cosmides, L., & Tooby, J. (2005). Neurocognitive adaptations designed for social exchange. In D. M. Buss (Ed.), *Evolutionary Psychology Handbook*. Wiley.

Costanza-Chock, S. (2020). *Design Justice: Community-Led Practices to Build the Worlds We Need.* The MIT Press.

Costigan, R. D., Iiter, S. S., & Berman, J. J. (1998). A multi-dimensional study of trust in organizations. *Journal of Managerial Issues*, 303–317.

Cox, J. (2022). Russia Says It Will Block Facebook. *Vice*, March 4. Retrieved March 11, 2022 from: www.vice.com/en/article/akva3g/russia-says-it-will-block-facebook.

Cox, J. R., & Griggs, R. A. (1982). The effects of experience on performance in Wason's selection task. *Memory & Cognition*, 10, 496–502.

Crain, M. (2018). The limits of transparency: Data brokers and commodification. *New Media & Society*, 20, 88–104.

Crandall, C. S., Eshleman, A., & O'brien, L. (2002). Social norms and the expression and suppression of prejudice: The struggle for internalization. *Journal of Personality and Social Psychology*, 82(3), 359–378.

Crawford, K (2021). *Atlas of AI: Power, Politics, and the Planetary Costs of Artificial Intelligence.*

Crossley, R. (2014). Mortal Kombat: Violent game that changed video games industry. *BBC*, June 2. Retrieved March 7, 2020 from: www.bbc.com/news/technology-27620071.

Curzer, H. (2012). *Aristotle and the Virtues.* Oxford University Press.

Damasio AR (1994). *Descartes' Error: Emotion, Reason, and the Human Brain.* Putnam.

Danielson, P. (1992). *Artificial Morality: Virtuous Robots for Virtual Games.* Routledge.

Darley, J. M., & Batson, C. D. (1973). 'From Jerusalem to Jericho': A study of situational and dispositional variables in helping behaviour. *Journal of Personality and Social Psychology*, 27, 100–108.

Dastin, J. (2018). Amazon scraps secret AI recruiting tool that showed bias against women. *Reuters*, October 10. Retrieved April 11, 2020 from: www.reuters.com/article/us-amazon-com-jobs-automation-insight/amazon-scraps-secret-ai-recruiting-tool-that-showed-bias-against-women-idUSKCN1MK08G.

Dautenhahn, K. (1998). The art of designing socially intelligent agents: Science, fiction, and the human in the loop. *Applied Artificial Intelligence*, 12, 573–617.

Davies, H. (2015). Ted Cruz using firm that harvested data on millions of unwitting Facebook users. *The Guardian*, December 11. Retrieved April 17, 2020 from: www.theguardian.com/us-news/2015/dec/11/senator-ted-cruz-president-campaign-facebook-user-data.

Dawkins, R. (1976/2017). The Selfish Gene. Oxford University Press.

De Bary, W. T., Chain. W.-T., & Watson, B. (1960). *Sources of Chinese Tradition* (Vol. 1). Columbia University Press.

De Cristofaro, V., Pellegrini, V., Giacomantonio, M., Livi, S., & van Zomeren, M. (2021). Can moral convictions against gender inequality overpower system justification effects? Examining the interaction between moral conviction and system justification. *British Journal of Social Psychology*, 60, 1279–1302.

De Dreu, C. K., & McCusker, C. (1997). Gain–loss frames and cooperation in two-person social dilemmas: A transformational analysis. *Journal of Personality and Social Psychology*, 72(5), 1093–1106.

Del Vicario, M., Vivaldo, G., Bessi, A., Zollo, F., Scala, A., Caldarelli, G., & Quattrociocchi, W. (2016). Echo chambers: Emotional contagion and group polarization on facebook. *Scientific Reports*, 6, 1–12.

de Oliveira, R., Karatzoglou, A., Concejero Cerezo, P., Armenta Lopez de Vicuña, A., & Oliver, N. (2011). Towards a psychographic user model from mobile phone usage. In *CHI'11 Extended Abstracts on Human Factors in Computing Systems* (pp. 2191–2196).

De Vries, A., & Stoll, C. (2021). Bitcoin's growing e-waste problem. *Resources, Conservation and Recycling*, 175, 105901.

DeVries, R. E. (2012). Personality predictors of leadership styles and the self–other agreement problem. *The Leadership Quarterly*, 23(5), 809–821.

De Vries, R. E., & Van Gelder, J. L. (2015). Explaining workplace delinquency: The role of Honesty–Humility, ethical culture, and employee surveillance. *Personality and Individual Differences*, 86, 112–116.

Deacon, T. W. (1998). *The Symbolic Species: The Co-evolution of Language and the Brain (No. 202)*. W. W. Norton & Company.

DeCew, J. (1997). *In Pursuit of Privacy: Law, Ethics, and the Rise of Technology*. Cornell University Press.

DeCew, J. (2006). Privacy. *Stanford Encyclopedia of Philosophy*. Retrieved April 11, 2020 from: http://plato.stanford.edu/entries/priva-cy/.

Defeyter, M. A., & German, T. P. (2003). Acquiring an understanding of design: Evidence from children's insight problem solving. *Cognition*, 89(2), 133–155.

DeGrave, A. J., Janizek, J. D., & Lee, S. I. (2021). AI for radiographic COVID-19 detection selects shortcuts over signal. Nature Machine Intelligence, 3, 610–619.

Dehaene, S. (2014). *Consciousness and the Brain: Deciphering How the Brain Codes our Thoughts*. Penguin.

Dennett, D. C. (1987). The Intentional Stance. MIT Press.

Dennett, D. C. (1995). *Darwin's Dangerous Idea: Evolution and the Meanings of Life*. Simon and Schuster.

Dennett, D. C. (2014). When HAL kills, who's to blame? Computer ethics. *Computer Ethics*, 203–214.

Deutsch, M. (1962). Cooperation and trust: Some theoretical notes. In M. R. Jones (Ed.), *Nebraska Symposium on Motivation* (pp. 275–320). University of Nebraska Press.

Devlin, H. (2016). Discrimination by algorithm: Scientists devise test to detect AI bias. *The Guardian*, December 18. Retrieved May 1, 2020 from: www.theguardian.com/technology/2016/dec/19/discrimination-by-algorithm-scientists-devise-test-to-detect-ai-bias.

DeWall, C. N., Baumeister, R. F., Gailliot, M. T., & Maner, J. K. (2008). Depletion makes the heart grow less helpful: Helping as a function of self-regulatory energy and genetic relatedness. *Personality and Social Psychology Bulletin*, 34, 1653–1662.

Dhar, P. (2020). The carbon impact of artificial intelligence. *Nature Machine Intelligence*, 2, 423–425.

Diener, E., Fraser, S. C., Beaman, A. L., & Kelem, R. T. (1976). Effects of deindividuation variables on stealing among Halloween trick-or-treaters. *Journal of Personality and Social Psychology*, 33, 178–183.

Dietvorst, B. J., Simmons, J. P., and Massey, C. (2015). Algorithm aversion: people erroneously avoid algorithms after seeing them err. *Journal of Experimental Psychology: General*, 144, 114–126.

DMV (2021). *Autonomous Vehicles*. Department of Motor Vehicles. Retrieved November 11, 2020 from: www.dmv.ca.gov/portal/dmv/detail/vr/autonomous/autonomousveh_ol316+.

Doi, T. (1973). *The Anatomy of Dependence*, trans. J. Bester. Kadansha.

Doi, T. (2005). *Understanding Amae: The Japanese Concept of Need-Love*. Brill.

Dombrowski, L., Harmon, E., & Fox, S. (2016, June). Social justice-oriented interaction design: Outlining key design strategies and commitments. In *Proceedings of the 2016 ACM Conference on Designing Interactive Systems* (pp. 656–671).

Domingos, P. (2012). A few useful things to know about machine learning. *Communications of the ACM*, 55(10), 78–87.

Domingos, P. (2015). *The Master Algorithm: How the Quest for the Ultimate Learning Machine will Remake our World*. Basic Books.

Döring, N., Mohseni, M. R., & Walter, R. (2020). Design, use, and effects of sex dolls and sex robots: Scoping review. *Journal of Medical Internet Research*, 22(7), e18551.

Dornan, C. (1990). Some problems in conceptualizing the issue of 'science and the media'. *Critical Studies in Media Communication*, 7(1), 48–71.

Dovidio, J. F., Piliavin, J. A., Schroeder, D. A., & Penner, L. (2006). *The Social Psychology of Prosocial Behavior*. Lawrence Erlbaum Associates.

Draper, N. A. (2019). *The Identity Trade*. New York University Press.

Dreyfus, H. L. (1979). *What Computers Can't Do: The Limits of Artificial Intelligence* (Revised Edition). Harper.

Duhem, P. (1954). *The Aim and Structure of Physical Theory*, trans. P. Wiener. Princeton University Press.

Dunbar, R. (1997). *Grooming, Gossip and the Evolution of Language*. Harvard University Press.

Duncker, K. (1945). On problem-solving. *Psychological Monographs*, 58(5, Whole No. 270).

Dunfield, K. A., & Kuhlmeier, V. A. (2010). Intention-mediated selective helping in infancy. *Psychological Science*, 21(4), 523–527.

Dunning, D. (2011). The Dunning–Kruger effect: On being ignorant of one's own ignorance. In *Advances in Experimental Social Psychology, Vol. 44*. (pp. 247–296). Academic Press.

Earle, T. (2000). Archaeology, property, and prehistory. Annual Review of Anthropology, 29(1), 39–60.

Easterbrook, N. (1992). The arc of our destruction: Reversal and erasure in cyberpunk. *Science Fiction Studies*, 19, 378–394.

Easterbrook, N. (2009). *Ethics and Alterity*. Routledge.

Eastwick, P. W., & Gardner, W. L. (2009). Is it a game? Evidence for social influence in the virtual world. *Social Influence*, 4(1), 18–32.

Edwards, K., & Smith, E. E. (1996). A disconfirmation bias in the evaluation of arguments. *Journal of Personality and Social Psychology*, 71, 5–24.

Ekelund, S., & Iskoujina, Z. (2019). Cybersecurity economics–balancing operational security spending. *Information Technology & People*, 32, 1318–1342.

Ellensheng, S. (2020). Facebook, Google discuss sharing smartphone data with government to fight coronavirus, but there are risks. *CNBC*, March 19. Available at: www.cnbc.com/2020/03/19/facebook-google-could-share-smartphone-data-to-fight-coronavirus.html.

Ellis, D. (1984). Video arcades, youth, and trouble. *Youth & Society*, 16, 47–65.

Ellison, N., Heino, R., & Gibbs, J. (2006). Managing impressions online: Self-presentation processes in the online dating environment. Journal of Computer-Mediated Communication, 11(2), 415–441.

Ensafi, R., Winter, P., Mueen, A., & Crandall, J. R. (2015). Analyzing the great firewall of China over space and time. *Proceedings on Privacy Enhancing Technology*, 61–76.

Ericsson, K. A., Hoffman, R. R., Kozbelt, A., & Williams, A. M. (Eds.) (2018). *The Cambridge Handbook of Expertise and Expert Performance*. Cambridge University Press.

Estache, A., Manacorda, M., Valletti, T. M., Galetovic, A., & Mueller, B. (2002). Telecommunications reform, access regulation, and Internet adoption in Latin America [with comments]. *Economia*, 2(2), 153–217.

Eubanks, V. (2018). *Automating Inequality: How High-Tech Tools Profile, Police, and Punish the Poor*. St. Martin's Press.

Evans, J. S. B., & Frankish, K. E. (2009). *In Two Minds: Dual Processes and Beyond*. Oxford University Press.

Evans, R. B. (2000). Psychological instruments at the turn of the century. *American Psychologist*, 55, 322–325.

Evers, K. (2001). *Standards for Ethics and Responsibility in Science*. Retrieved August 22, 2008 from: www.icsu.org/publications/reports-and-reviews/standards-responsibility-science/SCRES-Background.pdf.

Facjler, M. (2017). Six Years After Fukushima, Robots Finally Find Reactors' Melted Uranium Fuel. *The New York Times*, November 19. Retrieved January 11, 2020 from: www.nytimes.com/2017/11/19/science/japan-fukushima-nuclear-meltdown-fuel.html.

Fagan, L. M., Shortliffe, E. H., & Buchanan, B. G. (1980). Computer-based medical decision making: From MYCIN to VM. *Automedica*, 3, 97–108.

Fan, J., McCandliss, B. D., Sommer, T., Raz, A., & Posner, M. I. (2002). Testing the efficiency and independence of attentional networks. *Journal of Cognitive Neuroscience*, 14(3), 340–347.

Farley, J. D. (2006). The N.S.A.'s Math Problem. *The New York Times*, May 16. Retrieved April 3, 2020 from: www.nytimes.com/2006/05/16/opinion/16farley.html.

Fazio, L. (2020). Pausing to consider why a headline is true or false can help reduce the sharing of false news. *Harvard Kennedy School Misinformation Review*, 1(2).

Fechner, G.T. (1860/1964). *Elemente der Psychophysik* (2 vols.). E. J. Bonset.

Feeney, M. (2016). *Surveillance Takes Wing: Privacy in the Age of Police Drones. CATO Institute.* Policy Analysis No. 807. Retrieved February 21, 2022 from: www.cato.org/publications/policy-analysis/surveillance-takes-wing-privacy-age-police-drones.

Fehr, E., & Fischbacher, U. (2003). The nature of human altruism. *Nature*, 425(6960), 785–791.

FeldmanHall, O., Dalgleish, T., Thompson, R., Evans, D., Schweizer, S., & Mobbs, D. (2012). Differential neural circuitry and self-interest in real vs hypothetical moral decisions. *Social Cognitive and Affective Neuroscience*, 7, 743–751.

Feldstein, S. (2019). *The Global Expansion of AI Surveillance*. Carnegie Endowment for International Peace.

Ferguson, A. G. (2019). *The Rise of Big Data Policing: Surveillance, Race, and the Future of Law Enforcement*. NYU Press.

Ferguson, C. J., & Kilburn, J. (2010). Much ado about nothing: The misestimation and overinterpretation of violent video game effects in Eastern and Western nations: Comment on Anderson et al. *Psychological Bulletin*, 136(2), 174–178.

Ferguson, M. C., Coulson, M., & Barnett, J. (2011). A meta-analysis of pathological gaming prevalence and comorbidity with mental health, academic, and social problems. *Journal of Psychiatric Research*, 45, 1573–1578.

Financial Times (2021), Snap, Facebook, Twitter and YouTube lose nearly $10bn after iPhone privacy changes, *The Financial Times*. Retrieved June 22, 2021 from https://www.ft.com/content/4c19e387-ee1a-41d8-8dd2-bc6c302ee58e

Fischer, D. H. (1970). *Historians' Fallacies: Toward a Logic of Historical Thought*. New York: Harper and Row

Fiske, A. P. (1991). *Structures of Social Life: The Four Elementary Forms of Human Relations: Communal Sharing, Authority Ranking, Equality Matching, Market Pricing*. Free Press.

Fiske, A. P. (1992). The four elementary forms of sociality: Framework for a unified theory of social relations. Psychological Review, 99(4), 689–723.

Fiske, A. P., & Rai, T. S. (2014). *Virtuous Violence: Hurting and Killing to Create, Sustain, End, and Honor Social Relationships*. Cambridge University Press.

Fiske, S. T., Cuddy, A. J. C., Glick, P., & Xu, J. (2002). A model of (often mixed) stereotype content: Competence and warmth respectively follow from perceived status and competition. *Journal of Personality and Social Psychology*, 82(6), 878–902. Available at: https://doi.org/10.1037/0022-3514.82.6.878.

Fiske, S. T., Cuddy, A. J., & Glick, P. (2007). Universal dimensions of social cognition: Warmth and competence. Trends in Cognitive Sciences, 11(2), 77–83.

Fjeld, J., Achten, N., Hilligoss, H., Nagy, A. C., and Srikumar, M. (2020). Principled Artificial Intelligence: Mapping consensus in ethical and rights-based approaches to principles for AI. Berkman Klein Center for Internet & Society. Retrieved June 17, 2021 from: https://dash.harvard.edu/handle/1/42160420.

Flaherty, K. (2019). A RoboCop, a park and a fight: How expectations about robots are clashing with reality. NBC News, October 4. Retrieved February 21, 2022 from: www.nbcnews.com/tech/tech-news/robocop-park-fight-how-expectations-about-robots-are-clashing-reality-n1059671.

Fleck, L. (1935/2012). Genesis and Development of a Scientific Fact. University of Chicago Press.

Floridi, L., Cowls, J., Beltrametti, M., Chatila, R., Chazerand, P., Dignum, V., et al. (2018). AI4People – An ethical framework for a good AI society: Opportunities, risks, principles, and recommendations. Minds and Machines, 28, 689–707.

Fogel, S. (2012). Telltale Games: The majority of The Walking Dead players try to do the right thing. Venture Beat, August 15. Retrieved April 13, 2020 from: https://venturebeat.com/2012/08/15/telltale-games-the-walking-dead-statistics-trailer/.

Foot, P. (1978/2002). Virtues and Vices and Other Essays in Moral Philosophy. Oxford University Press on Demand.

Fowler, G. A. & Hunter, T. (2021). When you 'Ask app not to track,' some iPhone apps keep snooping anyway. The Washington Post. Retrieved February 17, 2021 from https://www.washingtonpost.com/technology/2021/09/23/iphone-tracking/

Fox, J., & Rooney, M. C. (2015). The Dark Triad and trait self-objectification as predictors of men's use and self-presentation behaviors on social networking sites. Personality and Individual Differences, 76, 161–165. Available at: http://dx.doi.org/10.1016/j.paid.2014.12.017.

Franke, U. E. (2014). Drones, drone strikes, and us policy: The politics of unmanned aerial vehicles. Parameters, 44, 121.

Frankel, M. S. (1989). Professional codes: Why, how, and with what impact? Journal of Business Ethics, 8, 109–115.

Franklin, S., & Patterson, F. G. Jr. (2006). The LIDA architecture: Adding new modes of learning to an intelligent, autonomous, software agent. IDPT-2006 Proceedings (Integrated Design and Process Technology), Society for Design and Process Science, San Diego, California.

French, P. A. (1979). The corporation as a moral person. American Philosophical Quarterly, 16(3), 207–215.

Friedman, B., & Kahn, P. H., Jr. (2007). Human values, ethics, and design. In The Human-Computer Interaction Handbook (pp. 1267–1292). CRC Press.

Friedman, B., & Nissenbaum, H. (1996). Bias in computer systems. ACM Transactions on Information Systems (TOIS), 14, 330–347.

Friedman, B., Millett, L., and Felten, E. (2000). Informed Consent Online: A Conceptual Model and Design Principles. University of Washington Computer Science & Engineering Technical Report 00–12–2.

Frohlich, N., & Oppenheimer, J. A. (1993). Choosing Justice: An Experimental Approach to Ethical Theory. University of California Press.

Frohlich, N., Oppenheimer, J. A., & Eavey, C. L. (1987). Choices of principles of distributive justice in experimental groups. American Journal of Political Science, X, 606–636.

Frost, L., Walshe, R., & Muscella, S. (2021). Landscape of AI standards. StandICT.eu 2023 Coordination and Support Action. Retrieved June 25, 2021 from: https://zenodo.org/record/5011179.

FTC (2019a). FTC imposes $5 billion penalty and sweeping new privacy restrictions on Facebook. *Federal Trade Commission*. Retrieved April 9, 2020 from: www.ftc.gov/news-events/press-releases/2019/07/ftc-imposes-5-billion-penalty-sweeping-new-privacy-restrictions.

FTC (2019b). Google and YouTube will pay record $170 million for alleged violations of children's privacy law. *Federal Trade Commission*. Retrieved April 9, 2020 from: www.ftc.gov/news-events/press-releases/2019/09/google-youtube-will-pay-record-170-million-alleged-violations.

FTC (2020). Equifax Data Breach Settlement. *Federal Trade Commission*, January. Retrieved February 6, 2020 from: www.ftc.gov/enforcement/cases-proceedings/refunds/equifax-data-breach-settlement.

Fukuyama, F. (1996). *Trust: Human Nature and the Reconstitution of Social Order*. Simon and Schuster.

Fullerton, J. (2018). China's 'social credit' system bans millions from travelling. *The Telegraph*. Retrieved April 9, 2020 from: www.telegraph.co.uk/news/2018/03/24/chinas-social-credit-system-bans-millions-travelling/.

Gabriel, I. (2020). Artificial intelligence, values, and alignment. *Minds and Machines*, 30(3), 411–437.

Gaertner, W., & Schokkaert, E. (2012). *Empirical Social Choice: Questionnaire-Experimental Studies on Distributive Justice*. Cambridge University Press.

Galison, P. (1987). *How Experiments End*. The University of Chicago Press.

Gantman, A. P., & Van Bavel, J. J. (2014). The moral pop-out effect: Enhanced perceptual awareness of morally relevant stimuli. *Cognition*, 132, 22–29.

Garbarino, E., & Lee, O. F. (2003). Dynamic pricing in internet retail: Effects on consumer trust. *Psychology & Marketing*, 20(6), 495–513.

Gardner, H. (1983). *Frames of Mind: The Theory of the Multiple Intelligences*. Basic Books.

Garg, N., Schiebinger, L., & Jurafsky. D, & Zou, J. (2018). Word embeddings quantify 100 years of gender and ethnic stereotypes. *Proceedings of the National Academy of Sciences*, 17, E3635–3644.

Garner, R. T., & Rosen, B. (1967). *Moral Philosophy: A Systematic Introduction to Normative Ethics and Meta-ethics*. Macmillan.

Ge, L., & Thomas, S. (2008). A cross-cultural comparison of the deliberative reasoning of Canadian and Chinese accounting students. Journal of Business Ethics, 82, 189–211.

Gee, J. (2007). Pleasure, learning, video games, and life: The projective stance. In M. Knobel & C. Lankshear (Eds.), *A New Literacies Sampler*. Peter Lang.

Gee, J. (2008). Video games and embodiment. *Games and Culture*, 3, 253–263.

Gelfand, M. J., Nishii, L. H., & Raver, J. L. (2006). On the nature and importance of cultural tightness-looseness. *Journal of Applied Psychology*, 91(6), 1225–1244.

Geraci, R. M. (2008). Apocalyptic AI: Religion and the promise of artificial intelligence. *Journal of the American Academy of Religion*, 76, 138–166.

German, T. P., & Barrett, H. C. (2005). Functional fixedness in a technologically sparse culture. *Psychological Science*, 16, 1–5.

German, T. P., & Defeyter, M. A. (2000). Immunity to functional fixedness in young children. *Psychonomic Bulletin & Review*, 7, 707–712.

Gescheider, G. A. (1997/2013). *Psychophysics: The Fundamentals*. Lawrence Erlbaum Associates.

Gibbs, J. C. (n.d.). *Moral Development and Reality: Beyond the Theories of Kohlberg*. Hoffman, and Haidt.

Gibson, J. J. (1977). The theory of affordances. In R. E. Shaw & J. Bransford (Eds.), *Perceiving, Acting, and Knowing: Toward an Ecological Psychology* (pp. 67–82). Lawrence Erlbaum Associates.

Gibson, J. J. (1979/2014). The Ecological Approach to Visual Perception. Psychology Press.

Gieryn, T. F. (1995). Boundaries of science. In *Science and the Quest for Reality* (pp. 293–332). Palgrave Macmillan.

Gigerenzer, G. (1991). From tools to theories: A heuristic of discovery in cognitive psychology. *Psychological Review*, 98, 254–267.

Gigerenzer, G., & Sturm, T. (2006). Tools = theories = data? On some circular dynamics in cognitive science. In M. G. Ash & T. Sturm (Eds.), *Psychology's Territories: Historical and Contemporary Perspectives from Different Disciplines* (pp. 305–342). Lawrence Erlbaum Associates.

Gilbert, D. T., & Malone, P. S. (1995). The correspondence bias. *Psychological Bulletin*, 117(1), 21–38.

Gilbert, G. N. (1977). Referencing as persuasion. *Social Studies of Science*, 7, 113–122.

Gilligan, C. (1982). *In a Different Voice: Psychological Theory and Women's Development*. Harvard University Press.

Gilmore, C. P. (1967, May). I used a computer at home… and so will you. *Popular Science*, 90–102.

Gilovich, T., Griffin, D., & Kahneman, D. (Eds.) (2002). *Heuristics and Biases: The Psychology of Intuitive Judgment*. Cambridge University Press.

Gino, F., Ayal, S., & Ariely, D. (2009). Contagion and differentiation in unethical behaviour: The effect of one bad apple on the barrel. *Psychological Science*, 20, 393–398.

Gips, J. (1991). Towards the ethical robot. In K. Ford, C. Glymour, & P. Hayes (Eds.), *Android Epistemology* (pp. 243–252). MIT Press.

Gips, J. (2005). Creating ethical robots: A grand challenge. *AAAI Symposium on Machine Ethics*, (pp. 18–21). IEEE.

Glasman, L. R., & Albarracin, D. (2006). Forming attitudes that predict future behaviour: A meta-analysis of the attitude-behaviour relation. *Psychological Bulletin*, 132, 778.

Glomb, T. M., & Miner, A. G. (2002). Exploring patterns of aggressive behaviors in organizations: Assessing model-data fit. In J. M. Brett, & F. Drasgow, (Eds.), The Psychology of Work: Theoretically Based Empirical Research (pp. 235–252). Lawrence Erlbaum Associates.

Gobet, F., & Simon, H. A. (1998). Expert chess memory: Revisiting the chunking hypothesis. *Memory*, 6, 225–255.

Gobet, F., & Waters, A. J. (2003). The role of constraints in expert memory. *Journal of Experimental Psychology: Learning, Memory, and Cognition*, 29, 1082–1094.

Gobry, G. A. (1973). Computer-assisted clinical decision making. *Methods of Information in Medicine* 12, 45–51.

Goebel, R., Chander, A., Holzinger, K., Lecue, F., Akata, Z., Stumpf, S., … & Holzinger, A. (2018, August). Explainable AI: The new 42? In *International Cross-Domain Conference for Machine Learning and Knowledge Extraction* (pp. 295–303). Springer.

Goldberg, L. R. (1970). Man versus model of man: A rationale, plus some evidence, for a method of improving on clinical inferences. *Psychological Bulletin*, 73(6), 422–432.

Goldstein, N. J., Griskevicius, V., & Cialdini, R. B. (2011). Reciprocity by proxy: A novel influence strategy for stimulating cooperation. *Administrative Science Quarterly*, 56(3), 441–473.

Golinski, J. (1992). *Science as public culture: Chemistry and enlightenment in Britain, 1760–1820*. Cambridge University Press.

Goodall, N. J. (2014). Ethical decision making during automated vehicle crashes. *Transportation Research Record*, 2424(1), 58–65.

Goodkind, A. L., Jones, B. A., & Berrens, R. P. (2020). Cryptodamages: Monetary value estimates of the air pollution and human health impacts of cryptocurrency mining. *Energy Research & Social Science*, 59, 101281.

Goodman, C. (2016a). *The Training Anthology of Śāntideva: A Translation of the* Śikṣā-samuccaya. Oxford University Press.

Goodman, C. (2016b). From Madhyamaka to Consequentialism. In *The Cowherds, Moonpaths: Ethics and Emptiness* (pp. 141–158). Oxford University Press.

Goodman, N. (1955). *Fact, Fiction, and Forecast*. Harvard University Press.

Google (2021). Publish your own StreetView. Retrieved October 11, 2021 from: https://developers.google.com/streetview/publish.

Gordon, D. F., Desjardins, M. (1995). Evaluation and selection of biases in machine learning. *Machine Learning*, 20, 5–22.

Gorner, J. (2016). With violence up, Chicago Police focus on a list of likeliest to kill, be killed. *Chicago Tribune*, July 22. Retrieved February 2, 2020 from: www.chicagotribune.com/news/ct-chicago-police-violence-strategy-met-20160722-story.html.

Gouldner, A. W. (1960). The norm of reciprocity: A preliminary statement. *American Sociological Review*, 25, 161–178.

Govindarajulu, N. S., & Bringsjord, S. (2015). Ethical regulation of robots must be embedded in their operating systems. In R. Trappl (Ed.), *A Construction Manual for Robot's Ethical Systems: Requirements, Methods, Implementations*. Springer.

Govindarajulu, N. S., & Bringsjord, S. (2017). On automating the doctrine of Double Effect. In *Proceedings of the Twenty-Sixth International Joint Conference on Artificial Intelligence (IJCAI-17)* (pp. 4722–4730).

Graham, J., Haidt, J., & Nosek, B. A. (2009). Liberals and conservatives rely on different sets of moral foundations. Journal of Personality and Social Psychology, 96(5), 1029.

Grasso, A. (2015). Will machines replace us or work with us? *Wired Magazine*. Available at: www.wired.com/insights/2015/01/will-machines-replace-us-or-work-with-us/.

Grau, C. (2006). There is no 'I' in 'robot': Robots and utilitarianism. *IEEE Intelligent Systems*, 21(4), 52–55.

Gray, C. M., Kou, Y., Battles, B., Hoggatt, J., & Toombs, A. L. (2018, April). The dark (patterns) side of UX design. In *Proceedings of the 2018 CHI Conference on Human Factors in Computing Systems* (pp. 1–14).

Greene, D., Hoffmann, A. L., & Stark, L. (2019, January). Better, nicer, clearer, fairer: A critical assessment of the movement for ethical artificial intelligence and machine learning. In *Proceedings of the 52nd Hawaii International Conference on System Sciences*.

Greene, J. D. (2013). *Moral Tribes: Emotion, Reason, and the Gap Between Us and Them*. Penguin.

Greene, J. D., & Paxton, J. M. (2009). Patterns of neural activity associated with honest and dishonest moral decisions. *Proceedings of the National Academy of Sciences*, 106(30), 12506–12511.

Greene, J., & Haidt, J. (2002). How (and where) does moral judgment work? Trends in Cognitive Sciences, 6(12), 517–523.

Greene, P. J., Durch, J. S., Horwitz, W., & Hooper, V. (1985). Policies for responding to allegations of fraud in research. *Minerva*, 23, 203–215.

Greenemeier, L. (2016). Driverless cars will face moral dilemmas. Scientific American, June. Retrieved March 10, 2021 from: www.scientificamerican.com/article/driverless-cars-will-face-moral-dilemmas/.

Greenwald, G. (2013a). NSA collecting phone records of millions of Verizon customers daily. *The Guardian*, June 6. Available at: www.theguardian.com/world/2013/jun/06/nsa-phone-records-verizon-court-order.

Greenwald, T. (2013b). Data won the U.S. election. now can it save the world? *MIT Technology Review*, May 29. Retrieved January 4, 2021 from: www.technologyreview.com/2013/05/29/178302/data-won-the-us-election-now-can-it-save-the-world/.

Griffin, E. (2010). Pro-Gun Russian bots flood Twitter after parkland shooting. *Wired*, February 15. Retrieved December 28, 2019 from: www.wired.com/story/pro-gun-russian-bots-flood-twitter-after-parkland-shooting/.

Griffiths, M. D., Kuss, D. J., & King, D. L. (2012). Video game addiction: Past, present and future. *Current Psychiatry Reviews*, 8(4), 308–318.

Grinberg, M., Hristova, E., & Borisova, M. (2012). Cooperation in Prisoner's Dilemma game: Influence of social relations. In *Proceedings of the Cognitive Science Society* (pp. 408–413).

Grizzard, M., Tamborini, R., Lewis, R. J., Wang, L., & Prabhu, S. (2014). Being bad in a video game can make us morally sensitive. *Cyberpsychology, Behavior, and Social Networking*, 17(8), 499–504.

Groch, S. (2019). ANU data breach: How hackers got inside Australia's top university. *The Canberra Times*, October 2. Retrieved March 3, 2020 from: www.canberratimes.com.au/story/6414841/like-a-diamond-heist-how-hackers-got-into-australias-top-uni/.

Grossman, D. (1995). *On Killing: The Psychological Cost of Learning to Kill in War and Society*. Little Brown.

Grove, W. M., Zald, D. H., Lebow, B. S., Snitz, B. E., & Nelson, C. (2000). Clinical versus mechanical prediction: A meta-analysis. *Psychological Assessment*, 12, 19–30.

Gruen, L. (2015). *Entangled Empathy: An Alternative Ethic for Our Relationship with Animals*. Lantern Books.

Guéguen, N. (2012). The sweet smell of … implicit helping: Effects of pleasant ambient fragrance on spontaneous help in shopping malls. *The Journal of Social Psychology*, 152(4), 397–400.

Gulshan, V., Peng, L., Coram, M., Stumpe, M. C., Wu, D., Narayanaswamy, A., … & Webster, D. R. (2016). Development and validation of a deep learning algorithm for detection of diabetic retinopathy in retinal fundus photographs. Journal of the American Medical Association, 316, 2402–2410.

Gunning, D. (2016). *DARPA XAI BAA*. DARPA. Retrieved August 19, 2020 from: www.darpa.mil/attachments/DARPA-BAA-16-53.pdf.

Gürer, D. (2002). Pioneering women in computer science. *ACM SIGCSE Bulletin*, 34, 175–180.

Gürses, S., & Del Alamo, J. M. (2016). Privacy engineering: Shaping an emerging field of research and practice. *IEEE Security & Privacy*, 14, 40–46.

Guston, D. H. (2007). *Between Politics and Science: Assuring the Integrity and Productivity of Reseach*. Cambridge University Press.

Guthrie, C., & Quinlan, M. (2007). *Just War: The Just War Tradition: Ethics in Modern Warfare*. Bloomsbury Publishing USA.

Hacking, I. (1992). The self-vindication of the laboratory sciences. In A. Pickering (Ed.), *Science as Practice and Culture* (pp. 29–64). University of Chicago Press.

Hagendorff, T. (2020). The ethics of AI ethics: An evaluation of guidelines. *Minds and Machines*, 30, 99–120.

Haidt, J. (2007). The new synthesis in moral psychology. *Science*, 316(5827), 998–1002.

Haidt, J., & Graham, J. (2007). When morality opposes justice: Conservatives have moral intuitions that liberals may not recognize. Social Justice Research, 20(1), 98–116.

Haidt, J., & Joseph, C. (2004). Intuitive ethics: How innately prepared intuitions generate culturally variable virtues. Daedalus, 133(4), 55–66.

Haile, T. (2015). What You Think You Know About the Web Is Wrong. *Time Magazine*, March 9. Retrieved March 24, 2010 from: https://time.com/12933/what-you-think-you-know-about-the-web-is-wrong/.

Hall, M., et al. (2021). 691 people have been charged in the Capitol insurrection so far. This searchable table shows them all. *Insider*, October 28. Retrieved October 29, 2021 from: www.insider.com/all-the-us-capitol-pro-trump-riot-arrests-charges-names-2021-1.

Halpern, D., Valenzuela, S., & Katz, J. E. (2016). 'Selfie-ists' or 'Narci-selfiers'? A cross-lagged panel analysis of selfie taking and narcissism. *Personality and Individual Differences*, 97, 98–101.

Hanisch, K. A., Hulin, C. L., & Seitz, S. T. (1996). Mathematical/computational modeling of organizational withdrawal processes: Benefits, methods, and results. In G. R. Ferris, A. Nedd, J. B. Shaw, J. E. Beck, P. S. Kirkbride, & K. M. Rowland (Eds.), Research in Personnel and Human Resources Management, Vol. 14 (pp. 91–142). JAI Press.

Hao, K. (2021). A horrifying new AI app swaps women into porn videos with a click. *MIT Technology Review*, September. Retrieved October 1, 2021 from: www.technologyreview.com/2021/09/13/1035449/ai-deepfake-app-face-swaps-women-into-porn/.

Hao, K. & Swart, H. (2022). South Africa's private surveillance machine is fueling a digital apartheid. *MIT Technology Review*, Retrieved May 1, 2022 from www.technologyreview.com/2022/04/19/1049996/south-africa-ai-surveillance-digital-apartheid/

Hardin, R. (2002). *Trust and trustworthiness*. Russell Sage Foundation.

Hardt, M., Prince, E., & Srebro, N. (2016). Equality of opportunity in supervised learning. In *Proceedings of the 30th International Conference on Neural Information Processing Systems* (pp. 3323–3331). Curran Associates Inc.

Hardwig, J. (1991). The role of trust in knowledge. *The Journal of Philosophy*, 88(12), 693–708.

Harman, G. (1973). *Thought*. Princeton University Press.

Harré, R. (2009). *Pavlov's Dog and Schrödinger's Cat*. Oxford University Press.

Harris, D. (2018). Deepfakes: False pornography is here and the law cannot protect you. *Duke Law & Technology Review*, 17, 99–128.

Harris, L. T., & Fiske, S. T. (2006). Dehumanizing the lowest of the low: Neuroimaging responses to extreme out-groups. Psychological Science, 17(10), 847–853.

Harris, L. T., & Fiske, S. T. (2009). Social neuroscience evidence for dehumanised perception. *European Review of Social Psychology*, 20, 192–231.

Harris, L. T., & Fiske, S. T. (2018). Dehumanizing the lowest of the low: Neuroimaging responses to extreme out-groups. In *Social Cognition* (pp. 215–226). Routledge.

Hartzog, W., & Stutzman, F. (2013). The case for online obscurity. *California Law Review*, 101, 1.

Harvey, A., & Jules, LaPlace (2019). MS-CELEB-1M. Exposing.ai. Retrieved: April 7, 2021 from https://exposing.ai/msceleb/

Haslam, N., & Loughnan, S. (2014). Dehumanization and infrahumanization. *Annual Review of Psychology*, 65, 399–423.

Haslam, N., Bastian, B., Laham, S., & Loughnan, S. (2012). *Humanness, Dehumanization, and Moral Psychology*.

Haslam, N., Bastian, B., Laham, S., & Loughnan, S. (2012). Humanness, dehumanization, and moral psychology. In M. Mikulincer & P. R. Shaver (Eds.), *The Social Psychology of Morality: Exploring the Causes of Good and Evil* (pp. 203–218). American Psychological Association.

Hatton, C. (2015). China 'social credit': Beijing sets up huge system. BBC News, October 26. Retrieved April 13, 2020 from: www.bbc.com/news/world-asia-china-34592186.

Hatton, L. (1997). The T experiments: Errors in scientific software. *IEEE Computational Science and Engineering*, 4, 27–38.

Hayden, B. (1998). Practical and prestige technologies: The evolution of material systems. *Journal of Archaeological Method and Theory*, 5(1), 1–55.

Hayduk, L., Cummings, G., Boadu, K., Pazderka-Robinson, H., & Boulianne, S. (2007). Testing! testing! one, two, three–Testing the theory in structural equation models! *Personality and Individual Differences*, 42(5), 841–850.

He, H. (2015). *Social Ethics in a Changing China: Moral Decay or Ethical Awakening*. Brookings.

Heenan, M., & Murray, S. (2006). *Study of Reported Rapes in Victoria 2000–2003: Summary Research Report*. State of Victoria (Australia), Department of Human Services. Retrieved February 21, 2022 from: www.ojp.gov/ncjrs/virtual-library/abstracts/study-reported-rapes-victoria-2000-2003-summary-research-report.

Heider, F. (1958). *The Psychology of Interpersonal Relations*. Psychology Press.

Heinlein, R. A. (1966). *The Moon is a Harsh Mistress*. Macmillan.

Helft, M. (2007). New privacy issues raises as Google's map service zooms in even closer. *The New York Times*, June 1. Retrieved January 7, 2020 from: www.nytimes.com/2007/06/01/business/worldbusiness/01iht-google.4.5965170.html.

Hellström, T. (2013). On the moral responsibility of military robots. *Ethics and Information Technology*, 15(2), 99–107.

Hemmadi, X (March 24, 2020). Toronto is gathering cellphone location data from telecoms to find out where people are still congregating amid coronavirus shutdown: Tory. *Financial Post*. Available at: https://business.financialpost.com/technology/city-of-toronto-gathering-cellphone-location-data-from-telecoms-in-bid-to-slow-spread-of-covid-19-tory.

Hempel, C. G., & Oppenheim, P. (1948). Studies in the logic of explanation. Philosophy of Science, 15, 135–175.

Herbst, P. G. (1959). *Task Structure and Work Relations*. (Document No. 528). Tavistock Institute of Human Relations.

Herz, J. C. (1997). *Joystick Nation: How Videogames Ate Our quarters, Won Our Hearts, and Rewired Our Minds*. Atlantic/Little, Brown.

Hibbard, B. (2001). *Super-Intelligent Machines*. Springer.

Hill, T. (1971). Kant on imperfect duty and supererogation, *Kant Studien*, 62, 55–76. Reprinted in his 1992 *Dignity and Practical Reason in Kant's Moral Theory*. Cornell University Press (p. 147–175).

Hill, K. (2020). The secretive company that might end privacy as we know it. *The New York Times*, Retrieved January 7, 2022 from: https://www.nytimes.com/2020/01/18/technology/clearview-privacy-facial-recognition.html

Hill, K. (2021). Clearview AI's facial recognition app called illegal in Canada. *The New York Times*, Retrieved January 7, 2022 from: https://www.nytimes.com/2021/02/03/technology/clearview-ai-illegal-canada.html?searchResultPosition=8

Hoeft, F., Watson, C. L., Kesler, S. R., Bettinger, K. E., Reiss, A. L. (2008). Gender differences in the mesocorticolimbic system during computer game-play. *Journal of Psychiatric Research*, 42, 253–258.

Hofstadter, D. R. (2007). *I Am a Strange Loop*. Basic Books.

Hogarth, R. M. (2001). *Educating Intuition*. University of Chicago Press.

Hollinger, R. C., & Adams, A. (2014). 2012 National Retail Security Survey Final Report. University of Florida.

Hollinger, R. C., & Davis, J. L. (2006). Employee theft and staff dishonesty. In M. Gill (Ed.), The Handbook of Security (pp. 203–228). Palgrave Macmillan.

Holvoet, C., Scola, C., Arciszewski, T., & Picard, D. (2016). Infants' preference for prosocial behaviours: A literature review. *Infant Behaviour & Development*, 45, 125–139.

Hong, Y., Chiu, C., 86 Kung, T. (1997). Bringing culture out in front: Effects of cultural meaning system activation on social cognition. In K. Leung, U. Kim, S. Yamaguchi, 86 Y. Kashima (Eds.), *Progress in Asian Social Psychology* (Vol. 1, pp. 135–146). Singapore: Wiley.

Horner, J. K., & Symons, J. (2019). Understanding error rates in software engineering: Conceptual, empirical, and experimental approaches. *Philosophy & Technology*, 32(2), 363–378.

Horowitz, M. C. (2019). When speed kills: Lethal autonomous weapon systems, deterrence, and stability. *Journal of Strategic Studies*, 42(6), 764–788.

Horty, J. (2001). *Agency and Deontic Logic*. Oxford University Press, New York.

Horwitz, J. (2021). Facebook says its rules apply to all. Company documents reveal a secret elite that's exempt. *The Wall Street Journal*, September 13. Retrieved September 17, 2021 from: www.wsj.com/articles/facebook-files-xcheck-zuckerberg-elite-rules-11631541353?mod=hp_lead_pos7.

Hoshino-Browne, E. (2004). Investigating attitudes cross-culturally: A case of cognitive dissonance among East Asians and North Americans. In *Contemporary Perspectives on the Psychology of Attitudes* (pp. 393–416). Psychology Press.

Hosie, R. (2017). The psychological reason you can't stop checking your phone. *The Independent*, February 10. Retrieved April 16, 2020 from: www.independent.co.uk/lifestyle/why-keep-checking-phone-psychology-smartphone-notifications-social-media-a7572916.html.

Howard, P. N., & Kollanyi, B. (2016). *Bots, #Strongerin, and #Brexit: Computational Propaganda During the UK–EU Referendum*. Research Note 2016.1. Project on Computational Propaganda.

Howard, P. N., Duffy, A., Freelon, D., Hussain, M. M., Mari, W., & Maziad, M. (2011). *Opening Closed Regimes: What Was the Role of Social Media during the Arab Spring?* Available at: SSRN 2595096.

Huang, H. M. (2006). The Autonomy Levels for Unmanned Systems (ALFUS) framework: Interim results. In *Performance Metrics for Intelligent Systems (PerMIS) Workshop*, Gaithersburg.

Huang, H. M. et al. (2005). A framework for Autonomy Levels For Unmanned Systems (ALFUS). In *Proceedings of the AUVSI's Unmanned Systems North America Symposium*.

Huang, H. M., Pavek, K., Ragon, M., Jones, J., Messina, E., & Albus, J. (2007). Characterizing unmanned system autonomy: Contextual autonomous capability and level of autonomy analyses. In *Unmanned Systems Technology IX* (Vol. 6561, p. 65611N, May). International Society for Optics and Photonics.

Huang, J., Li, Q., Xue, Y., Cheng, T., Xu, S., Jia, J., Feng, L. (2015). Teenchat: A chatterbot system for sensing and releasing adolescents' stress, *International Conference on Health Information Science* (pp. 133–145). Springer.

Huang, Y. Y., & Chou, C. (2010). An analysis of multiple factors of cyberbullying among junior high school students in Taiwan. *Computers in Human Behavior*, 26(6), 1581–1590.

Huesmann, L. R., Moise-Titus, J., Podolski, C. L., & Eron, L. D. (2003). Longitudinal relations between children's exposure to TV violence and their aggressive and violent behavior in young adulthood: 1977–1992. *Developmental Psychology*, 39, 201.

Human Rights Clinic (October 2012). *Counting Drone Strike Deaths*. Columbia Law School. Available at: https://web.law.columbia.edu/sites/default/files/microsites/human-rights-institute/COLUMBIACounting%20Drone%20Strike%20DeathsSUMMARY.pdf.

Hume, D. (1738–1740/2003). *A Treatise of Human Nature*. Courier Corporation.

Hume, D. (1748). *An Enquiry Concerning Human Understanding*.

Hurley, L. (2018). Supreme Court restricts police on cellphone location data. *Reuters*, June 22. Retrieved April 3, 2020 from: www.reuters.com/article/us-usa-court-mobilephone-idUSKBN1JI1WT.

IEEE (2016). Ethically Aligned Design. The IEEE Global Initiative for Ethical Considerations in Artificial Intelligence and Autonomous Systems.

Ikuenobe, P. (2020). African Communal Ethics. In *The Palgrave Handbook of African Social Ethics* (pp. 129–145). Palgrave Macmillan.

Information Commissioner's Office and the the Office of the Australian Information Commissioner (2021). Commissioner Initiated Investigation in Clearview AI, Inc. Retrieved January 7, 2022 from: https://www.oaic.gov.au/__data/assets/pdf_file/0016/11284/Commissioner-initiated-investigation-into-Clearview-AI,-Inc.-Privacy-2021-AICmr-54-14-October-2021.pdf

Inkster, B., Sarda, S., & Subramanian, V. (2018). An empathy-driven, conversational artificial intelligence agent (Wysa) for digital mental well-being: Real-world data evaluation mixed-methods study. *JMIR mHealth and uHealth*, 6(11), e12106. Available at: https://mhealth.jmir.org/2018/11/e12106.

Ireton, J. (2015). Twitter analysis during Canada election campaign helping parties build strategy. *CBC News*, October 15. Retrieved December 15, 2019 from: www.cbc.ca/news/canada/ottawa/data-analytics-campaign-strategy-1.3271381.

Isen AM, Clark M, Schwartz ME (1976). Duration of the effect of good mood on helping: Footprints in the sands of time. *Journal of Personality and Social Psychology*, 34(3), 385–393

Ishowo-Oloko, F., Bonnefon, J. F., Soroye, Z., Crandall, J., Rahwan, I., & Rahwan, T. (2019). Behavioural evidence for a transparency–efficiency tradeoff in human–machine cooperation. *Nature Machine Intelligence*. Available at doi: 10.1038/s42256-019-0113-5.

Jablonka, E., & Lamb, M. J. (2014). *Evolution in Four Dimensions, Revised Edition: Genetic, Epigenetic, Behavioral, and Symbolic Variation in the History of Life*. MIT Press.

Jacoby, L. L. (1991). A process dissociation framework: Separating automatic from intentional uses of memory. *Journal of Memory and Language*, 30(5), 513–541.

Janis, I. L., & Mann, L. (1977). *Decision Making: A Psychological Analysis of Conflict, Choice, and Commitment*. Free Press.

Jansen, P., Brey, P., et al. (2019). *D4.4: Ethical Analysis of AI and Robotics Technologies*. SIENNA Project.

Jensen, C. B., & Blok, A. (2013). Techno-animism in Japan: Shinto cosmograms, actor-network theory, and the enabling powers of non-human agencies. *Theory, Culture & Society*, 30, 84–115.

Jentzsch, S., Schramowski, P., Rothkopf, C., & Kersting, K. (2019). The moral choice machine: Semantics derived automatically from language corpora contain human-like moral choices. In Proceedings of the 2nd AAAI/ACM Conference on AI, Ethics, and Society. Association for the Advancement of Artificial Intelligence.

Jeong, M., Zo, H., Lee, C. H., & Ceran, Y. (2019). Feeling displeasure from online social media postings: A study using cognitive dissonance theory. *Computers in Human Behavior*, 97, 231–240.

Jia, W. (2001). *The Remaking of the Chinese Character and Identity in the 21st Century: The Chinese Face Practices*. Greenwood Publishing Group.

Jiang, F., Jiang, Y., Zhi, H., Dong, Y., Li, H., Ma, S., … & Wang, Y. (2017). Artificial intelligence in healthcare: Past, present and future. *Stroke and Vascular Neurology*, 2(4). Available at doi: 10.1136/svn-2017-000101.

Jiang, L., Hwang, J. D., Bhagavatula, C., Bras, R. L., Forbes, M., Borchardt, J., … & Choi, Y. (2021). Delphi: Towards Machine Ethics and Norms. *arXiv preprint* arXiv: 2110.07574.

Jiang, X., Coffee, M., …, & Huang, Y. (2020). Towards an artificial intelligence framework for data-driven prediction of coronavirus clinical severity. *Computers, Materials & Continua*, 63, 537–551. CMC. Available at doi: 10.32604/cmc.2020.010691.

Jin, D. Y. (2017). *Smartland Korea: Mobile Communication, Culture, and Society*. University of Michigan Press.

Jobin, A., Ienca, M., & Vayena, E. (2019). The global landscape of AI ethics guidelines. *Nature Machine Intelligence*, 1, 389–399.

Joeckel, S., Bowman, N. D., and Dogruel, L. (2012). Gut or game? The influence of moral intuitions on decisions in video games. *Media Psychology*, 15, 460–485.

Johnson, M. K., Rowatt, W. C., & Petrini, L. (2011). A new trait on the market: Honesty–Humility as a unique predictor of job performance ratings. *Personality and Individual Differences*, 50, 857–862.

Johnson, S. G., Valenti, J. J., & Keil, F. C. (2019). Simplicity and complexity preferences in causal explanation: An opponent heuristic account. *Cognitive Psychology*, 113, 101222.

Johnson-Laird, P. N., & Wason, P. C. (1970). A theoretical analysis of insight into a reasoning task. *Cognitive Psychology*, 1(2), 134–148.

Jonason, P. K., Slomski, S., & Partyka, J. (2012). The Dark Triad at work: How toxic employees get their way. *Personality and individual differences*, 52(3), 449–453.

Jones, D. N., & Paulhus, D. L. (2017). Duplicity among the dark triad: Three faces of deceit. *Journal of Personality and Social Psychology*, 113(2), 329–342.

Jones, N. (2018). How to stop data centres from gobbling up the world's electricity. *Nature*, 561, 163–167.

Jordan, J., Mullen, E., & Murnighan, J. K. (2011). Striving for the moral self: The effects of recalling past moral actions on future moral behavior. *Personality and Social Psychology Bulletin*, 37(5), 701–713.

Jorgensen, A. (1995). Survey shows policies on ethical issues still lacking enforcement mechanisms. *Professional Ethics Report*, 8, 1, 6.

Joseph, A. D., Laskov, P., Roli, F., Tygar, J. D., and Nelson, B. (2013). Machine Learning Methods for Computer Security (Dagstuhl Perspectives Workshop 12371). *Dagstuhl Manifestos*, 3, 1–30.

Jost, J. T. (1997). An experimental replication of the depressed-entitlement effect among women. *Psychology of Women Quarterly*, 21(3), 387–393.

Jost, J. T. (2018). A quarter century of system justification theory: Questions, answers, criticisms, and societal applications, *British Journal of Social Psychology*, 58, 263–314.

Jost, J. T., & Major, B. (Eds.) (2001). *The Psychology of Legitimacy: Emerging Perspectives on Ideology, Justice, and Intergroup Relations*. Cambridge University Press.

Kahneman, D. (2011). *Thinking, Fast and Slow*. Macmillan.

Kahneman, D., & Klein, G. (2009). Conditions for intuitive expertise: A failure to disagree. *American Psychologist*, 64(6), 515–526.

Kallgren, C. A., Reno, R. R., & Cialdini, R. B. (2000). A focus theory of normative conduct: When norms do and do not affect behavior. *Personality and Social Psychology Bulletin*, 26(8), 1002–1012.

Kandias, M., Stavrou, V., Bozovic, N., & Gritzalis, D. (2013, November). Proactive insider threat detection through social media: The YouTube case. In *Proceedings of the 12th ACM Workshop on Workshop on Privacy in the Electronic Society* (pp. 261–266).

Kandula, S., & Shaman, J. (2019). Reappraising the utility of Google flu trends. *PloS Computational Biology*, 15(8), e1007258.

Kane, M. T. (1992). An argument-based approach to validity. *Psychological Bulletin*, 112(3), 527–535.

Kang, J. (1998). Information privacy in cyberspace transactions. *Stanford Law Review*, 50, 1193–1294.

Kant, I. (1797/1991). *The Metaphysics of Morals*. Cambridge University Press.

Kara, Y., Boyacioglu, M. A., & Baykan, Ö. K. (2011). Predicting direction of stock price index movement using artificial neural networks and support vector machines: The sample of the Istanbul Stock Exchange. *Expert systems with Applications*, 38, 5311–5319.

Kardaras, N. (2016). It's 'digital heroin': How screens turn kids into psychotic junkies. *The New York Post*, August 27.

Kates, A. W., Wu, H., & Coryn, C. L. (2018). The effects of mobile phone use on academic performance: A meta-analysis. *Computers & Education*, 127, 107–112.

Katz, J. E., & Aakhus, M. (Eds.) (2002). *Perpetual Contact: Mobile Communication, Private Talk, Public Performance*. Cambridge University Press.

Kearns, M., & Roth, A. (2019). *The Ethical Algorithm: The Science of Socially Aware Algorithm Design*. Oxford University Press.

Keil, F. C., & Wilson, R. A. (2000). *Explanation and Cognition*. MIT press.

Kelley, H. H., & Thibaut, J. W. (1978). *Interpersonal Relations: A Theory of Interdependence*. Wiley.

Kelly, K. (2010). *What Technology Wants*. Penguin.

Kenny, D. A., Kaniskan, B., & McCoach, D. B. (2015). The performance of RMSEA in models with small degrees of freedom. *Sociological Methods & Research*, 44(3), 486–507.

Khan, F. U. (1995). The Ethics of Autonomous Learning Systems. In *Android Epistemology*, (pp. 253–265). ACM.

Khan, I. A., Brinkman, W. P., Fine, N., & Hierons, R. M. (2008, January). Measuring personality from keyboard and mouse use. In *Proceedings of the 15th European Conference on Cognitive Ergonomics: The Ergonomics of Cool Interaction* (pp. 1–8).

Kim, M. C. (2004). Surveillance technology, privacy and social control: With reference to the case of the electronic national identification card in South Korea. *International Sociology*, 19(2), 193–213.

Kim, S. S. H. C. (2017). Korean *han* and the postcolonial afterlives of 'the beauty of sorrow'. *Korean Studies*, 41, 253–279.

Kim, Y., & Yang, J. (2013). Impact of Chemyeon on Koreans' verbal aggressiveness and argumentativeness. *Korea Journal*, 53, 48–77.

Kimppa, K. K., Heimo, O. I., & Harviainen, J. T. (2016). First dose is always freemium. *ACM SIGCAS Computers and Society*, 45(3), 132–137

King, D. L., Delfabbro, P. H., & Griffiths, M. D. (2012). Clinical interventions for technology-based problems: Excessive Internet and video game use. *Journal of Cognitive Psychotherapy*, 26, 43–56.

King, D. L., Delfabbro, P. H., & Griffiths, M. D. (2013). Trajectories of problem video gaming among adult regular gamers: An 18-month longitudinal study. *Cyberpsychology, Behaviour and Social Networking*, 16, 72–76.

King, G., Pan, J., & Roberts, M. E. (2014). Reverse-engineering censorship in China: Randomized experimentation and participant observation. *Science*, 345(6199). Available at doi: 10.1126/science.1251722.

King, I. (2008). *How to Make Good Decisions and Be Right All the Time*. Continuum.

Kirchgaessner, Stephanie; Lewis, Paul; Pegg, David; Cutler, Sam; Lakhani, Nina; Safi, Michael (2021). Revealed: Leak uncovers global abuse of cyber-surveillance weapon. *The Guardian*, July 18. Retrieved July 20, 2021 from: www.theguardian.com/world/2021/jul/18/revealed-leak-uncovers-global-abuse-of-cyber-surveillance-weapon-nso-group-pegasus.

Kirchmair, L. (2019). Descriptive vs. prescriptive global legal pluralism: A gentle reminder of David Hume's is–ought divide. *The Journal of Legal Pluralism and Unofficial Law*, 51, 48–71.

Kitayama, S., Snibbe, A. C., Markus, H. R., & Suzuki, T. (2004). Is there any 'free' choice? Self and dissonance in two cultures. *Psychological Science*, 15(8), 527–533.

Kitson, J. (2020). The war in Nagorno-Karabakh has big lessons for the British Army. *CAPX*, November 18. Retrieved August 17, 2021 from: https://capx.co/the-war-in-nagorno-karabakh-has-big-lessons-for-the-british-army/.

Kizza, J. M. (Ed.) (2013). *Ethical and Social Issues in the Information Age*. Springer.

Klein, A. (2016). Tesla driver dies in first fatal autonomous car crash in US. *New Scientist*, July 1. Retrieved February 21, 2022 from: www.newscientist.com/article/2095740-tesla-driver-dies-in-first-fatal-autonomous-car-crash-in-us/.

Klein, G. (1998). *Sources of Power: How People Make Decisions*. MIT Press.

Klein, G. A. (1993). A recognition-primed decision (RPD) model of rapid decision making. *Decision Making in Action: Models and Methods*, 5(4), 138–147.

Knockel, J., et al. (2020). We Chat, they watch: How international users unwittingly build up WeChat's Chinese censorship apparatus. *Research Report #127*, May 7. Citizens Lab.

Kobie, N. (2019). The complicated truth about China's social credit system. *Wired* July 6. Retrieved April 15, 2020 from: www.wired.co.uk/article/china-social-credit-system-explained.

Koepp, M. J., Gunn, R. N., Lawrence, A. D., Cunningham, V. J., Dagher, A., Jones, T., Brooks, D. J., Bench, C. J., & Grasby, P. M. (1998). Evidence for striatal dopamine release during a video game. *Nature*, 21, 266–268.

Kogut, T., & Ritov, I. (2005). The singularity effect of identified victims in separate and joint evaluations. *Organizational Behavior and Human Decision Processes*, 97, 106–116.

Kohlberg, L. (1976). Moral stages and moralization: The cognitive-development approach. *Moral Development and Behaviour: Theory Research and Social Issues*, 31–53.

Kohlberg, L. (1981). *The Philosophy of Moral Development: Moral Stages and the Idea of Justice* (Vol. 1). Harper & Row.

Kokkinakis, A. V., Lin, J., Pavlas, D., & Wade, A. R. (2016). What's in a name? Ages and names predict the valence of social interactions in a massive online game. *Computers in Human Behaviour*, 55, 605–613.

Koriat, A., Lichtenstein, S., & Fischhoff, B. (1980). Reasons for confidence. *Journal of Experimental Psychology: Human Learning and Memory*, 6(2), 107–118.

Koriat, A., Sheffer, L., & Ma'ayan, H. (2002). Comparing objective and subjective learning curves: Judgments of learning exhibit increased underconfidence with practice. *Journal of Experiment Psychology: General*, 131, 147–162.

Kosinski, M., Stillwell, D., & Graepel, T. (2013). Private traits and attributes are predictable from digital records of human behavior. In *Proceedings of the National Academy of Sciences*, 110(15), 5802–5805.

Krieg, A., & Rickli, J. M. (2019). *Surrogate Warfare: The Transformation of War in the Twenty-First Century*. Georgetown University Press.

Krishnan, A. (2009). *Killer Robots: Legality and Ethicality of Autonomous Weapons*. Ashgate Publishing, Ltd.

Kruger, J., & Dunning, D. (1999). Unskilled and unaware of it: How difficulties in recognizing one's own incompetence lead to inflated self-assessments. *Journal of Personality and Social Psychology*, 77(6), 1121.

Kruikemeier, S., Sezgin, M., & Boerman, S. C. (2016). Political microtargeting: Relationship between personalized advertising on Facebook and voters' responses. *Cyberpsychology, Behaviour, and Social Networking*, 19, 367–372.

Krull, D. S., Loy, M. H. M., Lin, J., Wang, C. F., Chen, S., & Zhao, X. (1999). The fundamental attribution error: Correspondence bias in individualist and collectivist cultures. *Personality and Social Psychology Bulletin*, 25(10), 1208–1219.

Kteily, N., Hodson, G., & Bruneau, E. (2016). They see us as less than human: Metadehumanization predicts intergroup conflict via reciprocal dehumanization. *Journal of Personality and Social Psychology*, 110(3), 343–370.

Kuhn, T. (1962/2021). *The Structure of Scientific Revolutions*. Princeton University Press.

Kulms, P., & Kopp, S. (2018). A social cognition perspective on human–computer trust: The effect of perceived warmth and competence on trust in decision-making with computers. *Frontiers in Digital Humanities*, 5, 14. Available at: https://doi.org/10.3389/fdigh.2018.00014.

Kupferschmidt, K. (2017). Social media 'bots' tried to influence the U.S. Election. Germany may be next. *Science Magazine*. Retrieved January 4, 2021 from: www.sciencemag.org/news/2017/09/social-media-bots-tried-influence-us-election-germany-may-be-next.

Kurzweil, R. (2005). *The Singularity is Near: When Humans Transcend Biology*. Penguin.

Kuss, D. J., & Griffiths, M. D. (2012). Online gaming addiction in children and adolescents: A review of empirical research. *Journal of Behavioral Addictions*, 1, 3–22.

Kwon, S.Y. (2001). Codependence and interdependence: Cross-cultural reappraisal of boundaries and relationality. *Pastoral Psychology*, 50, 39–52.

LaFollette, M. C. (1990). *Making Science Our Own: Public Images of Science, 1910-1955*. University of Chicago.

Lakatos, I. (1963). *Proofs and Refutations*. Nelson.

Lange, S., Pohl, J., & Santarius, T. (2020). Digitalization and energy consumption. Does ICT reduce energy demand? *Ecological Economics*, 176, 106760.

Lara-Cabrera, R., Nogueira-Collazo, M., Cotta, C., & Fernández-Leiva, A. J. (2015). Game artificial intelligence: Challenges for the scientific community. In *Proceedings 2st Congreso de la Sociedad Española para las Ciencias del Videojuego* (pp. 1–12).

Laranjo, L., Dunn, A. G., Tong, H. L., Kocaballi, A. B., Chen, J., Bashir, R., ... & Coiera, E. (2018). Conversational agents in healthcare: A systematic review. *Journal of the American Medical Informatics Association*, 25, 1248–1258.

Larson, E. J. (2021). *The Myth of Artificial Intelligence: Why Computers Can't Think the Way We Do*. Harvard University Press.

Lavan, M. (2011). Slavishness in Britain and Rome in Tacitus' Agricola. *The Classical Quarterly*, 61(1), 294–305.

Law, J., & Williams, R. J. (1982). Putting facts together: A study of scientific persuasion. *Social Studies of Science*, 12, 535–558.

Lazer, D., Kennedy, R., King, G., & Vespignani, A. (2014). The parable of Google Flu: Traps in big data analysis. *Science*, 343(6176), 1203–1205.

Le Merrer, E., Morgan, B., & Trédan, G. (2021, May). Setting the Record Straighter on Shadow Banning. In *IEEE INFOCOM 2021-IEEE Conference on Computer Communications* (pp. 1–10). IEEE.

Lea, M., & Spears, R. (1991). Computer-mediated communication, de-individuation and group decision-making. Special Issue: Computer-supported cooperative work and groupware. *International Journal of Man Machine Studies*, 34, 283–301.

Leach, M. M., & Harbin, J. (1997). Psychological ethics codes: A comparison of twenty-four countries. *International Journal of Psychology*, 32, 181–192.

Leary, D. (1990). *Metaphors in the History of Psychology*. Cambridge University Press.

Lee, E., Lee, J. A., Moon, J. H., & Sung, Y. (2015). Pictures speak louder than words: Motivations for using Instagram. *Cyberpsychology, Behavior, and Social Networking*, 18(9), 552–556.

Lee, J. D., & See, K. A. (2004). Trust in automation: Designing for appropriate reliance. *Human Factors*, 46(1), 50–80.

Lee, K., & Ashton, M. C. (2004). Psychometric properties of the HEXACO personality inventory. *Multivariate Behavioural Research* 39(2), 329–358.

Lee, K., & Ashton, M. C. (2008). The HEXACO personality factors in the indigenous personality lexicons of English and 11 other languages. *Journal of Personality*, 76, 1001–1054.

Lee, K., Ashton, M. C., & De Vries, R. E. (2005). Predicting workplace delinquency and integrity with the HEXACO and five-factor models of personality structure. *Human Performance*, 18(2), 179–197.

Lee, K., Ashton, M. C., & Shin, K. H. (2005). Personality correlates of workplace anti-social behaviour. *Applied Psychology: An International Review*, 54(1), 81–98.

Lee, W. S., Ahn, S. M., Chung, J. W., Kim, K. O., Kwon, K. A., Kim, Y., … & Baek, J. H. (2018). Assessing concordance with Watson for Oncology, a cognitive computing decision support system for colon cancer treatment in Korea. *JCO Clinical Cancer Informatics*, 2, 1–8.

Leidner, B., Castano, E., & Ginges, J. (2013). Dehumanization, retributive and restorative justice, and aggressive versus diplomatic intergroup conflict resolution strategies. *Personality and Social Psychology Bulletin*, 39, 181–192.

Leiner, B. M., Cerf, V. G., Clark, D. D., Kahn, R. E., Kleinrock, L., Lynch, D. C., … & Wolff, S. (2003/2009). A brief history of the Internet. *ACM SIGCOMM Computer Communication Review*, 39(5), 22–31.

Leite, I., Pereira, A., Mascarenhas, S., Martinho, C., Prada, R., & Paiva, A. (2013). The influence of empathy in human–robot relations. *International Journal of Human-Computer Studies*, 71, 250–260.

Lemmens, J. S., Valkenburg, P. M., & Peter, J. (2009). Development and validation of a game addiction scale for adolescents. *Media Psychology*, 12, 77–95.

Lemmens, J. S., Valkenburg, P. M., & Peter, J. (2011). The effects of pathological gaming on aggressive behavior. *Journal of Youth and Adolescence*, 40, 38–47.

Lenton, A. P., & Francesconi, M. (2010). How humans cognitively manage an abundance of mate options. Psychological Science, 21, 528–533.

Levin, I. P., Rouwenhorst, R. M., & Trisko, H. M. (2005). Separating gender biases in screening and selecting candidates for hiring and firing. *Social Behavior and Personality: An International Journal*, 33(8), 793–804.

Lewis, J. D., & Weigert, A. (1985). Trust as a social reality. *Social Forces*, 63, 967–985.

Lewis, K., Gonzalez, M., & Kaufman, J. (2012). Social selection and peer influence in an online social network. *Proceedings of the National Academy of Sciences*, 109(1), 68–72.

Lewis, M., Yarats, D., Dauphin, Y. N., Parikh, D., & Batra, D. (2017). Deal or no deal? end-to-end learning for negotiation dialogues. In *Proceedings of the 2017 Conference on Empirical Methods in Natural Language Processing* (pp. 2433–2443). Association for Computational Linguistics.

Leyens, J. P., Demoulin, S., Vaes, J., Gaunt, R., & Paladino, M. P. (2007). Infra-humanization: The wall of group differences. *Social Issues and Policy Review*, 1(1), 139–172.

Li, C. (2008). The philosophy of harmony in classical Confucianism. *Philosophy Compass*, 3(3), 423–435.

Li, J., Bzdok, D., Chen, J., Tam, A., Ooi, L. Q. R., Holmes, A. J., … & Genon, S. (2022). Cross-ethnicity/race generalization failure of behavioral prediction from resting-state functional connectivity. *Science Advances*, 8(11), eabj1812.

Liang, F., Tan, Q., Zhan, Y., Wu, X., & Li, J. (2020). Selfish or altruistic? The influence of thinking styles and stereotypes on moral decision-making. *Personality and Individual Differences*, 110465.

Liang, H., Tsui, B. Y., Ni, H., Valentim, C., Baxter, S. L., Liu, G., … & Xia, H. (2019). Evaluation and accurate diagnoses of pediatric diseases using artificial intelligence. Nature Medicine, 25, 433–438.

Liberman, V., Samuels, S. M., & Ross, L. (2004). The name of the game: Predictive Reputations Versus Situational Labels in Determining Prisoner's Dilemma Game Moves. *Personality and Social Psychology Bulletin*, 30, 1175–1185.

Liedtke, M. (2007). Google hits streets, raises privacy concerns. *NBC News*, June 1. Retrieved December 17, 2019 from: www.nbcnews.com/id/wbna18987058.

Lin, L. Y., Sidani, J. E., Shensa, A., Radovic, A., Miller, E., Colditz, J. B., … & Primack, B. A. (2016). Association between social media use and depression among US young adults. *Depression and Anxiety*, 33(4), 323–331.

Lin, P., Abney, K., and Bekey, G. A. (Eds.) (2012). *Robot Ethics. The Ethical and Social Implications of Robotics*. The MIT Press.

Lin, P., Bekey, G., & Abney, K. (2008). *Autonomous Military Robotics: Risk, Ethics, and Design*. California Polytechnic State Univ San Luis Obispo.

Lind, R. A. (2005). Evaluating research misconduct policies at major research universities: A pilot study. *Accountability in Research*, 12, 241–262.

Lisak, D., Gardinier, L., Nicksa, S. C., & Cote, A. M. (2010). False allegations of sexual assault: An analysis of ten years of reported cases. *Violence Against Women*, 16, 1318–1334. Available at doi: 10.1177/1077801210387747.

Logan, G. D. (1988). Toward an instance theory of automatization. *Psychological Review*, 95, 492–527.

Lombrozo, T. (2007). Simplicity and probability in causal explanation. *Cognitive Psychology*, 55(3), 232–257.

Longoni, C., Bonezzi, A., & Morewedge, C. K. (2019). Resistance to medical artificial intelligence. *Journal of Consumer Research*, 46(4), 629–650.

Lonsway, K. A., Archambault, J., & Lisak, D. (2009). False reports: Moving beyond the issue to successfully investigate and prosecute non-stranger sexual assault. Available at: www.nsvrc.org/publications/articles/false-reports-moving-beyond-issue-successfully-investigate-and-prosecute-non-s.

Lorenz, T. (2022). Internet 'algospeak' is changing our language in real time, from 'nip nops' to 'le dollar bean'. *Washington Post*, Retrieved April 12, 2022 from https://www.washingtonpost.com/technology/2022/04/08/algospeak-tiktok-le-dollar-bean/

Loton, D. et al. (2016). Video game addiction, engagement and symptoms of stress, depression and anxiety: The mediating role of coping. *International Journal of Mental Health and Addiction*, 14, 565–578.

Loubier, A. (2017). How will the future of work affect women? *Forbes*, June 7. Retrieved February 21, 2022 from: www.forbes.com/sites/andrealoubier/2017/06/07/how-will-the-future-of-work-affect-women/#24443c4ec26e.

Lovelace, A. A. (1843) Notes by A.A.L. [August Ada Lovelace], Taylor's Scientific Memoirs, Vol. III. (pp. 666–731). London.

Lü, L., Medo, M., Yeung, C. H., Zhang, Y. C., Zhang, Z. K., & Zhou, T. (2012). Recommender systems. *Physics Reports*, 519, 1–49.

Luce, R. D., & Raiffa, H. (1957). *Games and Decisions: Introduction and Critical Survey*. Wiley.

Luchins, A. S. (1942). Mechanization in problem solving: The effect of Einstellung. Psychological Monographs, 54(6), Whole No. 248.

Luger, E., Moran, S., & Rodden, T. (2013, April). Consent for all: Revealing the hidden complexity of terms and conditions. In *Proceedings of the SIGCHI Conference on Human Factors in Computing Systems* (pp. 2687–2696).

Mac, R., & Frenkel, S. (2021). No more apologies: Inside Facebook's push to defend its image. *The New York Times*, September 21. Retrieved October 9, 2021 from: www.nytimes.com/2021/09/21/technology/zuckerberg-facebook-project-amplify.html.

MacIntyre, A. (1985/2004). *After Virtue*, 2nd Edn. Duckworth.

Mairesse, F., & Walker, M. (2006, June). Automatic recognition of personality in conversation. In *Proceedings of the Human Language Technology Conference of the NAACL, Companion Volume: Short Papers* (pp. 85–88).

Malle, B. F., Scheutz, M., Arnold, T., Voiklis, J., & Cusimano, C. (2015). Sacrifice one for the good of many? People apply different moral norms to human and robot agents. In *Proceedings of the Tenth Annual ACM/IEEE International Conference on Human-Robot Interaction (HRI '15)* (pp. 117–124). ACM.

Malmodin, J., & Lundén, D. (2018). The energy and carbon footprint of the global ICT and E&M sectors 2010–2015. *Sustainability*, 10, 3027.

Mann, L. (1981). The baiting crowd in episodes of threatened suicide. *Journal of Personality and Social Psychology*, 41, 703.

Manyika, J., et al. (November 28, 2017). *Jobs Lost, Jobs Gained: What the Future of Work will Mean for Jobs, Skills, and Wages*. McKinsey and Company.

Marchant, G. E., Allenby, B., Arkin, R., Barrett, E. T., Borenstein, J., Gaudet, L. M., ... & Silberman, J. (2011). International governance of autonomous military robots. *Columbia Science and Technology Law Review*, 12, 272–315.

Marcus, L. (2015, 13–17 July). Ecological space and cognitive geometry. In K. Karimi, L. Vaughan, K. Sailer, G. Palaiologou, & T. Bolton (Eds.), *Proceedings of the 10th International Space Syntax Symposium*. Space Syntax Laboratory.

Margoni, F., & Surian, L. (2018). Infants' evaluation of prosocial and antisocial agents: A meta-analysis. Developmental Psychology, 54, 1445–1455.

Markowitz, D. (2017). The future of online dating is unsexy and brutally effective. *Gizmodo*, October 25. Retrieved February 11, 2020 from: https://gizmodo.com/the-future-of-onl ine-dating-is-unsexy-and-brutally-effe-1819781116.

Marks, G., & Miller, N. (1987). Ten years of research on the false-consensus effect: An empirical and theoretical review. *Psychological Bulletin*, 102(1), 72–90.

Marlow, T., Miller, S., & Roberts, J. T. (2021). Bots and online climate discourses: Twitter discourse on President Trump's announcement of US withdrawal from the Paris Agreement. *Climate Policy*, 1–13.

Maronick, T. (2014). Do consumers read terms of service agreements when installing software? A two-study empirical analysis. *International Journal of Business and Social Research*, 4(6), 137–145.

Marvin, C. (1988). *When Old Technologies Were New: Thinking About Electric Communication in the Late Nineteenth Century*. Oxford University Press, USA.

Masolo, D. (2010). *Self and Community in a Changing World*. Indiana University Press.

Mason, M. (2003). Contempt as a moral attitude. *Ethics*, 113, 234–272.

Mason, R. O. (1986). Four ethical issues of the information age. *Management Information Systems Quarterly*, 10, 5–12.

Mathew, S., Petropoulos, M., Ngo, H. Q., & Upadhyaya, S. (2010, September). A data-centric approach to insider attack detection in database systems. In *International Workshop on Recent Advances in Intrusion Detection* (pp. 382–401). Springer.

Mattioli, D. (2019). Amazon changed search algorithm in ways that boost its own products. *The Wall Street Journal*, September 16. Retrieved September 2, 2020 from: www. wsj.com/articles/amazon-changed-search-algorithm-in-ways-that-boost-its-own-products-11568645345.

Mayer, R. C., Davis, J. H., & Schoorman, F. D. (1995). An integrative model of organizational trust. *Academy of Management Review*, 20, 709–734.

Maynard Smith, J. (1972). 'Game Theory and The Evolution of Fighting'. *On Evolution* (pp. 8–28). Edinburgh University Press.

Maynard Smith, J., & Price, G. R. (1973). The logic of animal conflict. *Nature*, 246, 15–18.

Mayor, A. (2020). *Gods and Robots: Myths, Machines, and Ancient Dreams of Technology*. Princeton University Press.

Mazar, N., & Zhong, C. B. (2010). Do green products make us better people? *Psychological Science*, 21(4), 494–498.

Mazar, N., Amir O., Ariely D. (2008). The dishonesty of honest people: A theory of self-concept maintenance. *Journal of Marketing Research*, 45, 633–644.

Mazarr, M. J., Casey, A., Demus, A., Harold, S. W., Matthews, L. J., Beauchamp-Mustafaga, N., & Sladden, J. (2019). *Hostile Social Manipulation: Present Realities and Emerging Trends*. RAND Corporation. Available at: www.rand.org/pubs/research_reports/RR2713.html.

Mbiti, J. (1989). *African Religions and Philosophy*. Heinemann.

McCabe, D. L., & Trevino, L. K. (1997). Individual and contextual influences on academic dishonesty: A multicampus investigation. *Research in Higher Education*, 38(3), 379–396.

McClelland, J. L., Rumelhart, D. E., & PDP Research Group. (1986). Parallel distributed processing. *Explorations in the Microstructure of Cognition*, 2, 216–271.

McCowan, T. C. (1981). Space Invaders' wrist. *The New England journal of medicine*, 304, 1368.

McCrae, N., Gettings, S., & Purssell, E. (2017). Social media and depressive symptoms in childhood and adolescence: A systematic review. *Adolescent Research Review*, 2(4), 315–330.

McDonald, A. M., & Cranor, L. F. (2008). The cost of reading privacy policies. *Isjlp*, 4, 543.

McLain, S. (2016). Toyota to sell 'cuddly companion' robot in Japan. *The Wall Street Journal*, October 3. Retrieved September 11, 2020 from: www.wsj.com/articles/toyota-to-sell-cuddly-companion-robot-in-japan-1475486949.

McNamara, R. S. (1995). In *Retrospect: the Tragedy and Lessons of Vietnam*. New York: Time Books.

McPherson, M., Smith-Lovin, L., & Cook, J. M. (2001). Birds of a feather: Homophily in social networks. *Annual Review of Sociology*, 27, 415–444.

McTear, M. F. (2002). Spoken dialogue technology: Enabling the conversational user interface. *ACM Comput Surv*, 34, 90–169.

McTear, M. F., Callejas, Z., & Griol, D. (2016). *The Conversational Interface: Talking to Smart Devices*. Springer.

Meehl, P. E. (1954). *Clinical versus Statistical Prediction: A Theoretical Analysis and a Review of the Evidence*. University of Minnesota Press.

Mehta, N. (2012). Knight 440 million loss sealed by new rules on canceling trades. *Bloomberg*, August 14. Retrieved April 7, 2020 from: www.bloomberg.com/news/articles/2012-08-14/knight-440-million-loss-sealed-by-new-rules-on-canceling-trades.

Meisenzahl, M. (2020a). This robot wanders New York City informing people about coronavirus, but it's already been banned from one park. *Business Insider*, March 5. Available at: www.businessinsider.com/robot-teaches-about-coronavirus-covid-19-symptoms-new-york-city-2020-3.

Meisenzahl, M. (2020b). These robots are fighting the coronavirus in China by disinfecting hospitals and making meals. *Business Insider*, March 8. Available at: www.businessinsider.co.za/see-chinese-robots-fighting-the-coronavirus-in-photos-2020-3.

Melis, A. P., Hare, B., & Tomasello, M. (2006). Chimpanzees recruit the best collaborators. *Science*, 311(5765), 1297–1300.

Merritt, A. C., Effron, D. A., & Monin, B. (2010). Moral self-licensing: When being good frees us to be bad. *Social and Personality Psychology Compass*, 4, 344–357.

Merton, R. K. (1942). The Normative Structure of Science. In Storer, N.W. (1973) *The Sociology of Science*. University of Chicago Press, 267–278.

Merton, R. K. (1957). Priorities in scientific discovery: A chapter in the sociology of science. *American Sociological Review*, 22, 635–659.

Merton, R. K. (1968). The Matthew effect in science: The reward and communication systems of science are considered. *Science*, 159(3810), 56–63.

Mesoudi, A., Whiten, A., & Laland, K. N. (2006). Towards a unified science of cultural evolution. *Behavioral and Brain Sciences*, 29, 329–383. Available at doi: 10.1017/S0140525X06009083.

Messick, S. (1995). Validation of inferences from persons' responses and performances as scientific inquiry into score meaning. *American Psychologist*, 50, 741–749.

Metcalfe, J., & Mischel, W. (1999). A hot/cool-system analysis of delay of gratification: Dynamics of willpower. *Psychological Review*, 106(1), 3–19.

Metz, Thaddeus. 2007. Ubuntu as a moral theory: A reply to four critics. *South African Journal of Philosophy*, 26(4), 369–387.

Mill, J. S. (1998). *Utilitarianism*. Oxford University Press.

Miller, C., Wu, P., Funk, H., Wilson, P., & Johnson, L. (2006, May). A computational approach to etiquette and politeness: Initial test cases. In *Proceedings of 2006 BRIMS Conference* (pp. 15–18).

Millington, S. J., Arntfield, R. T., Guo, R. J., Koenig, S., Kory, P., Noble, V., Mallemat, H., & Schoenherr, J. R. (2018). Expert agreement in the interpretation of lung ultrasound studies performed on mechanically ventilated patients. *Journal of Ultrasound in Medicine*, 37, 2659–65.

Milmer, D. (2022). Anonymous: The hacker collective that has declared cyberwar on Russia, The Guardian, February 27. Retrieved March 3, 2022 from: www.theguardian.com/world/2022/feb/27/anonymous-the-hacker-collective-that-has-declared-cyberwar-on-russia.

Milmo, D. (2022). Amateur hackers warned against joining Ukraine's 'IT army'. The *Guardian*, February 27. Retrieved March 11, 2022 from: https://amp.theguardian.com/world/2022/feb/27/anonymous-the-hacker-collective-that-has-declared-cyberwar-on-russia.

Mitani, J. C. (2006). Reciprocal exchange in chimpanzees and other primates. In *Cooperation in Primates and Humans* (pp. 107–119). Springer.

Mithen, S. J. (1996). *The Prehistory of the Mind a Search for the Origins of Art, Religion and Science*. Orion Publishing Group.

Mitroff, I. I. (1974). Norms and counter-norms in a select group of the Apollo moon scientists: A case study of the ambivalence of scientists. *American sociological review*, 39, 579–595.

Mittelstadt, B. (2017). Ethics of the health-related Internet of Things: A narrative review. Ethics and Information Technology, 19, 157–175.

Mohamed, S., Png, M. T., & Isaac, W. (2020). Decolonial AI: Decolonial theory as sociotechnical foresight in artificial intelligence. *Philosophy & Technology*, 33(4), 659–684.

Molek-Kozakowska, K. (2013). Towards a pragma-linguistic framework for the study of sensationalism in news headlines. *Discourse & Communication*, 7, 173–197.

Molla, R. (2019). Google, Amazon, and Facebook all spent record amounts last year lobbying the US government. *Vox*, January 23. Retrieved March 10, 2020 from: www.vox.com/2019/1/23/18194328/google-amazon-facebook-lobby-record.

Monsell, S. (2003). Task switching. *Trends in Cognitive Sciences*, 7, 134–140.

Moody, T. C. (1993). *Philosophy and Artificial Intelligence*. Prentice Hall.

Moon, H. (2014). Genealogy of the modern theological understanding of *Han*. *Pastoral Psychology*, 63(4), 419–435.

Moor, J. (2009). Four kinds of ethical robots. *Philosophy Now*, 72, 12–14.

Moore, A. D. (Ed.) (2005). *Information Ethics: Privacy, Property, and Power*. University of Washington Press.

Moore, B., Jr. (1984/2017). *Privacy: Studies in Social and Cultural History: Studies in Social and Cultural History*. Routledge.

Moore, D. A., & Healy, P. J. (2008). The trouble with overconfidence. *Psychological Review*, 115(2), 502–517.

Moore, G. E. (1903/1993). *Principia Ethica*. Foreword by T. Baldwin. Cambridge University Press.

Moore, T. (2010). The economics of cybersecurity: Principles and policy options. International *Journal of Critical Infrastructure Protection*, 3(3–4), 103–117.

More, D. (2018). Amazon admits Alexa device eavesdropped on Portland family. *Huffington Post*, May 25. Retrieved December 17, 2019 from: www.huffpost.com/entry/alexa-eavesdropping-portland-familiy_n_5b0727cae4b0fdb2aa51b23e.

More, M. (2013). The philosophy of transhumanism. *The Transhumanist Reader: Classical and Contemporary Essays on the Science, Technology, and Philosophy of the Human Future*, 3–17.

Morgan, J. (2014). Privacy is completely and utterly dead, and we killed it. Forbes, August 19. Retrieved April 17, 2021 from: www.forbes.com/sites/jacobmorgan/2014/08/19/privacy-is-completelyand-utterly-dead-and-we-killed-it/.

Morgenstern, M. (2016). Automation and anxiety: Will smarter machines cause mass unemployment. *The Economist*, June 23. Retrieved February 21, 2022 from: www.economist.com/special-report/2016/06/23/automation-and-anxiety.

Mori, M. (1970). Bukimi no tani [The uncanny valley]. *Energy*, 7, 33–35.

Mozur, P., Zhoing, R., & Krolik, A. (2020). In coronavirus fight, China gives citizens a color code, with red flags. *The New York Times*, March 1. Retrieved March 13, 2020 from: www.nytimes.com/2020/03/01/business/china-coronavirus-surveillance.html.

Mullen, B., Atkins, J. L., Champion, D. S., Edwards, C., Hardy, D., Story, J. E., & Vanderklok, M. (1985). The false consensus effect: A meta-analysis of 115 hypothesis tests. *Journal of Experimental Social Psychology*, 21(3), 262–283.

Müller, V. C. (Ed.) (2016). *Risks of Artificial Intelligence*. Chapman & Hall – CRC Press.

Mumford, L. (1934/2010). *Technics and Civilization*. University of Chicago Press.

Munson, L. J., Hulin, C., & Drasgow, F. (2000). Longitudinal analysis of dispositional influences and sexual harassment: Effects on job and psychological outcomes. Personnel Psychology, 53, 21–46.

Murakami, Y. (2004). Utilitarian deontic logic. In *Proceedings of the Fifth International Conference on Advances in Modal Logic (AiML 2004)* (pp. 288–302).

Muria, M. & Yang, Y. (2019). Microsoft worked with Chinese military university on artificial intelligence. *Financial Post*, April 10, 2019. Retrieved April 7, 2021 from: https://www.ft.com/content/9378e7ee-5ae6-11e9-9dde-7aedca0a081a

Muris, P., Merckelbach, H., Otgaar, H., & Meijer, E. (2017). The malevolent side of human nature: A meta-analysis and critical review of the literature on the dark triad (narcissism, Machiavellianism, and psychopathy). *Perspectives on Psychological Science*, 12(2), 183–204.

Murphy, R, Woods, D. D. (2009). Beyond Asimov: The three laws of responsible robotics. *IEEE Intelligent Systems*, 24, 14–20.

Myers West, S. (2018). Censored, suspended, shadowbanned: User interpretations of content moderation on social media platforms. *New Media & Society*, 20(11), 4366–4383.

Nagel, T. (1989). *The View from Nowhere*. Oxford University Press.

Nagel, T. (1997). Justice and Nature. *Oxford Journal of Legal Studies*, 17, 303–321.

Nakamura, K. (2011). A closer look at the moral dilemma: Exploration of the latent structure and meaning of 'emotional' and 'rational'. In *Proceedings of the Thirty-Third Annual Conference of the Cognitive Science Society* (pp. 1084–1089).

Nakanishi, H. (2019). Modern society has reached its limits. Society 5.0 will liberate us. *World Economic Forum*, January. Retrieved November 14, 2021 from: www.weforum.org/agenda/2019/01/modern-society-has-reached-its-limits-society-5-0-will-liberate-us.

Nareyek, A. (2004). AI in computer games. *Queue*, 1, 58–65.

Näsi, M., & Koivusilta, L. (2013). Internet and everyday life: The perceived implications of internet use on memory and ability to concentrate. *Cyberpsychology, Behavior, and Social Networking*, 16, 88–93.

Nasser, T. (2014). Modern war crimes by the United States: Do drone strikes violate international law? Questioning the legality of US drone strikes and analyzing the United States' response to international reproach based on the realism theory of international relations. *S. Cal. Interdisc. LJ*, 24, 289.

Nay, J. L., & Zagal, J. P. (2017). Meaning without consequence: Virtue ethics and inconsequential choices in games. In *Proceedings of the 12th International Conference on the Foundations of Digital Games* (pp. 1–8).

Nazarian, S., Glover, B., Ashrafian, H., Darzi, A., & Teare, J. (2021). Diagnostic accuracy of artificial intelligence and computer-aided diagnosis for the detection and characterization of colorectal polyps: Systematic review and meta-analysis. Journal of Medical Internet Research, 23(7), e27370.

Nelson, T. O., & Narens, L. (1994). Why investigate metacognition? *Metacognition: Knowing about Knowing*, 13, 1–25.

Neshat, M., Sepidnam, G., Sargolzaei, M., & Toosi, A. N. (2014). Artificial fish swarm algorithm: A survey of the state-of-the-art, hybridization, combinatorial and indicative applications. *Artificial Intelligence Review*, 42(4), 965–997.

Newman, M. Z. (2017). *Atari Age: The Emergence of Video Games in America*. MIT Press.

Newman, M. Z. (2017). Children of the '80s never fear: Video games did not ruin your life. *Smithsonian Magazine*, May 25. Retrieved February 21, 2022 from: www.smithsonianmag.com/history/children-80s-never-fear-video-games-did-not-ruin-your-life-180963452/.

Newport, F. (2013). *Americans Disapprove of Government Surveillance Programs*. *Gallup*. Retrieved February 28, 2014 from: www.gallup.com/poll/163043/americans-disapprove-government-surveillance-programs.aspx.

Newton, K. (2021). Using research to improve your experience. *Instagram*, September 12. Retrieved November 1, 2021 from: https://about.instagram.com/blog/announcements/using-research-to-improve-your-experience.

Ng, A. (2019). Chinese facial recognition company left database of people's locations exposed. CNET.com, February 13. Retrieved February 3, 2020 from: www.cnet.com/tech/services-and-software/chinese-facial-recognition-company-left-database-of-peoples-location-exposed/.

Ni, V. (2021). China cuts amount of time minors can spend playing online video games. *The Guardian*, August 30. Retrieved February 21, 2022 from: www.theguardian.com/world/2021/aug/30/china-cuts-amount-of-time-minors-can-spend-playing-video-games.

Nickerson, R. S. (1998). Confirmation bias: A ubiquitous phenomenon in many guises. *Review of General Psychology*, 2, 175–220.

Nickerson, D. W., & Rogers, T. (2014). Political campaigns and big data. *Journal of Economic Perspectives*, 28(2), 51–74.

Nietzsche, F. W. (1997). *Beyond Good and Evil*. Dover Thrift Edition.

Nisbett, R. (2004). *The Geography of Thought: How Asians and Westerners Think Differently... and Why*. Simon and Schuster.

Nishida, K. (1990). *An Inquiry Into the Good*. M. Abe and C. Ives (trans.). Yale University Press.

Noble, S. U. (2018). *Algorithms of Oppression: How Search Engines Reinforce Racism*. NYU Press.

Norman, D. A. (1999). Affordance, conventions, and design. *Interactions*, 6, 38–43.

Norman, D. A. (2005). Human-centered design considered harmful. *Interactions*, 12(4), 14–19.

Norman, D. A. (2013). *The Design of Everyday Things: Revised and Expanded Edition*. Basic Books.

Norman, D. A., & Shallice, T. (1980). *Attention to Action. Willed and Automatic Control of behavior*. University of California San Diego CHIP Report 99.

Norman, D. A., & Shallice, T. (1986). Attention to action: Willed and automatic control of behaviour. In R. J. Davidson, G. E. Schwarts, & D. Shapiro (Eds.), *Consciousness and Self-regulation: Advances in Research and Theory, Vol. 4* (pp. 1–18). Plenum.

Norman, G. R., Grierson, L. E. M., Sherbino, J., Hamstra, S. J., Schmidt, H. G., & Mamede, S. (2018). Expertise in medicine and surgery. In K. A. Ericsson, R. R. Hoffman, A. Kozbelt, & A. M. Williams (Eds.), The Cambridge Handbook of Expertise and Expert Performance (pp. 331–355). Cambridge University Press.

Notario, N., Crespo, A., Martín, Y. S., Del Alamo, J. M., Le Métayer, D., Antignac, T., … & Wright, D. (2015, May). PRIPARE: Integrating privacy best practices into a privacy engineering methodology. In *2015 IEEE Security and Privacy Workshops* (pp. 151–158). IEEE.

Nussbaum, M. C. (1993). Non-relative virtues: An Aristotelian approach. In M. C. Nussbaum and A. Sen (Eds.), *The Quality of Life* (pp. 242–270). Oxford University Press.

Nye, J. S. (2011). Nuclear Lessons for Cyber Security? *Strategic Studies Quarterly*, 5, 18–38.

O'Boyle, E. H., Jr., Forsyth, D. R., Banks, G. C., & McDaniel, M. A. (2012). A meta-analysis of the dark triad and work behavior: A social exchange perspective. *Journal of Applied Psychology*, 97(3), 557–579.

O'Connor, C. (2017). Earning power: Here's how much top influencers can make on Instagram and Youtube. *Forbes*. Retrieved April 19, 2020 from: www.forbes.com/sites/clareoconnor/2017/04/10/earning-power-heres-how-much-top-influencers-can-make-on-instagram-and-youtube/#5ee121c824db.

O'Neil, C. (2016). *Weapons of Math Destruction: How Big Data Increases Inequality and Threatens Democracy*. Broadway Books.

O'Neill, O. (1975). *Acting on Principle*. Columbia University Press.

Obar, J. A., & Oeldorf-Hirsch, A. (2020). The biggest lie on the internet: Ignoring the privacy policies and terms of service policies of social networking services. *Information, Communication & Society*, 23, 128–147.

OECD (2021). *OECD Framework for the Classification of AI systems – Public Consultation on Preliminary Findings*. Organisation for Economic Cooperation and Develop. Retrieved October 16, 2021 from: https://aipo-api.buddyweb.fr/app/uploads/2021/06/Report-for-consultation_OECD.AI_Classification.pdf.

Office of the Inspector General (2020). *OIG releases advisory on the Chicago Police Department's predictive risk models*, January 23. Retrieved 3 February, 2020 from: https://igchicago.org/2020/01/23/oig-releases-advisory-on-the-chicago-police-departments-predictive-risk-models/.

Office of the Privacy Commissioner of Canada (2021). Joint investigation of Clearview AI, Inc. by the Office of the Privacy Commissioner of Canada, the Commission d'accès à l'information du Québec, the Information and Privacy Commissioner for British Columbia, and the Information Privacy Commissioner of Alberta. Retrieved January 7, 2022 from: https://www.priv.gc.ca/en/opc-actions-and-decisions/investigations/investigations-into-businesses/2021/pipeda-2021-001/

OKCupid (2010). The case for an older woman. *OK Trends*, February 16. Retrieved February 26, 2020 from: https://theblog.okcupid.com/the-case-for-an-older-woman-99d8cabacdf5.

Oliver, A. (2015). Nudging, shoving, and budging: Behavioural economic-informed policy. *Public Administration*, 93, 700–714.

Omohundro, S. M. (2008). The basic AI drives. *Artificial General Intelligence*, 171, 483–492.

Ortutay, B. (2021). Gardening Group Has A 'Hoe' Lotta Problems With Facebook's Algorithms. *The Huffington Post*, August 30. Retrieved September 12, 2021 from: www.huffpost.com/entry/facebook-algorithm-hoe-gardening-group_n_60f718aee4b07c153fb9c529.

Ouellet, M., Hashimi, S., Gravel, J., & Papachristos, A. V. (2019). Network exposure and excessive use of force: Investigating the social transmission of police misconduct. *Criminology & Public Policy*, 18, 675–704.

Pagani, L. S., Harbec, M. J., & Barnett, T. A. (2019). Prospective associations between television in the preschool bedroom and later bio-psycho-social risks. *Pediatric Research*, 85(7), 967–973.

Paiva, A., Dias, J., Sobral, D., Aylett, R., Woods, S., Hall, L., & Zoll, C. (2005). Learning by feeling: Evoking empathy with synthetic characters. *Applied Artificial Intelligence*, 19, 235–266.

Palaus, M., et al. (2017). Neural basis of video gaming: A systematic review. *Frontiers of Human Neuroscience*, 11. 248.

Panova, T., & Carbonell, X. (2018). Is smartphone addiction really an addiction? *Journal of Behavioral Addictions*, 7, 252–259.

Parasuraman, R., & Riley, V. (1997). Humans and automation: Use, misuse, disuse, abuse. *Human Factors*, 39(2), 230–253.

Parasuraman, R., Molloy, R., & Singh, I. L. (1993). Performance consequences of automation-induced 'complacency'. International Journal of Aviation Psychology, 3, 1–23.

Parasuraman, R., Sheridan, T. B., & Wickens, C. D. (2000). A model for types and levels of human interaction with automation. *IEEE Transactions on systems, man, and cybernetics-Part A: Systems and Humans*, 30(3), 286–297.

Park, J. Y. (2016). Wisdom, compassion, and Zen social ethics: The case of Jinul, Seongcheol. Retrieved January 17, 2021 from: www.buddhism.org/wisdom-compassion-and-zen-social-ethics-the-case-of-jinul-seongcheol/.

Park, J., Song, Y., Teng, C.-I. (2011). Exploring the links between personality traits and motivations to play online games. *Cyberpsychology, Behaviour and Social Networking*, 14, 747–751.

Pasmore, W., Francis, C., Haldeman, J., & Shani, A. (1982). Sociotechnical systems: A North American reflection on empirical studies of the seventies. *Human Relations*, 35(12), 1179–1204.

Paulhus, D. L., & Williams, K. M. (2002). The dark triad of personality: Narcissism, Machiavellianism, and psychopathy. *Journal of Research in Personality*, 36, 556–563.

Paulhus, D. L., Harms, P. D., Bruce, M. N., & Lysy, D. C. (2003). The over-claiming technique: Measuring self-enhancement independent of ability. *Journal of Personality and Social Psychology*, 84(4), 890–904.

Paxton, A., & Griffiths, T. L. (2017). Finding the traces of behavioral and cognitive processes in big data and naturally occurring datasets. *Behavior Research Methods*, 49, 1630–1638.

Payton, L. (2012). Robocalls linked to Guelph Tory campaign worker's computer. *CBC News*, May 4. Retrieved February 5, 2020 from: www.cbc.ca/news/politics/robocalls-linked-to-guelph-tory-campaign-worker-s-computer-1.1223417.

Pelley, S. (2021). Whistleblower: Facebook is misleading the public on progress against hate speech, violence, misinformation Frances Haugen says in her time. *CBS News*, October 4. Retrieved October 10, 2021 from: www.cbsnews.com/news/facebook-whistleblower-frances-haugen-misinformation-public-60-minutes-2021-10-03/.

Peng, W., Lee, M., & Heeter, C. (2010). The effects of a serious game on role-taking and willingness to help. *Journal of Communication*, 60, 723–742.

Peng, K., Mathur, A., & Narayanan, A. (2021). Mitigating dataset harms requires stewardship: Lessons from 1000 papers. arXiv preprint arXiv:2108.02922.

Penrose, R. (1989). *The Emperor's New Mind: Concerning Computers, Minds and the Laws of Physics*. Oxford University Press.

Perez, C. C. (2019). *Invisible Women: Exposing Data Bias in a World Designed for Men*. Random House.

Perez, S. (2021). TikTok just gave itself permission to collect biometric data on US users, including 'faceprints and voiceprints'. *TechCrunch*, Retrieved February 17, 2021 from https://www.washingtonpost.com/technology/2021/09/23/iphone-tracking/

Perlow, L., & Weeks, J. (2002). Who's helping whom? Layers of culture and workplace behavior. *Journal of Organizational Behavior: The International Journal of Industrial, Occupational and Organizational Psychology and Behavior, 23*(4), 345–361.

Perry, R., & Greber, L. (1990). Women and computers: An introduction. *Signs: Journal of Women in Culture and Society, 16,* 74–101.

Petitte, O. (2013). Mass Effect 3 by the numbers: 4 percent of players like shooting doctors in the face. *PC Gamer.* Retrieved February 25, 2014 from: www.pcgamer.com/2013/03/25/mass-effect-3-infographic.

Petras, K., ten Oever, S., & Jansma, B. M. (2016). The effect of distance on moral engagement: Event related potentials and alpha power are sensitive to perspective in a virtual shooting task. *Frontiers in Psychology, 6,* 2008.

Pew Research Center (June 16, 2021). *Experts Doubt Ethical AI Design Will Be Broadly Adopted as the Norm in the Next Decade.* Retrieved June 21, 2021 from: file:///C:/Users/12024/Downloads/PI_2021.06.16_Ethical-AI-Design_FINAL.pdf.

Pew Research Center. (2013). Majority Views NSA Phone Tracking as Acceptable Antiterror Tactic. *Pew Research.* Retrieved February 28, 2014 from: www.peoplepress.org/2013/06/10/majority-views-nsa-phone-tracking-asacceptable-anti-terror-tactic/.

Piaget, J. (1932). *The Moral Judgment of Children.* Routledge & Kegan-Paul.

Pillutla, M. M., & Chen, X.-P. (1999). Social norms and cooperation in social dilemmas: The effects of context and feedback. *Organizational Behavior and Human Decision Processes, 78,* 81–103.

Pinto, M. D., Hickman, R. L. Jr., Clochesy, J., & Buchner, M. (2013). Avatar-based depression self-management technology: Promising approach to improve depressive symptoms among young adults. *Applied Nursing Research, 26,* 45–48.

Plaut, V. C., & Bartlett III, R. P. (2012). Blind consent? A social psychological investigation of non-readership of click-through agreements. *Law and Human Behaviour, 36,* 1–23.

Pollina, E., & Busvine, D. (2020). European Mobile Operators Share Data for Coronavirus Fight. *U.S. News & World Report,* March 18. Available at: www.usnews.com/news/technology/articles/2020-03-18/european-mobile-operators-share-data-for-coronavirus-fight.

Pope, D. G., & Sydnor, J. R. (2011). Implementing anti-discrimination policies in statistical profiling models. *American Economic Journal: Economic Policy, 3*(3), 206–231.

Popper, N. (2012). Knight Capital says trading glitch cost it $440 million. The New York Times, August. Retrieved October 17, 2020 from: https://dealbook.nytimes.com/2012/08/02/knight-capital-says-trading-mishap-cost-it-440-million/.

Postmes, T., & Spears, R. (1998). Deindividuation and antinormative behaviour: A meta-analysis. *Psychological bulletin, 123,* 238.

Postmes, T., Spears, R., Sakhel, K., & De Groot, D. (2001). Social influence in computer-mediated communication: The effects of anonymity on group behaviour. *Personality and Social Psychology Bulletin, 27,* 1243–1254.

Prentice, D. A., & Miller, D. T. (1996). Pluralistic ignorance and the perpetuation of social norms by unwitting actors. In *Advances in Experimental Social Psychology, Vol. 28* (pp. 161–209). Academic Press.

Prescott, T., & Szollosy, M. (2017). Ethical principles of robotics, *Connection Science, 29*(2), 119–123.

Price, D. K. (1965). *The Scientific Estate.* Harvard University Press.

Primack, B. A., Shensa, A., Sidani, J. E., Escobar-Viera, C. G., & Fine, M. J. (2021). Temporal associations between social media use and depression. *American Journal of Preventive Medicine, 60*(2), 179–188.

Puente, M. (2019). LAPD ends another data-driven crime program touted to target violent offenders. *LA Times,* April 12. Retrieved December 19, 2019 from: www.latimes.com/local/lanow/la-me-laser-lapd-crime-data-program-20190412-story.html.

Purves, D., Jenkins, R., & Strawser, B. J. (2015). Autonomous machines, moral judgment, and acting for the right reasons. *Ethical Theory and Moral Practice*, 18(4), 851–872.

Putnam, R. D. (2000). *Bowling Alone: The Collapse and Revival of American Community*. Simon and schuster.

Putnam-Hornstein, E., & Needell, B. (2011). Predictors of child protective service contact between birth and age five: An examination of California's 2002 birth cohort. *Children and Youth Services Review*, 33, 1337–1344.

Putnam-Hornstein, E., Needell, B., King, B., & Johnson-Motoyama, M. (2013). Racial and ethnic disparities: A population-based examination of risk factors for involvement with child protective services. *Child Abuse & Neglect*, 37, 33–46.

Pyke, A., Schoenherr, J. R., & Thomson, R. (2022). Ethical dimensions of organizational assessment for work roles: The promises and perils of artificial intelligence. In J. DeFalco & A. Hampton (Eds.), *The Frontlines of AI Ethics: Human-Centric Perspectives on Technology's Advance*. Routledge.

Quattrociocchi, W., Scala, A., & Sunstein, C. R. (2016). *Echo chambers on Facebook*. SSRN 2795110.

Quine, W. V. O. (1951). Two dogmas of empiricism. *Philosophical Review*, 60, 20–43.

Quittner, J. (1997). Invasion of Privacy. *Time Magazine*, August 25.

Radin, M. J. (2012). *Boilerplate: The Fine Print, Vanishing Rights, and the Rule of Law*. Princeton University Press.

Rai, T. S., & Holyoak, K. J. (2013). Exposure to moral relativism compromises moral behavior. *Journal of Experimental Social Psychology*, 49(6), 995–1001.

Ramirez, A., Jr., Sumner, E. M., Fleuriet, C., & Cole, M. (2015). When online dating partners meet offline: The effect of modality switching on relational communication between online daters. *Journal of Computer-Mediated Communication*, 20, 99–114.

Rand, D. G., Brescoll, V. L., Everett, J. A., Capraro, V., & Barcelo, H. (2016). Social heuristics and social roles: Intuition favors altruism for women but not for men. *Journal of Experimental Psychology: General*, 145(4), 389–396.

Rapoport, A. C. (1965). *Prisoner's Dilemma: A Study in Conflict and Cooperation*. University of Michigan Press.

Rasmussen Report (2013). 59% oppose government's secret collecting of phone records. *Rasmussen Reports*. Retrieved October 1, 2020 from: www.rasmussenreports.com/public_content/politics/.

Rasmussen Report (2018). Five years later, many say Snowden is neither hero nor traitor. *Rasmussen Reports*. Retrieved October 1, 2020 from: www.rasmussenreports.com/public_content/politics/general_politics/august_2018/five_years_later_many_say_snowden_is_neither_hero_nor_traitor.

Rawls, J. (1971a). *A Theory of Justice*. Belknap Press of Harvard University Press.

Rawls, J. (1971b). Justice as reciprocity. In S. Gorovitz (Ed.), John Stuart Mill, Utilitarianism (pp. 244–245).

Rayburn, J. M., & Rayburn, L. G. (1996). Relationship between Machiavellianism and type A personality and ethical-orientation. *Journal of Business Ethics*, 15(11), 1209–1219.

Rayson, S. J., Hachamovitch, D. J., Kwatinetz, A. L., & Hirsch, S. M. (1998). *Autocorrecting Text Typed into a Word Processing Document*. U.S. Patent No. 5,761,689. U.S. Patent and Trademark Office.

Reddy, S., Fox, J., & Purohit, M. P. (2019). Artificial intelligence-enabled healthcare delivery. *Journal of the Royal Society of Medicine*, 112(1), 22–28.

Reeves, B., Ram, N., Robinson, T. N., Cummings, J. J., Giles, C. L., Pan, J., … & Yeykelis, L. (2021). Screenomics: A framework to capture and analyze personal life experiences and the ways that technology shapes them. *Human–Computer Interaction*, 36(2), 150–201.

Reniers, R. L., Corcoran, R., Drake, R., Shryane, N. M., & Völlm, B. A. (2011). The QCAE: A questionnaire of cognitive and affective empathy. *Journal of Personality Assessment*, 93(1), 84–95.

RescueTime (March 21, 2019). Screen time stats 2019: Here's how much you use your phone during the workday. *Rescue Time Blog*. Retrieved January 19, 2020 from: https://blog.rescuetime.com/screen-time-stats-2018/.

Rest, J. R. (1986). *Moral Development: Advances in Research and Theory*. Praeger.

Rest, J. R., Bebeau, M. J., & Thoma, S. J. (1999). *Postconventional Moral Thinking: A Neo-Kohlbergian Approach*. Lawrence Erlbaum Associates.

Richardson, K. (2016). The asymmetrical 'relationship' parallels between prostitution and the development of sex robots. *ACM SIGCAS Computers and Society*, 45(3), 290–293.

Richens, J. G., Lee, C. M., & Johri, S. (2020). Improving the accuracy of medical diagnosis with causal machine learning. *Nature Communications*, 11, 1–9.

Ridgeway, C. L. (2011). *Framed by Gender: How Gender Inequality Persists in the Modern World*. Oxford University Press.

Rigby, M. J. (2019). Ethical dimensions of using artificial intelligence in health care. *AMA Journal of Ethics*, 21(2), 121–124.

Roach, J. A. (1983). Rules of engagement. *Naval War College Review*, 36(1), 46–55.

Roberts, J. A., & David, M. E. (2020). Boss phubbing, trust, job satisfaction and employee performance. *Personality and Individual Differences*, 155, 109702.

Roberts, M., Driggs, D., Thorpe, M., Gilbey, J., Yeung, M., Ursprung, S., … & Schönlieb, C. B. (2021). Common pitfalls and recommendations for using machine learning to detect and prognosticate for COVID-19 using chest radiographs and CT scans. *Nature Machine Intelligence*, 3(3), 199–217.

Robinette, P., Li, W., Allen, R., Howard, A. M., & Wagner, A. R. (2016, March). Overtrust of robots in emergency evacuation scenarios. In *2016 11th ACM/IEEE International Conference on Human-Robot Interaction (HRI)* (pp. 101–108). IEEE.

Rocha, B., & Yates, J. (2019). Twitter trolls stoked debates about immigrants and pipelines in Canada, data show. *CBC News*, February 12. Retrieved December 12, 2019 from: www.cbc.ca/news/canada/twitter-troll-pipeline-immigrant-russia-iran-1.5014750.

Roose, K. (2021). Inside Facebook's data wars. The New York Times, July 14. Retrieved January 9, 2021 from: www.nytimes.com/2021/07/14/technology/facebook-data.html.

Rosen, L. D., Whaling, K., Rab, S., Carrier, L. M., & Cheever, N. A. (2013). Is Facebook creating 'iDisorders'? The link between clinical symptoms of psychiatric disorders and technology use, attitudes, and anxiety. *Computers in Human Behavior*, 29(3), 1243–1254.

Rosenbaum, E. (2020). Robotic medicine may be the weapon the world needs to combat the coronavirus. *CNBC*, February 26. Available at: www.cnbc.com/2020/02/26/robotic-medicine-may-be-the-weapon-needed-to-combat-the-coronavirus.html.

Rosenberg, M., Confessore, N., & Cadwalladr, C. (2018). How Trump consultants exploited the Facebook data of millions. *The New York Times*, March 17. Retrieved April 17, 2020 from: www.nytimes.com/2018/03/17/us/politics/cambridge-analytica-trump-campaign.html.

Rosenberg, S. et al. (1968). A multidimensional approach to the structure of personality impressions. *Journal of Personality & Social Psychology*, 9, 283–294.

Rosenberg, Y. (2008). *The Golem and the Wondrous Deeds of the Maharal of Prague*. Yale University Press.

Rosenblatt, F. (1958). The perceptron: A probabilistic model for information storage and organization in the brain. *Psychological Review*, 65, 386–408.

Rosenthal, R. (1979). The file drawer problem and tolerance for null results. *Psychological Bulletin*, 86, 638.

Rosin, P. L., Lai, Y. K., Liu, C., Davis, G. R., Mills, D., Tuson, G., & Russell, Y. (2018). Virtual recovery of content from x-ray micro-tomography scans of damaged historic scrolls. *Scientific Reports*, 8, 1–10.

Ross, C. (Sept. 5, 2017). IBM pitched its Watson supercomputer as a revolution in cancer care. It's nowhere close. *STAT*. Retrieved January 26, 2020 from: www.statnews.com/2017/09/05/watson-ibm-cancer/.

Ross, L. (1977). The intuitive psychologist and his shortcomings: Distortions in the attribution process. In *Advances in Experimental Social Psychology* (Vol. 10, pp. 173–220). Academic Press.

Rousseau, D. M., Sitkin, S. B., Burt, R. S., & Camerer, C. (1998). Not so different after all: A cross-discipline view of trust. *Academy of Management Review*, 23, 393–404.

Royce, W. W. (1970). Managing the development of large software systems: Concepts and techniques. In *Proceedings, WESCON*, August, 29170.

Rudder, C. (2014). Race and Attraction, 2009–2014. *OK Trends*, September 10. Retrieved September 10, 2021 from: www.gwern.net/docs/psychology/okcupid/raceandattraction20092014.html.

Rumelhart, D. E., Hinton, G. E., & McClelland, J. L. (1986). A general framework for parallel distributed processing. *Parallel Distributed processing: Explorations in the Microstructure of Cognition*, 1(45–76), 26.

Rumelhart, D. E., McClelland, J. L., & PDP Research Group (1988). *Parallel Distributed Processing, Vol. 1* (pp. 354–362). IEEE.

Ruse, M., & Wilson, E.O. (1986). Moral philosophy as applied science. *Philosophy*, 61, 173–192.

Russell, S., & Norvig, P. (1995/2010). *Artificial Intelligence: A Modern Approach*. Prentice Hall.

Ryder, R. D. (1989). *Animal Revolution: Changing Attitudes Toward Speciesism*, Basil Blackwell.

Saati, B., Salem, M., & Brinkman, W. P. (2005). Towards customized user interface skins: Investigating user personality and skin colour. In *Proceedings of HCI 2005*, 2, 89–93.

Sainato, M. (2015). *Stephen Hawking, Elon Musk, and Bill Gates Warn About Artificial Intelligence*, August 19. Retrieved January 7, 2020 from: https://observer.com/2015/08/stephen-hawking-elon-musk-and-bill-gates-warn-about-artificial-intelligence/.

Salmon, W. C. (1989). *Four Decades of Scientific Explanation*. University of Minnesota Press.

Sanders, S D (2011). Privacy is dead: The birth of social media background checks. *SUL Review*, 39, 243–264.

Saucier, G. (2009). What are the most important dimensions of personality? Evidence from studies of descriptors in diverse languages. Social and Personality Psychology Compass, 3, 620–637.

Saucier, G., Thalmayer, A. G., Payne, D. L., Carlson, R., Sanogo, L., Ole-Kotikash, L., … & Szirmák, Z. (2014). A basic bivariate structure of personality attributes evident across nine languages. *Journal of Personality*, 82, 1–14.

Saunders, J., Hunt, P., & Hollywood, J. S. (2016). Predictions put into practice: A quasi-experimental evaluation of Chicago's predictive policing pilot. *Journal of Experimental Criminology*, 12(3), 347–371.

Savage, J. (2004). Does viewing violent media really cause criminal violence? A methodological review. *Aggression and Violent Behaviour*, 10, 99–128. Available at doi: 10.1016/j.avb.2003.10.001.

Schacter, D. L., & Addis, D. R. (2007). The cognitive neuroscience of constructive memory: Remembering the past and imagining the future. *Philosophical Transactions of the Royal Society B: Biological Sciences*, 362, 773–786.

Schaffer, D. (1995). Shocking secrets revealed! The language of tabloid headlines. *ETC: A Review of General Semantics*, 52, 27–46.

Schane, S. A. (1986). Corporation is a person: The language of a legal fiction. *Tulane Law Review*, 61, 563–609.

Scharre, P. (2018). *Army of None: Autonomous Weapons and the Future of War*. WW Norton & Company.

Scheck, P., & Nelson, T. (2005). Lack of pervasiveness of the underconfidence-with-practice-effect: Boundary conditions and an explanation via anchoring. *Journal of Experimental Psychology: General*, 134, 124–128.

Scherer, M. (2012). How Obama's data crunchers helped him win. *CNN*. Retrieved January 7, 2020 from: www.cnn.com/2012/11/07/tech/web/obama-campaign-tech-team/index.html.

Scheutz, M., & Arnold, T. (2016, March). Are we ready for sex robots? In *2016 11th ACM/IEEE International Conference on Human-Robot Interaction (HRI)* (pp. 351–358). IEEE.

Schirner, G., Erdogmus, D., Chowdhury, K., & Padir, T. (2013). The future of human-in-the-loop cyber-physical systems. *Computer*, 46, 36–45.

Schmandt-Besserat, D. (1978). The earliest precursor of writing. *Scientific American*, 238, 50–59.

Schneider, W., & Shiffrin, R. M. (1977). Controlled and automatic human information processing: I. Detection, search, and attention. *Psychological Review*. 84, 1–66.

Schoenherr, J. R. (2017). Prestige technology in the evolution and social organization of early psychological science. *Theory & Psychology*, 27, 6–33.

Schoenherr, J. R. (2019a). Moral economies and codes of conduct: The social organization of Canadian experimental psychology. *Scientia Canadensis*, 41, 31–54.

Schoenherr, J. R. (2019b). Metacognitive assessments of performance: The psychometric properties of confidence scales and confidence models. In Proceedings of the 35th Annual Meeting of the International Society for Psychophysics, Turkey.

Schoenherr, J. R. (2020a). Understanding surveillance societies: Social cognition and the adoption of surveillance technologies. In *2020 IEEE International Symposium on Technology and Society (ISTAS)* (pp. 346–357). IEEE.

Schoenherr, J. R. (2020b). Black boxes and the computational mind: From psychophysics to explainable artificial intelligence. In *Proceedings of the 36th Annual Meeting of the International Society for Psychophysics*.

Schoenherr, J. R. (2021a). The adoption of surveillance technologies: Data openness, privacy, and cultural tightness. *IEEE Transactions on Technology and Society*, 2, 122–127.

Schoenherr, J. R. (2021b). Building ethical agency into adaptive instructional systems: The FATE of assessment. In *International Conference on Human-Computer Interaction* (pp. 265–283). Springer.

Schoenherr, J. R. (2021c). Trust and explainability in A/IS-mediated healthcare: Operationalizing the Therapeutic Alliance in a distributed system. In *Proceedings of IEEE ISTAS2021*, (pp. 1–8). IEEE.

Schoenherr, J. R. (2022a). Whose privacy, what surveillance? Dimensions of the mental models for privacy and security. IEEE Technology and Society Magazine, 41, 54–65.

Schoenherr, J. R. (2022b). The currency of the attentional economy: The uses and abuses of attention in our world. IEEE Technology and Society Magazine, 41, 11–14.

Schoenherr, J. R. (2022c). Learning engineering is ethical, In G. Goodale (Ed.), *Learning Engineering Toolkit*. Routledge Publishing.

Schoenherr, J. R. (in press). Factors related to intentional and unintentional insider threat behaviours. *IEEE Transactions on Technology and Society*.

Schoenherr, J. R. (submitted a). Beyond human: Extending Stereotype Content Model of social categories to nonhuman categories. Applied Social Psychology.

Schoenherr, J. R. (submitted b). Trust and reliability in the sociotechnical systems of healthcare. *IEEE Transactions on Technology and Society Magazine*.

Schoenherr, J. R., & Burleigh, T. J. (2015). The uncanny valley and social categories. *Frontiers in Psychology*, 5, 1456. Available at: https://doi.org/10.3389/fpsyg.2014.01456.

Schoenherr, J. R., & Burleigh, T. J. (2020). Dissociating affective and cognitive dimensions of uncertainty by altering regulatory focus. *Acta Psychologica*, 205, 103017.

Schoenherr, J. R., & DeFalco, J. (2021). *Moral Education and A/IS Standardization: Responsible and Ethical Design Through Education*. ISTAS.

Schoenherr, J. R., & Hamstra, S. J. (2016). Psychometrics and its discontents: An historical perspective on the discourse of the measurement tradition. *Advances in Health Care Education*, 21, 719–729.

Schoenherr, J. R., & Lis, J (in press). Sensemaking Ethical Evaluation Matrix (SEEM) for ethical design and process evaluation. In G. Goodale (Ed.), *Learning* Engineering Toolkit. Routledge Publishing.

Schoenherr, J. R., & Nguyen, K. (2018). Multi-Agent Accumulator-Based Decision-Making Model of Incivility (MADI). In *Proceedings of the International Conference on Social Computing, Behavioral-Cultural Modeling & Prediction and Behaviour Representation in Social Modeling and Simulation* (pp. 76–81). Washington, DC.

Schoenherr, J. R., & Nguyen, K. (2019). Modelling the workplace incivility with prosocial and antisocial cues to predict psychological and organizational exit. In *Proceedings of the International Conference on Social Computing, Behavioral-Cultural Modeling & Prediction and Behaviour Representation in Social Modeling and Simulation*. Washington, DC.

Schoenherr, J. R., & Thomson, R. (2020a). Beyond the prisoner's dilemma: The social dilemmas of cybersecurity. In *2020 International Conference on Cyber Situational Awareness, Data Analytics and Assessment (CyberSA)* (pp. 1–7). IEEE.

Schoenherr, J. R., & Thomson, R. (2020b). Insider Threat detection: A solution in search of a problem. *IEEE CyberScience 2020*. In *2020 International Conference on Cyber Security and Protection of Digital Services (Cyber Security)* (pp. 1–7). IEEE.

Schoenherr, J. R., & Thomson, R. (2020c). Health information seeking behaviour, risk communication, and mobility during COVID-19. In *2020 IEEE International Symposium on Technology and Society (ISTAS)* (pp. 283–289). IEEE.

Schoenherr, J. R., & Thomson, R. (2021a). The Cybersecurity (CSEC) Questionnaire: Individual differences in unintentional insider threat behaviours. In *2021 International Conference on Cyber Situational Awareness, Data Analytics and Assessment (CyberSA)* (pp. 1–8). IEEE.

Schoenherr, J. R., & Thomson, R. (2021b). Persuasive features of scientific explanations: Explanatory schemata of physical and psychosocial phenomena. *Frontiers in Psychology*, 12. Available at doi: 10.3389/fpsyg.2021.644809.

Schoenherr, J. R., & Thomson, R. (in press). Ethical frameworks for cybersecurity: Applications for human and artificial agents. In Defalco, J., & Hampton, A. *The Frontlines of AI Ethics: Human-Centric Perspectives on Technology's Advance*.

Schoenherr, J. R., Månsson, K., & Gioe, D.V. (submitted). Multiple Approach Paths to Insider Threat (MAP-IT): Intentional, ambivalent, and unintentional insider threats. *International Journal of Intelligence and Counterintelligence*.

Schoenherr, J. R., Waechter, J., & Millington, S. J. (2018). Subjective awareness of ultrasound expertise development: Individual experience as a determinant of overconfidence. *Advances in Health Science Education*, 23, 749–765.

Schoenherr, J., & Williams-Jones, B. (2011). Research Integrity/Misconduct Policies of Canadian Universities. *Canadian Journal of Higher Education*, 41(1), 1–17.

Schultz, P. W., Nolan, J. M., Cialdini, R. B., Goldstein, N. J., & Griskevicius, V. (2007). The constructive, destructive, and reconstructive power of social norms. *Psychological Science*, 18(5), 429–434.

Schwartz, R., Vassilev, A., Greene, K., Perine, L., Burt, A., & Hall, P. (2022). *Towards a Standard for Identifying and Managing Bias in Artificial Intelligence*, NIST Special Publication 1270. National Institute of Standards and Technology. https://doi.org/10.6028/NIST. SP.1270

Schwitzgebel, E., & Rust, J. (2014). The self-reported moral behavior of ethics professors, *Philosophical Psychology*, 27, 293–327.

Scott, M. (2017). Google fined record $2.7 Billion in E.U. antitrust ruling. The New York Times, June 27. Retrieved March 16, 2022 from: www.nytimes.com/2017/06/27/technology/eu-google-fine.html.

Seales, W. B., Parker, C. S., Segal, M., Tov, E., Shor, P., & Porath, Y. (2016). From damage to discovery via virtual unwrapping: Reading the scroll from En-Gedi. *Science Advances*, 2, e1601247.

Secord, J. A. (2004). Knowledge in transit, *Isis*, 95, 654–672.

Senarath, A., & Arachchilage, N. A. (2018, June). Why developers cannot embed privacy into software systems? An empirical investigation. In *Proceedings of the 22nd International Conference on Evaluation and Assessment in Software Engineering 2018* (pp. 211–216).

Senarath, A., Grobler, M., & Arachchilage, N. A. G. (2019). Will they use it or not? Investigating software developers' intention to follow privacy engineering methodologies. *ACM Transactions on Privacy and Security (TOPS)*, 22(4), 1–30.

Sengers, P., Boehner, K., David, S., & Kaye, J. J. (2005, August). Reflective design. In Proceedings of the 4th Decennial Conference on Critical Computing: Between Sense and Sensibility (pp. 49–58).

Sengupta, E., Garg, D., Choudhury, T., & Aggarwal, A. (2018, November). Techniques to eliminate human bias in machine learning. In *2018 International Conference on System Modeling & Advancement in Research Trends (SMART)* (pp. 226–230). IEEE.

Severson, R. J. (1997). *The Principles of Information Ethics*. M. E. Sharpe.

Shahbaz, A., & Funk, A. (2021). The global drive to control big tech. *Freedom House*. Available at: https://freedomhouse.org/report/freedom-net/2021/global-drive-control-big-tech#Internet.

Shahbazov, F. (November 3, 2020). Tactical reasons behind military breakthrough in Karabakh conflict. *The Jamestown Foundation*. Retrieved August 17, 2021 from: https://jamestown.org/program/tactical-reasons-behind-military-breakthrough-in-karabakh-conflict/.

Shalev-Shwartz, S., & Ben-David, S. (2014). *Understanding Machine Learning: From Theory to Algorithms*. Cambridge University Press.

Shallice, T. (1982). Specific impairments of planning. *Philosophical Transactions of the Royal Society London*, B, 298, 199–209.

Shapin, S. (1989). The invisible technician. American Scientist, 77, 554–563.

Shapin, S. (1994). A Social History of Truth: Civility and Science in Seventeenth-Century England. University of Chicago Press.

Shapin, S., & Schaffer, S. (1985). *Leviathan and the Air Pump: Hobbes, Boyle, and the Experimental Life*. Princeton University Press.

Sharabi, L. L., & Caughlin, J. P. (2017). What predicts first date success? A longitudinal study of modality switching in online dating. Personal Relationships, 24, 370–391.

Shariff, A. F., Greene, J. D., Karremans, J. C., Luguri, J. B., Clark, C. J., Schooler, J. W., ... & Vohs, K. D. (2014). Free will and punishment: A mechanistic view of human nature reduces retribution. *Psychological Science*, 25, 1563–1570.

Shariff, A. F., & Norenzayan, A. (2007). God is watching you: Priming God concepts increases prosocial behaviour in an anonymous economic game. *Psychological Science*, 18, 803–809.

Sharkey, A. J. (2006). Robots, insects and swarm intelligence. *Artificial Intelligence Review*, 26(4), 255–268.

Sheridan, T. B., & Verplank, W. L. (1978). *Human and Computer Control of Undersea Teleoperators*. Massachusetts Inst of Tech Cambridge Man-Machine Systems Lab.

Shettleworth, S. J. (2009). *Cognition, Evolution, and Behavior*. Oxford University Press.

Shiffrin, R. M., & Schneider, W. (1977). Controlled and automatic human information processing: II. Perceptual learning, automatic attending, and a general theory. *Psychological Review*, 84, 127–190.

Sholes, E. (2007, March). Evolution of a UAV autonomy classification taxonomy. In *2007 IEEE Aerospace Conference* (pp. 1–16). IEEE.

Shortliffe, E. H. (1976). *Computer-based Medical Consultations: MYCIN*. Elsevier/North Holland.

Shropshire, J. (2009). A canonical analysis of intentional information security breaches by insiders. *Information Management & Computer Security*, 17, 296–310.

Shrout, P. E., & Bolger, N. (2002). Mediation in experimental and nonexperimental studies: New procedures and recommendations. *Psychological Methods*, 7(4), 422–445.

Shrum, L. J. (Ed.) (2012). *The Psychology of Entertainment Media: Blurring the Lines between Entertainment and Persuasion*. Taylor & Francis.

Siau, K., & Wang, W. (2018). Building trust in artificial intelligence, machine learning, and robotics. *Cutter Business Technology Journal*, 31(2), 47–53.

Sidanius, J., & Pratto, F. (2011). Social dominance theory. *Handbook of Theories of Social Psychology*, 2, 418–438.

Siegel, J. (11 December, 2015). Gun control and the no-fly list: All you need to know. *Newsweek*. Retrieved February 21, 2022 from: www.newsweek.com/gun-control-and-no-fly-list-all-you-need-know-403821.

Silver, D. L, & Yang, Q, Li, L. (2013). Lifelong machine learning systems: Beyond learning algorithms. In *2013 AAAI Spring Symposium Series*.

Simon, H. (1956). Rational choice and the structure of the environment. Psychological Review, 63, 129–138.

Simon, H. A., & Gilmartin, K. (1973). A simulation of memory for chess positions. *Cognitive Psychology*, 5, 29–46.

Simon, H., & Schaeffer, J. (1992). The game of chess. In R. Aumann & S. Hart (Eds.), Handbook of Game Theory, Vol. 1 (pp. 1–17). North-Holland.

Simonite, T. (2018). AI is the future – but where are the women? *Wired*. Retrieved January 17, 2020 from: www.wired.com/story/artificial-intelligence-researchers-gender-imbalance/.

Simonsen, J., & Robertson, T. (2012). *Routledge International Handbook of Participatory Design*. Routledge.

Singer, P. (1995). *Animal Liberation*. Random House.

Slater, M. D. (2007). Reinforcing spirals: The mutual influence of media selectivity and media effects and their impact on individual behaviour and social identity. *Communication Theory*, 17, 281–303.

Slovic, P. (2007). 'If I look at the mass, I will never act': Psychic numbing and genocide. *Judgment and Decision Making*, 2, 79–95.

Slovic, P. (2010). If I look at the mass I will never act: Psychic numbing and genocide. In *Emotions and Risky Technologies* (pp. 37–59). Springer.

Small, D. A., & Loewenstein, G. (2003). Helping a victim or helping the victim: Altruism and identifiability. *Journal of Risk and Uncertainty*, 26, 5–16.

Smith, B. (2022). Digital technology and the war in Ukraine. February 28. Retrieved March 11, 2022 from: https://blogs.microsoft.com/on-the-issues/2022/02/28/ukraine-russia-digital-war-cyberattacks/.

Smith, H. (2003). *Orthogonal Unit Differentiation*. Presentation at Game Developers Conference, 2003.

Snarey, J. R. (1985). Cross-cultural universality of social-moral development: A critical review of Kohlbergian research. *Psychological Bulletin*, 97, 202–232.

Sobel, R. (1981). *IBM-Colossus in Transition*. The Free Press.

Sober, E., & Wilson, D. S. (1997). Unto Others: The Evolution of Altruism. Harvard University Press.

Society for Human Resource Management (2022). *Automation and AI in HR*. Retrieved April 16, 2021 from: https://advocacy.shrm.org/SHRM-2022-Automation-AI-Research.pdf

Somashekhar, S. P., Kumarc, R., Rauthan, A., Arun, K. R., Patil, P., & Ramya, Y. E. (2017). Abstract S6-07: Double blinded validation study to assess performance of IBM artificial intelligence platform, Watson for oncology in comparison with Manipal multidisciplinary tumour board–First study of 638 breast cancer cases. *Cancer Research*, 77, 10.1158/1538-7445.SABCS16-S6-07.

Soni, S. (2011). Applications of ANNs in stock market prediction: A survey. *International Journal of Computer Science & Engineering Technology*, 2, 71–83.

Soper, P. (2002). The Ethics of Deference: Learning from Law's Morals. Cambridge University Press.

Sorokowski, P., Sorokowska, A., Frackowiak, T., Karwowski, M., Rusicka, I., & Oleszkiewicz, A. (2016). Sex differences in online selfie postings behaviors predict histrionic personality scores among men but not women. *Computers in Human Behavior*, 59, 368–373.

Sorokowski, P., Sorokowska, A., Oleszkiewicz, A., Frackowiak, T., Huk, A., & Pisanski, K. (2015). Selfie posting behaviors are associated with narcissism among men. *Personality and Individual Differences*, 85, 123–127.

Sparrow, B., Liu, J., & Wegner, D. M. (2011). Google effects on memory: Cognitive consequences of having information at our fingertips. *Science*, 333, 776–778.

Spears, R., Lea, M., & Lee, S. (1990). De-individuation and group polarization in computer-mediated communication. *British Journal of Social Psychology*, 29, 121–134.

Sperber, D. (1994). The modularity of thought and the epidemiology of representations. In J. Tooby et al. (Eds.), *Mapping the Mind: Domain Specificity in Cognition and Culture*, 39–67.

Sperber, D., & Hirschfeld, L. A. (2004). The cognitive foundations of cultural stability and diversity. *Trends in Cognitive Sciences*, 8(1), 40–46.

Sperber, D., & Wilson, D. (1986). *Relevance: Communication and Cognition*. Blackwell, Oxford and Harvard University Press.

Spinella, M. (2005). Prefrontal substrates of empathy: Psychometric evidence in a community sample. *Biological Psychology*, 70(3), 175–181.

Sporns, O. (2011). The human connectome: A complex network. *Annals of the New York Academy of Sciences*, 1224(1), 109–125.

Stamatellos, G. (2007). *Computer Ethics: A Global Perspective*. Jones and Bartlett Publishers.

Stamatellos, G. (2012). Self-determination and information privacy: A Plotinian virtue ethics approach. In *Values and Freedoms in Modern Information Law and Ethics* (pp. 779–791).

Standing, G. (2011). Behavioural conditionality: Why the nudges must be stopped-an opinion piece. *Journal of Poverty and Social Justice*, 19, 27–38.

Stanovich, K. E. (2005). *The Robot's Rebellion: Finding Meaning in the Age of Darwin*. University of Chicago Press.

Steinfeld, N. (2016). 'I agree to the terms and conditions': (How) do users read privacy policies online? An eye-tracking experiment. *Computers in Human Behaviour*, 55, 992–1000.

Sternberg, R. J. (Ed.) (2000). *Handbook of Intelligence*. Cambridge University Press.

Stevens, J. R., & Hauser, M. D. (2004). Why be nice? Psychological constraints on the evolution of cooperation. *Trends in Cognitive Sciences*, 8(2), 60–65.

Stevens, S. S. (1946). On the theory of scales of measurement. *Science*, 103, 677–80.

Stibel, J. (July 3, 2017). Why you're addicted to your phone ... and what to do about it. *USA Today*. Retrieved April 16, 2020 from: www.usatoday.com/story/money/columnist/2017/07/03/why-youre-addicted-your-phone-and-what-do/443448001/.

Stiff, J. B., & Mongeau, P. A. (2016). *Persuasive Communication*. Guilford Publications.

Stockdale, L., & Coyne, S. M. (2018). Video game addiction in emerging adulthood: Cross-sectional evidence of pathology in video game addicts as compared to matched healthy controls. *Journal of Affective Disorders*, 225, 265–272.

Strevens, M. (2008). Depth: An Account of Scientific Explanation. Harvard University Press.

Strickland, E. (2019). IBM Watson, heal thyself: How IBM overpromised and underdelivered on AI health care. IEEE Spectrum, 56(4), 24–31.

Strubel, J., & Petrie, T. A. (2017). Love me Tinder: Body image and psychosocial functioning among men and women. *Body Image*, 21, 34–38.

Strubell, E., Ganesh, A., & McCallum, A. (2020, April). Energy and policy considerations for modern deep learning research. In *Proceedings of the AAAI Conference on Artificial Intelligence, Vol. 34, No. 9* (pp. 13693–13696).

Sturm, T., & Ash, M. G. (2005). The role of instruments. *History of Psychology*, 8, 3–34.

Subiaul, F., Vonk, J., Okamoto-Barth, S., & Barth, J. (2008). Do chimpanzees learn reputation by observation? Evidence from direct and indirect experience with generous and selfish strangers. *Animal Cognition*, 11(4), 611–623.

Suler, J. (2004). Computer and cyberspace 'addiction'. *International Journal of Applied Psychoanalytic Studies*, 1(4), 359–362.

Suler, J. R., & Phillips, W. L. (1998). The bad boys of cyberspace: Deviant behavior in a multimedia chat community. *CyberPsychology & Behavior*, 1(3), 275–294.

Sullivan, D. (October 27, 2021). Giving kids and teens more control over their images in Search. *Google Blog*. Retrieved October 29, 2021 from: https://blog.google/products/search/giving-kids-and-teens-more-control-over-their-images-search/.

Suwajanakorn, S., Seitz, S. M., & Kemelmacher-Shlizerman, I. (2017). Synthesizing Obama: Learning lip sync from audio. *ACM Transactions on Graphics (ToG)*, 36(4), 1–13.

Sweeney, L. (2002). k-anonymity: A model for protecting privacy. *International Journal of Uncertainty, Fuzziness and Knowledge-Based Systems*, 10, 557–570.

Symons, J., & Alvarado, R. (2016). Can we trust Big Data? Applying philosophy of science to software. *Big Data & Society*, 3, 2053951716664747.

Symons, J., & Horner, J. K. (2020). Why there is no general solution to the problem of software verification. *Foundations of Science*, 25, 541–557.

Sze, V., Chen, Y. H., Yang, T. J., & Emer, J. S. (2017). Efficient processing of deep neural networks: A tutorial and survey. *Proceedings of the IEEE*, 105(12), 2295–2329.

Tabassum, M., Kosinski, T., & Lipford, H. R. (2019). 'I don't own the data': End user perceptions of smart home device data practices and risks. In *Fifteenth Symposium on Usable Privacy and Security ({SOUPS} 2019)*.

Tajfel, H., Billig, M. G., Bundy, R. P., & Flament, C. (1971). Social categorization and intergroup behaviour. *European Journal of Social Psychology*, 1(2), 149–178.

Tanash, R. S., Chen, Z., Thakur, T., Wallach, D. S., & Subramanian, D. (2015, October). Known unknowns: An analysis of Twitter censorship in Turkey. In *Proceedings of the 14th ACM Workshop on Privacy in the Electronic Society* (pp. 11–20).

Tannenbaum, D., Fox, C. R., & Rogers, T. (2017). On the misplaced politics of behavioural policy interventions. *Nature Human Behaviour*, 1, 0130.

Taplin, J. (2017). Why is Google spending record sums on lobbying Washington? *The Guardian*, July 30. Retrieved December 11, 2019 from: www.theguardian.com/technology/2017/jul/30/google-silicon-valley-corporate-lobbying-washington-dc-politics.

Tau, B., & Hackman, M. (2020). Federal agencies use cellphone location data for immigration enforcement. *The Wall Street Journal*, February 7. Retrieved March 2, 2020 from: www.wsj.com/articles/federal-agencies-use-cellphone-location-data-for-immigration-enforcement-11581078600.

Taub, L. (2011). Introduction: Reengaging with instruments. *Isis*, 102, 689–696.

Tavani, T. H. (2007). *Ethics and Technology: Ethical Issues in an Age of Information and Communication Technology*. Wiley.

Taylor, J. (2021). Why is Facebook shutting down its facial recognition system and deleting 'faceprints'? The Guardian, November 3. Retrieved November 4, 2021 from: www.theguardian.com/technology/2021/nov/03/why-is-facebook-shutting-down-its-facial-recognition-system-and-deleting-faceprints.

Teeny, J., Briñol, P., & Petty, R. E. (2017). The elaboration likelihood model: Understanding consumer attitude change. In C. V. Jansson-Boyd & M. J. Zawisza (Eds.), *Routledge International Handbook of Consumer Psychology* (pp. 390–410). Routledge/Taylor & Francis Group.

Tenbrunsel, A. E., & Messick, D. M. (1999). Sanctioning systems, decision frames, and cooperation. *Administrative Science Quarterly*, 44, 684–707

Teng, C.-I. (2008). Personality differences between online game players and nonplayers in a student sample. *Cyberpsychology & Behaviour*, 11, 232–234.

Tetsurō, W. (2011). *Purifying Zen: Watsuji Tetsurō's Shamōn Dōgen*. Steve Bein (trans.). University of Hawai'i Press.

Thaler, R., & Sunstein, C. (2008). *Nudge*. Penguin Books.

Thelwall, M. (2009). Homophily in myspace. *Journal of the American Society for Information Science and Technology*, 60, 219–231.

Thibaut, J. W., & Kelley, H. H. (1959). *The Social Psychology of Groups*. Wiley.

Thoreau, H. D. (1854/2008). Walden (annotated edition). Yale University Press.

Thorstensen, E. (2017). Creating golems: Uses of golem stories in the ethics of technologies. *NanoEthics*, 11, 153–168.

Till, B. D., & Busler, M. (2000). The match-up hypothesis: Physical attractiveness, expertise, and the role of fit on brand attitude, purchase intent and brand beliefs. *Journal of Advertising*, 29, 1–13.

Tiwald, J., & Van Norden, B. W. (2014). *Readings in Later Chinese Philosophy: Han to the Twentieth Century*. Hackett Publishing.

Topham, J. R. (1998). Beyond the 'common context': The production and reading of the *Bridgewater Treatise*, Isis, 89, 233–262.

Torresen, J. (2018). A review of future and ethical perspectives of robotics and AI. *Frontiers in Robotics and AI*, 4, 75. Available at: https://doi.org/10.3389/frobt.2017.00075.

Torres-Huitzil, C., & Girau, B. (2017). Fault and error tolerance in neural networks: A review. *IEEE Access*, 5, 17322–17341.

Towhey, M. (2008). Second Life could sexually exploit children via Internet, Rep. Mark Kirk says. *Chicago Tribune*, May 6. Retrieved June 22, 2008 from: https://archive.is/20130628214703/www.chicagotribune.com/news/local/chi-online-predator-alert-06-may06,0,4087619.story.

Tran, T. (2021). Scientists built an AI to give ethical advice, but it turned out super racist. *Futurism*, October 22. Retrieved October 23, 2021 from: https://futurism.com/delphi-ai-ethics-racist.

Trivers, R. (1971). The evolution of reciprocal altruism. *Quarterly Review of Biology*, 46, 35–57.

Trocmé et al. (1998). *Canadian Incidence Study of Reported Child Abuse and Neglect 1998 (CIS-1998): Final Report. Minister of Public Works and Government Services*, Canada, Ottawa.

Tschannen-Moran, M., & Hoy, W. K. (2000). A multidisciplinary analysis of the nature, meaning, and measurement of trust. *Review of Educational Research*, 70, 547–593.

Tsui, J. S. (1996). Auditors' ethical reasoning: Some audit conflict and cross cultural evidence. *The International Journal of Accounting*, 31(1), 121–133.

Tsui, J. S., & Windsor, C. (2001). Some cross-cultural evidence on ethical reasoning. *Journal of Business Ethics*, 31(2), 143–150.

Turiel, E. (2002). *The Culture of Morality: Social Development, Context, and Conflict*. Cambridge University Press.

Turner, M. E., Pratkanis, A. R., Probasco, P., & Leve, C. (1992). Threat, cohesion, and group effectiveness: Testing a social identity maintenance perspective on groupthink. *Journal of Personality and Social Psychology*, 63(5), 781–796.

Turow, J., Feldman, L., & Meltzer, K. (2005). *Open to Exploitation: American Shoppers Online and Offline*. Report of the Annenberg Public Policy Center, University of Pennsylvania.

Turse, N. (2013). *Kill Anything that Moves: The Real American War in Vietnam*. Macmillan.

Twenge, J. M. (2017). Have smartphones destroyed a generation? *The Atlantic*, September. Retrieved April 16, 2020 from: www.theatlantic.com/magazine/archive/2017/09/has-the-smartphone-destroyed-a-generation/534198/.

UNESCO. (2002). *Standards for Ethics and Responsibility in Science: An Empirical Study*. UNESCO.

UNESCO. (2005). *Universal Declaration on Bioethics and Human Rights*. UNESCO.

Uri, J. (2019). Fifty years ago: Nearly one month to boots in lunar dust. *Roundup Reads*, June 14. Retrieved March 7, 2020 from: https://roundupreads.jsc.nasa.gov/pages.ashx/1184/Fifty%%20Month %20to%20Boots%20in%20Lunar%20Dust.

Vaithianathan, R. (2016). Big Data should shrink bureaucracy big time. *Stuff*, October 17. Retrieved February 21, 2022 from: www.stuff.co.nz/national/politics/opinion/85416929/rhema-vaithianathan-big-data-should-shrink-bureaucracy-big-time.

Vaithianathan, R., Maloney, T., Putnam-Hornstein, E., & Jiang, N. (2013). Children in the public benefit system at risk of maltreatment: Identification via predictive modeling. *American Journal of Preventive Medicine*, 45, 354–359.

Vaithianathan, R., Putnam-Hornstein, E., Jiang, N., Nand, P., & Maloney, T. (2017). Developing predictive models to support child maltreatment hotline screening decisions: Allegheny County methodology and implementation. *Center for Social data Analytics*.

Valente, T. W. (1995). *Network Models of the Diffusion of Innovations*. Hampton Press.

Valentino-DeVries, J., Singer, N., Keller, M. H., Krolik, A. (2018). Your apps know where you were last night, and they're not keeping it secret. *The New York Times*, December 10. Retrieved December 17, 2019 from: www.nytimes.com/interactive/2018/12/10/business/location-data-privacy-apps.html?mtrref=undefined&gwh=4A7EE73F98FA4C8A226FF32091C4F241&gwt=pay&assetType=PAYWALL.

Vallor, S. (2016). *Technology and the Virtues: A Philosophical Guide to a Future Worth Wanting*. Oxford University Press.

van de Poel, I. (2020). Core values and value conflicts in cybersecurity: Beyond privacy versus security. In M. Christen, B. Gordijn, & M. Loi (Eds.), *The Ethics of Cybersecurity* (pp. 45–71). Springer.

Van den Hoven, J. (2013). Internet of Things Factsheet Ethics. *European Commission*. Retrieved February 11, 2020 from: https://people.cs.pitt.edu/~mosse/courses/cs3720/IOT-ethics.pdf.

Van Dijck, J. (2014). Datafication, dataism and dataveillance: Big Data between scientific paradigm and ideology. *Surveillance & Society*, 12, 197–208.

Van Gelder, J. L., & De Vries, R. E. (2012). Traits and states: Integrating personality and affect into a model of criminal decision making. Criminology, 50, 637–671.

Van Lange, P. A., & Rusbult, C. E. (2011). Interdependence theory. *Handbook of Theories of Social Psychology*, 2, 251–272.

Van Lier, J., Revlin, R., & De Neys, W. (2013). Detecting cheaters without thinking: Testing the automaticity of the cheater detection module. *PloS One*, 8(1), e53827.

Van Norden, B. W. (2008). *Mengzi: With Selections from Traditional Commentaries*. Hackett Publishing.

Vanderelst, D., & Winfield, A. (2018). An architecture for ethical robots inspired by the simulation theory of cognition. *Cognitive Systems Research*, 48, 56–66.

Verheij, B. (2016). Formalizing value-guided argumentation for ethical systems design. *Artificial Intelligence and Law*, 24, 387–407.

Verschuere, B., Meijer, E. H., Jim, A., Hoogesteyn, K., Orthey, R., McCarthy, R. J., ... & Yıldız, E. (2018). Registered replication report on Mazar, Amir, and Ariely (2008). Advances in Methods and Practices in Psychological Science, 1(3), 299–317.

Veruggio, G. (2005). The birth of roboethics. In *Proceedings of the IEEE International Conference on Robotics and Automation (ICRA)*. Workshop on Robo-Ethics.

Vilone, G., & Longo, L. (2020). *Explainable Artificial Intelligence: A Systematic Review*. arXiv preprint arXiv:2006.00093.

Vitak, J., Zube, P., Smock, A., Carr, C. T., Ellison, N., & Lampe, C. (2011). It's complicated: Facebook users' political participation in the 2008 election. *Cyberpsychology, Behaviour & Social Networking*, 14, 107–114. Available at doi: 10.1089/cyber.2009.0226.

Vohs, K. D., Mead, N. L., & Goode, M. R. (2006). The psychological consequences of money. Science, 314, 1154–1156.

Vohs, K. D., & Schooler, J. W. (2008). The value of believing in free will: Encouraging a belief in determinism increases cheating. *Psychological Science*, 19, 49–54.

Von Borzyskowski, I., Mazumder, A., Mateen, B., Wooldridge, M. (2021). *Data Science and AI in the Age of COVID-19: Reflections on the Response of UK's Data Science and AI Community to the COVID-19 Pandemic*. The Alan Turing Institute.

Vosoughi, S., Roy, D., & Aral, S. (2018). The spread of true and false news online. Science, 359, 1146–1151.

Wakeling, R. (2020). Mass Effect dev reveals most players refused to be the bad guy. *Gamespot*, February 28. Retrieved February 7, 2020 from: www.gamespot.com/articles/mass-effect-dev-reveals-most-players-refused-to-be/1100-6474033/.

Walker, G. H., Stanton, N. A., Salmon, P. M., & Jenkins, D. P. (2008). A review of sociotechnical systems theory: A classic concept for new command and control paradigms. *Theoretical Issues in Ergonomics Science*, 9(6), 479–499.

Wall Street Journal (2021). The Facebook files. Retrieved November 1, 2021 from: www.wsj.com/articles/the-facebook-files-11631713039.

Wallach, W. (2008). Implementing moral decision making faculties in computers and robots. *AI & Society*, 22, 463–475.

Wallach, W., & Allen, C. (2008). *Moral Machines: Teaching Robots Right from Wrong*. Oxford University Press.

Wallach, W., Franklin, S., & Allen, C. (2010). A conceptual and computational model of moral decision making in human and artificial agents. *Topics in Cognitive Science*, 2, 454–485.

Walter, A. (2006). The anti-naturalistic fallacy: Evolutionary moral psychology and the insistence of brute facts. *Evolutionary Psychology*, 4, 3–48.

Walther, J. B. (1996). Computer-mediated communication impersonal, interpersonal, and hyperpersonal interaction. *Communication Research*, 23, 3–43.

Walther, J. B. (2007). Selective self-presentation in computer-mediated communication: Hyperpersonal dimensions of technology, language, and cognition. *Computers in Human Behavior*, 23, 2538–2557.

Walton, A. G. (2018). How too much screen time affects kids' bodies and brains. *Forbes*, April 16. Retrieved April 11, 2020 from: www.forbes.com/sites/alicegwalton/2018/04/16/how-too-much-screen-time-affects-kids-bodies-and-brains/#7f1175c71549.

Wang, C. C., & Wang, C. H. (2008). Helping others in online games: Prosocial behavior in cyberspace. *CyberPsychology & Behavior*, 11, 344–346.

Wang, C. J., Ng, C. Y., & Brook, R. H. (2020). Response to COVID-19 in Taiwan: Big data analytics, new technology, and proactive testing. *JAMA*. Published online March 3, 2020. Available at doi: 10.1001/jama.2020.3151.

Wang, C., & Yu, G. (2017). The relationship between player's value systems and their in-game behaviour in a massively multiplayer online role-playing game. *International Journal of Computer Games Technology*, 2017, 1–8.

Wang, D., Khosla, A., Gargeya, R., Irshad, H., & Beck, A. H. (2016). Deep learning for identifying metastatic breast cancer. *arXiv preprint* arXiv:1606.05718.

Wang, L., Von Laszewski, G., Younge, A., He, X., Kunze, M., Tao, J., & Fu, C. (2010). Cloud computing: A perspective study. *New Generation Computing*, 28(2), 137–146.

Wang, R. (June 10, 2013). Beware trading privacy for convenience. *Harvard Business Review*. Available at: https://hbr.org/2013/06/beware-trading-privacy-for-con.

Warren, S., & Brandeis, L. (1890). The Right to Privacy. *Harvard Law Review*, 4, 193–220.

Washington, M. C., Okoro, E. A., Cardon, P. W. (2014). Perceptions of civility for mobile phone use in formal and informal meetings. *Business and Professional Communication Quarterly*. 77, 52–64.

Wason, P. C. (1966). Reasoning. In B. Foss (Ed.), *New Horizons in Psychology*. Penguin.

Watling, J., & Kaushal, S. (2020). The democratisation of precision strike in the Nagorno-Karabakh conflict. *RUSI*, October 22. Retrieved September 11, 2021 from: https://rusi.org/explore-our-research/publications/commentary/democratisation-precision-strike-nagorno-karabakh-conflict.

Weaver, A. J., & Lewis, N. L. (2012). Mirrored morality: An exploration of moral choice in video games. *Cyberpsychology, Behavior, & Social Networking*, 15, 610–614.

WEF & Boston Consulting Group (2019). *Towards a Reskilling Revolution Industry-Led Action for the Future of Work*. World Economic Forum. Available at: www3.weforum.org/docs/WEF_Towards_a_Reskilling_Revolution.pdf.

WEF (2016). *The Future of Jobs Employment, Skills and Workforce Strategy for the Fourth Industrial Revolution*. World Economic Forum. Available at: www3.weforum.org/docs/WEF_Future_of_Jobs.pdf.

Wegner, D. M. (1987). Transactive memory: A contemporary analysis of the group mind. In B. Mullen & G. R. Goethals (Eds.), *Theories of Group Behavior* (pp. 185–208). Springer.

Wegner, D. M., Erber, R., & Raymond, R. (1991). Transactive memory in close relationships. *Journal of Personality and Social Psychology*, 61, 923–929.

Weick, K. (1979). *The Social Psychology of Organizing*. McGraw-Hill.

Weick, K., Sutcliffe, K. M., & Obstfeld, D. (2005). Organizing and the process of sensemaking. *Organization Science*, 16, 409–421.

Weisbaum, H. (2018). Trust in Facebook has dropped by 66 percent since the Cambridge Analytica scandal. *NBC News*, April 18. Retrieved October 17, 2018 from: www.nbcnews.com/business/consumer/trust-facebook-has-dropped-51-percent-cambridge-analytica-scandal-n867011.

Weiser, E. B. (2015). # Me: Narcissism and its facets as predictors of selfie-posting frequency. *Personality and Individual Differences*, 86, 477–481.

Weiss, B. (2018). Meet the renegades of the intellectual Dark Web. *The New York Times*, May 8. Retrieved April 17, 2020 from: www.nytimes.com/2018/05/08/opinion/intellectual-dark-web.html.

Weizenbaum J. (1966). ELIZA – a computer program for the study of natural language communication between man and machine. *Communications of the ACM*, 9, 36–45.

Wells, G., Horwitz, J., & Seetharaman, D. (2021). Facebook knows Instagram is toxic for teen girls, company documents show. *The Wall Street Journal*, September 14. Retrieved November 1, 2021 from: www.wsj.com/articles/facebook-knows-instagram-is-toxic-for-teen-girls-company-documents-show-11631620739.

Wells, W. D. (1975). Psychographics: A critical review. *Journal of Marketing Research*, 12(2), 196–213.

Weng, L., Flammini, A., Vespignani, A., & Menczer, F. (2012). Com-petition among memes in a world with limited attention. *Scientific Reports*, 2, 335. Available at: http://dx.doi.org/10.1038/srep00335.

Westerlund, M. (2019). The emergence of deepfake technology: A review. *Technology Innovation Management Review*, 9(11), 39–52.

Westin, A. (1967). *Privacy and Freedom*. Atheneum.

Wheaton, S. (March 31, 2007). Obama Is First in Their Second Life. *The New York Times*. Available at: https://thecaucus.blogs.nytimes.com/2007/03/31/obama-is-first-in-their-second-life/.

Whitbeck, C. (1996). Ethics as design: Doing justice to moral problems. Hastings Center Report, 26, 9–16.

Whitehill, J. (2000). Buddhism and the Virtues. In *Contemporary Buddhist Ethics*, edited by Damien Keown, 17–36. Curzon Press.

WHO (2021). *Ethics and Governance of Artifical Intelligence for Health*. World Health Organization.

Wickens, C. D., Mavor, A., Parasuraman, R., & McGee, J. (1998). *The Future of Air Traffic Control: Human Operators and Automation*. National Academy Press.

Wilkes, M. A. (2007). 10th Vintage Computer Festival Panel Presentation, minutes 28–40, Mountain View, CA. YouTube, November 5.

Wilkinson-Ryan, T. (2013). A psychological account of consent of fine print. *Iowa Law Review*, 99, 1745–1784.

Wilkinson-Ryan, T. (2017). The perverse consequences of disclosing standard terms. *Cornell Law Review*, 103, 117–176.

Wilmer, H. H., Sherman, L. E., & Chein, J. M. (2017). Smartphones and cognition: A review of research exploring the links between mobile technology habits and cognitive functioning. *Frontiers in Psychology*, 8, 605.

Wilson, D. S., & Wilson, E. O. (2008). Evolution 'for the Good of the Group': The process known as group selection was once accepted unthinkingly, then was widely discredited; it's time for a more discriminating assessment. *American Scientist*, 96(5), 380–389.

Wilson, D. S., Near, D., & Miller, R. R. (1996). Machiavellianism: A synthesis of evolutionary and psychological literatures. *Psychological Bulletin*, 119(2), 285–299.

Winfield, A. F. (2014). Robots with internal models: A route to self-aware and hence safer robots. In J. Pitt (Ed.), *The Computer after Me: Awareness and Self-Awareness in Autonomic Systems*, 1st Edn (pp. 237–225). Imperial College Press.

Winfield, A. F., & Jirotka, M. (2017). The case for an ethical black box. In Y. Gao (Ed.), *Towards Autonomous Robot Systems* (pp. 1–12). Springer.

Winfield, A. F., & Jirotka, M. (2018). Ethical governance is essential to building trust in robotics and artificial intelligence systems. *Philosophical Transactions of the Royal Society A: Mathematical, Physical and Engineering Sciences*, 376, 20180085.

Winfield, A. F., Blum, C., & Liu, W. (2014). Towards an ethical robot: Internal models, consequences and ethical action selection. In M. Mistry, A. Leonardis, M. Witkowski, & C. Melhuish (Eds.), *Advances in Autonomous Robotics Systems* (pp. 85–96). Springer.

Winkler, R., & Mullins, B. (2015). How Google skewed search results. *The Wall Street Journal*, March 19. Retrieved September 2, 2020 from: www.wsj.com/articles/how-google-skewed-search-results-1426793553.

Winter, S. J., Stylianou, A. C., & Giacalone, R. A. (2004). Individual differences in the acceptability of unethical information technology practices: The case of Machiavellianism and ethical ideology. *Journal of Business Ethics*, 54, 279–230

Wittkower, D. E. (2016). Principles of anti-discriminatory design. In 2016 IEEE International Symposium on Ethics in Engineering, Science and Technology (ETHICS), May. (pp. 1–7). IEEE.

Wong, D. B. (2000). Xunzi on Moral Motivation. In T. C. Kline and P. J. Ivanhoe (Eds.), *Virtue, Nature and Moral Agency in the Xunzi* (pp. 135–154). Hackett Publishing Company.

Wong, D. B. (2005). Zhuangzi and the Obsession with Being Right. *History of Philosophy Quarterly*, 22, 91–107.

Wong, D. B. (2015). Growing virtue: The theory and science of developing compassion from a Mencian perspective. In B. Bruya (Ed.), *The Philosophical Challenge from China* (pp. 23–58). MIT Press.

Woods, H. C., & Scott, H. (2016). # Sleepyteens: Social media use in adolescence is associated with poor sleep quality, anxiety, depression and low self-esteem. *Journal of Adolescence*, 51, 41–49.

Woods, J. (2008). Avatars and Second Life adultery: A tale of online cheating and real-world heartbreak. *The Telegraph*, Retrieved January 5, 2020 from: www.telegraph.co.uk/technology/3457828/Avatars-and-Second-Life-adultery-A-tale-of-online-cheating-and-real-world-heartbreak.html.

Worth, N. C., & Book, A. S. (2014). Personality and behaviour in a massively multiplayer online role-playing game. *Computers in Human Behaviour*, 38, 322–330.

Wright, D. (2012). The state of the art in privacy impact assessment. *Computer Law & Security Review*, 28, 54–61.

Wulff, D. U., Mergenthaler-Canseco, M., & Hertwig, R. (2018). A meta-analytic review of two modes of learning and the description-experience gap. Psychological Bulletin, 144(2), 140–176.

Wynants, L., Van Calster, B., Collins, G. S., Riley, R. D., Heinze, G., Schuit, E., … & van Smeden, M. (2020). Prediction models for diagnosis and prognosis of covid-19: Systematic review and critical appraisal. *British Medical Journal*, 369. Available at: https://doi.org/10.1136/bmj.m1328.

Xiao, M., Wang, R., & Chan-Olmsted, S. (2018). Factors affecting YouTube influencer marketing credibility: A heuristic-systematic model. *Journal of Media Business Studies*, 15(3), 188–213.

Yakowitz, J. (2011). Tragedy of the data commons. *Harvard Journal of Law & Technology*, 25, 1–68.

Yan, L., Zhang, H. T., Xiao, Y., Wang, M., Sun, C., Liang, J., … & Tang, X. (2020). Prediction of survival for severe Covid-19 patients with three clinical features: Development of a machine learning-based prognostic model with clinical data in Wuhan. *medRxiv*. Available at: https://doi.org/10.1101/2020.02.27.20028027.

Yang, G. Z., Cambias, J., Cleary, K., Daimler, E., Drake, J., Dupont, P. E., … & Taylor, R. H. (2017). Medical robotics – Regulatory, ethical, and legal considerations for increasing levels of autonomy. *Science Robotics*, 2, 8638.

Yannakakis, G. N. (2012, May). Game AI revisited. In *Proceedings of the 9th Conference on Computing Frontiers* (pp. 285–292).

Yankelovich, D. (1972). *Corporate Priorities: A Continuing Study of the New Demands on Business.* Stanford, CT: Yankelovich Inc.

Yardi, S., & Boyd, D. (2010). Dynamic debates: An analysis of group polarization over time on twitter. *Bulletin of Science, Technology & Society*, 30, 316–327.

Yee, N., Ducheneaut, N., Nelson, L., & Likarish, P. (2011). Introverted elves & conscientious gnomes: The expression of personality in world of warcraft. In *Proceedings of the SIGCHI Conference on Human Factors in Computing Systems* (pp. 753–762). ACM.

Young, L., & Durwin, A. J. (2013). Moral realism as moral motivation: The impact of meta-ethics on everyday decision-making. *Journal of Experimental Social Psychology*, 49(2), 302–306.

Youyou, W., Kosinski, M., & Stillwell, D. (2015). Computer-based personality judgments are more accurate than those made by humans. *Proceedings of the National Academy of Sciences*, 112(4), 1036–1040.

Yu, E., & Cysneiros, L. (2002, October). Designing for privacy and other competing requirements. In *2nd Symposium on Requirements Engineering for Information Security (SREIS'02), Raleigh, North Carolina* (pp. 15–16).

Yu, K. H., Beam, A. L., & Kohane, I. S. (2018). Artificial intelligence in healthcare. *Nature Biomedical Engineering*, 2(10), 719–731.

Yuan, K. H. (2005). Fit indices versus test statistics. *Multivariate Behavioral Research*, 40(1), 115–148.

Yuasa, Y. (1987). The Body: *Toward an Eastern Mind-Body Theory*, T. P. Kasulis (Ed.), N. Shigenori and T. P. Kasulis (trans.). State University Press of New York.

Yudkowsky, E. (2008). Artificial intelligence as a positive and negative factor in global risk. In Bostrom, N., & Cirkovic, M. M. *Global Catastrophic Risks* (pp. 308–345). Oxford University Press.

Zaki, J., & Mitchell, J. P. (2013). Intuitive prosociality. *Current Directions in Psychological Science*, 22(6), 466–470. Available at: https://doi.org/10.1177/09637214134927.

Zanna, M. P., & Cooper, J. (1974). Dissonance and the pill: An attribution approach to studying the arousal properties of dissonance. Journal of Personality and Social Psychology, 29(5), 703.

Zeine, H. (2017). The problems with smart cities. *Forbes*, July 19. Retrieved Decemeber 17, 2019 from: www.forbes.com/sites/forbestechcouncil/2017/06/19/the-problems-with-smart-cities/#5cf693806067.

Zeng, Y., Lu, E., & Huangfu, C. (2018). *Linking Artificial Intelligence Principles.* arXiv.

Zhang, Y., & Wu, L. (2009). Stock market prediction of S&P 500 via combination of improved BCO approach and BP neural network. *Expert Systems with Applications*, 36, 8849–8854.

Zhao, J., Khashabi, D., Khot, T., Sabharwal, A., & Chang, K. W. (2021). *Ethical-Advice Taker: Do Language Models Understand Natural Language Interventions?* arXiv preprint arXiv:2106.01465.

Zhao, J., Wang, T., Yatskar, M., Ordonez, V., & Chang, K. W. (2017). *Men also like shopping: Reducing gender bias amplification using corpus-level constraints. arXiv preprint* arXiv:1707. 09457. 2017 Jul 29.

Ziman, J. (2000). *Real Science: What It Is and What It Means.* Cambridge University Press.

Zimmer, F., Scheibe, K., Stock, M., & Stock, W. G. (2019). Fake news in social media: Bad algorithms or biased users? *Journal of Information Science Theory and Practice*, 7, 40–53.

Zuboff, S. (2019). *The Age of Surveillance Capitalism: The Fight for a Human Future at the New Frontier of Power.* Profile Books.

Zwick, D., & Dholakia, N. (2004). Whose identity is it anyway? Consumer representation in the age of database marketing. *Journal of Macromarketing*, 24, 31–43.

INDEX